Contents

Preface

Four hundred and eighty one primary care groups (PCGs) covering the entire population of England were launched on 1 April 1999. They represent the most dramatic experiment in the history of the NHS. They are founded on the premise that local health professionals, managers and people know best what they require and how to provide it; better than the more remote systems of the past, which were also hampered by strong and vested professional interests.

The success of PCGs and their successor PCTs will depend on the motivation and ability of 'the few', the relatively small number of movers and shakers within each group. They will be the unsung heroes of this quiet revolution. A revolution that the general public has yet to understand or appreciate.

The contributing authors of this book include more than 30 of these heroes, who have willingly given yet more of their free time to describe the experiences and the lessons learnt. This is, therefore, a book *for* PCGs and *on* PCGs, but above all, this is a book *by* PCGs. The authors are all frontline GPs, nurses, managers, lay people, social service representatives and pharmacy advisors. It could not have been otherwise.

Those at the grass roots of primary care have been provided with a unique opportunity to plan and shape the modern NHS. It is they alone who have the authority to tell the rest of us how to do it when it comes to PCGs or PCTs. Their dedication and inspiration, in spite of the many challenges, are evident on every page. That is what makes this book unique.

Michael Dixon
Kieran Sweeney
August 2000

Who is this book for?

This book is aimed primarily at those working within PCGs and PCTs at any level, and those whose work involves and relates to them. We hope, however, that it will also be of interest to policy makers and planners, as well as the general public.

The NHS belongs to us all and this book is not simply a handbook showing how to do it and how some are doing it, though this is part of its function. It also demonstrates the immense potential of PCGs and PCTs to reshape the NHS, so that our local patients get what they need, how they need it and in as cost effective a way as possible. Thus, some of the chapters are as relevant to ordinary people, patients and observers as they are to those of us working within the 'new' NHS.

List of contributors

Graham Archard
General Practitioner, Christchurch
Governance Lead, Christchurch Primary Care Group
National Governance Lead, NHS Alliance

Jill Ashton
Chief Officer, Exeter Primary Care Group

Sarah Baker
Service Manager, Croydon & Surrey Downs Community Trust
Nurse Board Member and Clinical Governance Lead, Croydon South
Primary Care Group

John Bewick
Director of Health Improvement, North & East Devon Health Authority

Nick Bradley
General Practitioner, Exeter
Clinical Governance Lead, Exeter Primary Care Group

Ruth Chambers
General Practitioner, Staffordshire
Professor of Primary Care Development, Staffordshire University

Mark Couldrick
General Practitioner, Hemyock, Devon
IT Lead, Mid-Devon Primary Care Group

Donna Covey
Director, Association of Community Health Councils for England and
Wales

Geraint Davies
Chief Executive, Hayes & Harlington Primary Care Group

Andrew Edgar
Director, Centre for Applied Ethics, Cardiff University

Debbie Fleming
Chief Executive, Bournemouth Central Primary Care Group

Debbie Freake
General Practitioner, Newcastle
Chair, Newcastle West Primary Care Group

Steve Gillam
Director, Primary Care Programme, King's Fund, London

Barbara Hakin
General Practitioner, Bradford
Chair, Bradford South and West Primary Care Group

Tim Hind
Assistant Chief Social Services Officer (Community Care), Slough
Borough Council
Social Services Representative, Slough Primary Care Group

Chris James
General Practitioner, Southampton
Chair, Central Southampton Primary Care Group
Secretary, NHS Alliance

David Jenner
General Practitioner, Cullompton, Devon
Chair of mid-Devon Primary Care Group
Policy Advisor, NHS Alliance

David Kernick
General Practitioner, Exeter

Roy Latham
Lay Member, Kent Weald Primary Care Group

Martin Marshall
Clinical Senior Research Fellow, NPCRDC, University of Manchester

Ruth McDonald
Senior Research Fellow, University of Leeds
Health Economist, Mersey Live Primary Care Group

Mike North
General Practitioner, Essex
GP Board Member, Maldon and South Chelmsford Primary Care Group

David Paynton
General Practitioner, Southampton
Chair, Southampton East Healthcare Primary Care Group

Mark Robinson
Prescribing Manager, Croydon Primary Care Group

Helen Tanner
Practice Manager, Crediton
Co-opted Board Member, Mid-Devon Primary Care Group

Liz Titheridge
Nurse Representative, Woking Primary Care Group

Chris Town
Chief Executive, North Peterborough Primary Care Group

Alex Trompetas
General Practitioner, Surrey
Chairman, Central Croydon Primary Care Group

John Wood
General Practitioner, Leicester
Chair, Leicester City East Primary Care Group

Ian Wylie
Director of Corporate Affairs, King's Fund, London

Acknowledgements

We would like to thank all the authors who contributed to this book. Most of them are at the leading edge of the New NHS and have two or three daytime jobs already. Their commitment to this project has been absolute.

We would also like to thank all the wives and families not only of the authors but also of all those who are leading PCGs and trusts throughout the country. Every revolution has its casualties and many families have suffered from the midnight oil that has been burnt in the name of a new and better NHS.

We would particularly like to thank our own families for their patience and support. Michael Dixon would like to thank Joanna, whose own successful artistic career is so frequently interrupted by having to be a single mother during his frequent absences on behalf of the NHS. Also his neglected children, Finn, May and Liberty, who never complain but have also paid the price.

Michael would also like to thank his ever-patient personal assistant, Christine Quinn, who has become an expert in picking up the mess that he leaves behind. Finally, thanks are due to Radcliffe Medical Press and in particular to Paula Moran, who has been the guardian angel of this book. Her lot has been one of missed deadlines, *ad hoc* changes in direction and editorial sloth. She has borne this all with great equanimity and if there is any brilliance in this book, apart from the contributing authors, then it is entirely due to her.

Kieran Sweeney thanks his long-suffering wife Barbara, who has developed her career, run the house and tended to the children during his absences preparing the book, and to Patrick, Michael, Kieran and Louise, who often wondered what precisely he was doing during these absences.

And very finally. Thank you the reader, you must be either a participant in or an observer of the New NHS. You are without doubt the most vital link, as nothing will kill off the NHS faster than apathy.

To the writers, who contributed to this book.

To the NHS Alliance National Executive and all its members.

To all those who are working towards a fairer, better and more accountable National Health Service.

Introduction

Kieran Sweeney

Quality is the defining theme of the New NHS. Accountability comes a close second. Together they formed the central plank in a succession of government documents which set out the Labour Party's agenda for modernising the NHS, based on the Third Way, a strategy for government which emerged from a debate between the traditionalists and the modernisers of the newly elected administration.[1,2] Linking the history of the much-loved NHS with an urge to modernise it was the main health policy for the politicians. 'Creating the National Health Service was the greatest act of modernisation ever achieved by a Labour Government', proclaimed the Prime Minister in his foreword to the 1997 White Paper. 'But I know', he continued, 'that one of the main reasons people elected a new Government on May 1st was their concern that the NHS was failing them and their families'.[1]

Historical background

Failing them it may have been, but the real root of the Labour Party's concern with the NHS lay elsewhere – in the way the health service had evolved generally during its first half century. The early decades of the health service show it to have been an organisation which was administered, not managed, with an uneasy mixture of organisational tensions, statutory regulations, local freedoms and occasional political changes of direction.[3] Not long after the heady days of its introduction, cost containment became an increasing concern; by the 1980s it was the main item on the agenda. This is what the then managing director of Sainsbury's was asked to address in his eponymous Griffiths Report.[4] Introduce a more robust management structure, he suggested – perhaps not surprising, given his background.

Although far-reaching for its day, Griffiths' report was clearly not enough to placate the then prime minister, Margaret Thatcher, who caught the world unprepared when she announced her far-reaching health service reforms live on prime-time BBC, during an interview on

Panorama. The central planks of these reforms, namely the internal market, splitting the purchaser and the provider, and the introduction of fundholding, divided the medical profession. They were anathema to the Labour Party too, who remained uneasy about an internal market in a publicly funded system; the costs needed to sustain the system were huge, and issues of quality were rarely addressed.[5] Quality was to become the central issue: the idea was written into the 1997 government White Paper, curiously prepared when the hearings into the Bristol paediatric surgery debacle were underway. A statutory duty to improve quality in every locality was introduced. It was given the name clinical governance. And if quality and accountability were central to clinical governance, the addition of the description 'statutory' left no one in doubt that this time the NHS was to be changed and changed utterly.

The new NHS, said the Labour administration, was to be built on part-nerships driven by performance: it would remain a national service, fulfilling the promise that 'if you are ill or injured, there will be an national health service there to help'.[1] A greater degree of local responsi-bility would ensure efficiency, lead towards excellence and rebuild public confidence.

The introduction of PCGs

But how was this all to operate? In primary care, the new (statutory) roles and responsibilities would fall to the PCGs, comprising GPs, community nurses, representatives of social services and lay people. PCGs would take responsibility for commissioning services for the community, and could operate at any of four levels, from merely acting in support of health authorities in commissioning care (level 1), to the highest level, at which PCGs would be freestanding but accountable to the health author-ity for commissioning care, with added responsibility for the provision of community services (level 4). Initially, all operated at either level 1 or level 2, at which the PCG would accept responsibility for dispensing 40% of its unified budget, which covered general medical services, prescrib-ing, community hospitals and community services. This would increase to 60% for those PCGs wishing to remain at level 2 in their second year.

Three sets of guidance outline the main tasks for these groups.[6-8] They would undertake primary and community health service develop-ment, deciding what resources were available and how they should best be dispersed, retaining wherever possible the principle of equity. Such plans would be set out in the primary care investment plan, which covers services, staff, premises, and information and technology require-ments. Second, from April 1999, all PCGs would take charge of a limited indicative prescribing budget, which would extend to introducing incentive schemes for prescribing in which every practice would be obliged to participate. The fact the PCGs operated with a unified budget allowed for much greater innovation. They could, for example, decide to increase prescribing in one area, say for hypercholesterolaemia, while saving, albeit later, on surgical intervention for coronary heart disease in secondary care. Third, PCGs would commission community services through long-term service agreements (LTSAs), which would focus on conditions or patient groups, for example dementia, rather than on organisational preferences. Finally, and crucially, PCGs would develop and publish annually a Health Improvement Plan (HImP) by which they would set out their plans to improve the health of their community in the global sense, including those aspects previously the domain of social services or the local authority. Exciting collaboration with housing agencies, educational authorities and citizens' groups were to become possible, relegating the frustrating parallel planning of these organisations to history. And HImPs were to have clout: the chair of each PCG would sign up to it, binding the group to an accountability agreement with the health authority for any commitments contained in it. The reforms meant business: new business, collaboration and innovative partnerships underpinned with accountability. Quality was everything, shaped, supported, implemented and demonstrated (to the public, not just the powers that be) through the mechanism of clinical governance.

The constitution of PCGs

So it was with an air of great anticipation that in April 1999, 481 PCGs came into existence in England. They served populations of roughly 100 000: the smallest half that, the biggest over twice as many. All started at either level 1 or 2, but there was a barely concealed desire from the centre that many would progress up the ladder of responsibility before too long. The membership included GPs in the majority, community nurses, representatives of social services and lay people, brought together under a chair, usually a GP, and directed by a chief officer.

GP members of a PCG are elected from the local GP community, usually in a way that reflects the dispersal of practices served by the group. The two nurse representatives are similarly elected from their professional community, while the social service member is more often a senior professional. The lay member provides the 'reality check', and can provide the useful function of developing the public's interest in the work of the group. In addition to these core members, groups can co-opt others, for example a practice manager, or someone from a trust. Alongside the elected general practice members, a clinical governance lead sits on the PCG. This person is charged with the work of implementing clinical governance, assessing and recording baseline quality measurements for the group, and ensuring that recommendations from the central government bodies, the National Institute of Clinical Excellence (NICE), and the non-departmental statutory Commission for Health Improvement (CHI) were implemented. The remit of these two organisations is set out later in this introduction.

Clinical governance

Seven pillars support the concept of clinical governance. Clinical audit is central, combining with significant event auditing and evidence-based practice to ensure quality standards. Risk management, learning from complaints, near misses or adverse incidents, reduces both the medical and legal implications of errors. Workforce issues, including regular meaningful appraisal, personal development plans and clinical supervision are aimed to produce a workforce dedicated to improving their own and the organisation's standards. Linked to this are educational strategies, developing a culture of life-long learning and continuing professional development, which in turn need good information technology (IT) support and the acquisition of computer literacy. All of this can and should be underpinned by relevant, robust research, looking at ways of evaluating what's going on, always seeking to answer the 'so what' question. And finally, the patient experience, at which all of this is aimed, should be part and parcel of a decent clinical governance strategy. PCGs should ensure that wherever possible the patient or citizen's voice is heard, listened to and incorporated into governance, for example at the research level or in the risk management programme, or even more radically in evaluating certain key aspects of healthcare professionals' skills.

Such is the broad remit of clinical governance that attempts to capture its essence in a succinct definition have so far proved pretty elusive. Scally and Donaldson led the way with an introductory effort. 'Clinical governance', they announced, 'is a system through which NHS organisations are accountable for continuously improving the quality of their services and safeguarding high standards of care by creating an environment in which excellence flourishes'.[9] Patrick Pietroni offered a refinement, describing clinical governance as 'the means by which organisations ensure the provision of quality clinical care by making individuals accountable for setting, maintaining and monitoring performance standards'.[10] Whichever way you looked at it, quality was at the centre of clinical governance. To succeed, good clinical governance strategies would require new ways of working right across organisations, skilled leadership and a positive shift in culture in the NHS. But for those at the coalface, the issue which provokes the greatest concern is poor performance.

Reforms with clout: the role of NICE and CHI

If the Conservative-inspired funding policy was what made the incoming Labour politicians see red in the NHS, the strategists in the Department of Health had a more precise concern – postcode availability of services. The fact that some services, such as subfertility treatment or certain forms of cancer treatment, were available in some districts and not in others was simply unacceptable to the civil servants, and the public too, no doubt. It had to change. Even within fairly standard services there were well-documented and worrying variations in the quality of provision. The nineties seemed awash with medical catastrophies – we have already noted the irony of the simultaneity of the Bristol heart surgery hearings and the publication of the 1997 White Paper (modern and dependable, eh?). System-wide failures in breast cancer screening services and cervical screening services jostled for media coverage with reports of personal indiscretions by doctors, including one notorious fight between an anaesthetist and a surgeon during an operation in which one of the two suffered a broken nose! The government's response was predictable: what was needed was a body which would provide national guidance on reliable evidence of clinical and cost-effectiveness, providing clear national standards of what patients could expect to receive. Enter NICE.

The National Institute for Clinical Excellence was introduced to produce and disseminate clinical guidelines based on best evidence, advice on clinical audit methodologies, information on good practice, and appraisal of new and existing interventions. Its staff was drawn from the great and the good of the medical academic hierarchy (though the word on the street was that some positions were hard to fill, on the poisoned chalice ticket). NICE was to bring together the four established National Confidential Enquiries – into perioperative deaths, stillbirths, maternal deaths, and suicides and homicides by people with mental illness – to add focus, coherence and status to their respective findings. As a result of their appraisal and clarification, it should prove easier to set clinical standards. But whether these standards were being adhered to was another matter. This was to be the remit of NICE's sister organisation, the Commission for Health Improvement.

Commission for Health Improvement

A curious beast, CHI is defined as a statutory non-departmental public body. The very definition sets out its two important characteristics: it exists at arm's length from the government, is not a part of the Department of Health and has statutory powers under the Health Act, 1999. These powers extend to fining individuals who obstruct its proper business. The broad responsibility of CHI is to oversee the adequacy of implementation of clinical governance; its day-to-day work will revolve around visiting trusts and PCGs (or PCTs) to review arrangements to support, promote, develop and deliver high-quality services. To do this CHI will link regularly with Regional Executive Offices, each of which with regional responsibility for clinical governance. CHI's role will be to strengthen and support regional efforts and to act as an independent review mechanism. It also has a role in two other areas. It can act rapidly to assess and, where necessary, intervene in an organisation where persistent and serious concerns have been uncovered. And, over time, it will assume responsibility for overseeing and assisting with external incident inquiries.

CHI has a tall order to fulfil: 25 reviews in its first year, and all NHS trusts and PCG/Ts within a four-year cycle. To do this it has to develop an assessment template and handbook transparent to all, robust in its methodology and fair in its application. Clearly CHI's approach will evolve over time, and its very early site visits to secondary care organisations will be developmental. And although there are understandable concerns over CHI's potentially inspectorial role, the organisation is dedicated to a positive approach, uncovering successes, encouraging a developmental view of clinical governance and hoping to help shape quality arrangements through its work (Jocelyn Cornwell, Director of Policy and Development, CHI, personal communication). The patient experience will be central to its evaluations, a welcome and long-overdue innovation in health service research and development programmes.

From rhetoric to reality: early views on the reforms

The rhetoric of the NHS reforms has a universal appeal. Who could argue against the need for reform given the serious concerns about the way the health service was going and the number of catastrophic public failures in the service delivery? Who could argue against a body like NICE, with its central remit the clarification of evidence and the production of guidance on best practice? And was there not an unarguable case for an independent body to ensure that these things just could not happen again?

Critics abounded. 'Meaningless rhetoric' was how Neville Goodman described Scally and Donaldson's definition of clinical governance, 'a mixture of the blindingly obvious (people should lead well and work well in teams) and the unproved (clinical audit)'.[11] Doctors had concerns about the ultimate responsibility for clinical governance: did it lie with clinicians or managers?[12] Scally and Donaldson had tried to tease apart strategic and operational issues in governance, proposing that daily responsibility lay with clinicians while overall accountability rests with the chief executive officer. Given the statutory importance of clinical governance, this was more than a matter of semantics.

Goodman launched another attack on the whole basis of the reforms, arguing against the narrowness of evidence-based medicine, the denominator of all the reforms.[13] Too much reliance on statistics, randomised controlled trials and meta-analyses, he argued. And while the publication of guidelines might be a welcome product from NICE, Professor Gene Feder, speaking at a conference on the reforms at the Royal College of Physicians in September 1999, said 'we should not put too much faith in them, and be aware of continuing problems with their construction, dissemination and implementation'.[14] Other commentators, presenting at the same conference took a different tack. Terms like evidence, standards, guidelines, authority or equity had not been defined, argued Dr Michael Loughlin, a philosopher at Manchester University, yet they formed the basis of the documents describing the reforms. So how was the poor clinician or manager to know she was doing the right thing? Anyway, this is not how science as an intellectual commodity proceeds and develops. Good science has never been the property of a single body, especially a government-associated body such as NICE, which then pronounces on what is and is not acceptable. It just does not work that way. The evaluation work of NICE could stifle pharmaceutical research in the UK, if companies felt that their licences might be refused by NICE on the grounds that the NHS could not afford their products.

The existence of a body like NICE might also alter the legal status of the guidelines it produces. In 1995, Hurwitz had pointed out that written guidelines could not be cross-examined, they were classified as hearsay evidence and a court could not decide what was reasonable and proper simply by referring to them.[15] Given the association between NICE and the Secretary of State for Health proposed in the NHS reforms, the legal status of such material might now change, becoming more like commercial products, for which producers have to describe satisfactory competence for the manufacture of the product.

While many of these concerns remained theoretical, and many of the worries speculative, work on the ground proceeded apace. PCGs were set up, clinical governance leads girded their loins (after negotiating their contracts with their health authorities), lay people took their place at table and the reforms were under way. What happened?

From rhetoric to reality: the first year's experience

The first three parts of this book describe the early experience of PCGs as they got to grips with the work of implementing the reforms, developing clinical governance and working on the fresh collaborations required in the new NHS. It deals first with the theory underpinning day-to-day practice in PCGs, before discussing how some groups rose to their major operational challenges, and ending with a 'how to' section, in which particular members of a board tell it as they saw it. The purpose pervading the whole book is not to demonstrate *how* to do it, but rather, *this is how some groups did it*, with varying levels of success. We are deeply grateful for the honesty with which our contributing authors have written.

Andrew Edgar leads us off in his review of the ethical issues implicit in the workings of the new NHS, looking particularly at the concept of 'need' in relation to rationing. Like it or not, Edgar argues, PCGs have a moral role. They are required to address the perceived inadequacies of the 'old' NHS (that is, the NHS as it existed under the previous Conservative government). Edgar examines the two principal inadequacies, inefficiency and unfair allocation. While the former really meant the NHS bureaucracy, the latter derived more precisely from the system of GP fundholding. Edgar unpicks the ethical issues which infuse this debate. Chapter 2 extends this analysis, reflecting on how societal values relate to and influence the working of the new NHS.

Part 1 concludes with chapters on health economics and quality markers. David Kernick and Ruth McDonald lead us through a crisp, comprehensive introduction to the principles of health economics. They take up Andrew Edgar's point about fairness and efficiency, arguing that PCGs have a responsibility to maximise healthcare at the population level by taking decisions that are transparently fair. They will do so within a context of scarce resources and will be required to make judgements about the relative merits of different interventions. What services should they produce? How? Who should receive them? A basic grasp of health economics is a *sine qua non* for this task, and the authors set out the principles succinctly.

It is all very well demanding quality, but will we recognise it when we see it? Politicians' demands for greater efficiency increase the pressure on managers and clinical governance leads to judge whether clinicians are providing value for money. Drawing on his experience as a Harkness Fellow with the RAND group in California, Martin Marshall reviews the main types of quality markers relevant to primary care. Starting with the National Performance Assessment Framework classification, which lists health improvement, fair access, effective delivery, efficiency, patient experience and outcomes, Marshall takes the reader through the relative merits of each set of indicators. And if we are all busy collating this quality data, won't there be a demand to bring it into the public domain? What happens then? Marshall draws on the American literature to suggest some of the consequences of what he sees as an inevitable (and not undesirable) trend.

Part 2 shifts the perspective. Here, our contributors share with us their candid views on how their particular responsibilities developed over the first 12 months of activity. How are HImPs drawn up? How do they relate to and inform other aspects of PCG work? With what effect? John Bewick answers these questions in Chapter 5, and Chris James explains how these plans are converted into care pathways and long-term service agreements in Chapter 6. The relationship of the HImP to clinical governance is developed next by Gillam and Bradley, who describe their progress to date and their main challenges. How does one tackle the tension between the utilitarianism of public health and the individualism of general practice? The authors adopt a postmodern perspective in which to frame their views. 'Recognition of the multiple realities informing future clinical decision making lie at the heart of the called for cultural revolution', they argue. All changed, and changed utterly. This changed environment is illustrated by Helen Tanner in her description of how to draw up primary care investment plans. Part 2 ends with a chapter by Alex Trompetas (one of a growing number of GPs with a MBA) on managing human resources in PCGs.

Part 3 is the hands on, how to, section of the book. Liz Titheridge, nurse board member for Woking PCG has strong views on the matter: 'PCGs are about cultural change, and it is often up to the nurse to influence the shift in power, control and authority' she asserts. Roy Latham's experience as the lay member for Kent Weald PCG leads him to make a series of recommendations about training for lay people in NHS policy, strategy and structure. Other authors look at how to involve the public, represent social services and how to operate as chair or chief officer. Again the emphasis is on how it was, not do it this way at all costs.

Part 4 looks at many of the difficult tasks facing PCGs and provides hints on how to go about them. Proper involvement of the local community, patients and other primary care professionals is what PCGs are all about, but success calls for careful planning and innovative thinking. Debbie Freake, Ruth Chambers, Alex Trompetas and Sara Baker certainly know far more about these subjects than anyone else in primary care at present. The same can also be said of Barbara Hakin and David Paynton, who have written landmark chapters on intermediate care that may well prove to be the king-pin of the future NHS.

Proper communication, information and IT are vital to every PCG's success and Ian Wylie and David Jenner approach their subject with all the communication skills that one might expect. Mark Cloudrick discusses the complex subject of information and IT in a way that even the most Luddite of us will understand.

In Chapter 24, Debbie Fleming brings us down to earth with the realities, but also the potential, of each PCG and future PCT to hold its own budget. That will become ever more crucial as PCGs become PCTs.

PCTs are the subject of Part 5 and the last two chapters by Geraint Davis of Hillingdon PCT and Chris Town of North Peterborough PCT – both of whom are at the leading edge of the first wave of 17 PCTs. Their description of PCTs and how to go about them is optimistic and inspiring. Some primary care professionals, particularly GPs, have been less than positive about PCTs, but Chris Town provides plenty of reassurance: 'PCTs, like their forerunners, are based on practice populations and success relies heavily on the active participation of GPs, as well as other clinical professionals. We are fortunate to have enjoyed willing input so far and to ensure that this spirit continues, we will need to demonstrate clear advantages from this new way of working'.

At the time the NHS reforms described in this book were being laid out in a White Paper in 1997, the hearings into the Bristol children's heart surgery scandal were under way. As this book is being edited, Dr Harold Shipman is beginning 15 life sentences for murdering 15 women patients who chose to register with him as their family doctor; he is about to be charged with about 25 more murders. Is there any clearer justification for a book like this? As this book goes to press, the NHS Plan tells us that all PCGs are expected to become PCTs by 2004.

The NHS is changing beyond all recognition. The imperative to change is overwhelming, justified, appropriate and overdue. Healthcare professionals must get the direction of the reforms right, must have the skills to implement them honourably, must know for sure that they are developing quality strategies that are going to make a difference for their patients and must do so in an uncertain financial climate. This book offers us a unique insight into the reconfiguration of the new NHS. We are grateful to our contributors for allowing us access to their experience of the early workings of the reforms, warts and all.

References

1 Secretary of State for Health (1997) *The New NHS: modern, dependable.* Cm 3807. The Stationery Office, London.

2 Ham C (1999) The Third way in healthcare reform: does the emperor have any clothes? *Journal of Health Services Research and Policy.* **4**(3): 168–73.

3 Sweeney KG (1996) The use of focus groups to assess consumers' views on miscarriage and minor surgery. MPhil thesis, University of Exeter.

4 Griffiths R (1983) *NHS Management Enquiry.* Department of Health and Social Security, London.

5 Gray JD, Donaldson LJ (1996) Improving the quality of health care through contracting: a study of health authority practice. *Quality in Health Care.* **5**: 201–5.

6 Health Service Circular 1998/065. NHSE, Leeds.

7 Health Service Circular 1998/139. NHSE, Leeds.

8 Health Service Circular 1998/228. NHSE, Leeds.

9 Scally G, Donaldson L (1998) Clinical governance and the drive for quality in the new NHS in England. *BMJ.* **317**: 61–3.

10 Pietroni P (1998) Clinical governance in primary care groups. Address to clinical governance leads. RHA Conference Dillington House, November, 1998.

11 Goodman N (1998) Clinical governance. *BMJ.* **317**: 1725–7.

12 Beecham L (1999) Consultants receive guidance on clinical governance. *BMJ.* **318**: 1081.

13 Goodman N (1999) Who will challenge evidence based medicine? *Journal of the Royal College of Physicians.* **33**: 249–51.

14 Feder G (1999) NICE, CHI and the reforms. Presentation to conference at the Royal College of Physicians, September.

15 Hurwitz B (1995) Guidelines and the law (editorial). *BMJ.* **311**: 1517–18.

PART 1

Theory

CHAPTER 1

Ethics, rationing and the NHS

Andrew Edgar

The New NHS

It is widely argued, and generally accepted, that state provision of health-care suffers from an unavoidable and worsening shortfall in available resources. As economists would put it, there is a scarcity relative to the demand that is placed on those resources. Three reasons for this scarcity are given: ageing populations entail an ever-increasing burden of illness within the population; the costs of providing medical interventions, both in terms of new technologies and labour costs, increase more rapidly than the general rate of inflation; the very success of healthcare provision increases the population's expectations of what can be provided. If these reasons are valid, not all of the claims that are made on the resources of the healthcare system can be met immediately. It therefore becomes increasingly important, not simply to introduce or devise mechanisms that will serve to allocate resources among the competing claims made on them – for such mechanisms will undoubted already exist – but rather to scrutinise existing mechanisms. Such scrutiny may focus on two issues: the efficiency with which existing resources are used and the fairness with which they are allocated.

The New NHS, the White Paper published by the Labour Party after winning the 1997 election, attempts to play down the pressures on the NHS.[1] It argues that technological and demographic factors will not lead to challenges of a size that the NHS has not already dealt with, routinely, in the past; and expectations are to be channelled into shaping services to make them 'more responsive to the needs and preferences of the people who use them' (para 1.19–21). Arguments in favour of rationing, and thus the claim that the NHS can no longer be a 'universal health service' providing care 'to all on the basis of need', are therefore found to be unconvincing (para 1.18). These counter-claims are significant not for their validity, for it is perhaps too early to say whether the reforms have justified their optimism, but rather for what they imply about the interpretation of the concept of 'rationing' and the moral role of the NHS. Crucially, the implication is that 'to ration' is to allocate resources by any criteria other than need. This is reasserted throughout *The New NHS*. For example:

> *The Government has committed itself anew to the historic principle of the NHS: that if you are ill or injured there will be a national health service there to help; and access will be based on need and need alone – not on your ability to pay, or on who your GP happens to be or on where you live (para 1.5.)*

The New NHS thus responds to what were widely accepted to be the inadequacies of the NHS under the previous Conservative administration: inefficiency and unfair allocation. Charges of inefficiency are primarily laid against the workings of the NHS bureaucracy, not least as it developed in response to the internal market, but also in the proliferation of purchasing bodies with diverse remits and operating principles (para 2.10ff). Unfairness in the allocation of resources, or perhaps more precisely, the unfairness of access to the healthcare system, is seen to result in large part from the workings of GP fundholding (para 2.12). A GP fundholder is perceived to have been able to secure a wider range of services, more rapid service and services of higher quality than could a non-fundholder. An unfairness is therefore identified, precisely insofar as the treatment of any particular patient is not dependent on what might be termed intrinsically medical factors (which is to say, their 'need'), but on accidents of birth, residence or income.

On this analysis, the pivotal position of PCGs as purchasers with the new NHS bestows on the groups a significant *moral* role. They are heralded as being at once efficient and fair. The efficiency of the PCGs lies in their lower management costs, compared to GP fundholders. The PCG system is seen to reduce the number of commissioning bodies, to remove inefficient, short-term contracts, and to allow management costs to be shared across larger populations (para 5.20f), while the PCGs remain free to develop innovative, high-quality services and to share these throughout the NHS (para 5.2). In terms of fairness, the two-tier system of GP fundholders and non-fundholders is replaced by a single form of primary care organisation for all patients. Ideally, there would be no incentives for GPs to discriminate between patients because of the potential burden they might place on budgets, so that all suspicions of cherry-picking will be eliminated and no PCG will be able to secure privileged access to services at the expense of another group. In addition, it is asserted that, '[l]ocal doctors and nurses ... are in the best position to know what patients need', so that the commissioning of services by PCGs comes to be focused on the needs of a local community (albeit within broad national standards) (para 2.4). Indeed, this communal aspect of the PCGs is taken further: 'The intention is that Primary Care Groups should develop around natural communities' (para 5.16). PCGs therefore seek to ensure that all patients have the same access to services, determined 'according to need and need alone', and yet be able to commission services appropriate to the epidemiological profile of the local community.

Needs, outcomes and values

While *The New NHS* does much to respond to the perceived inequities of the old NHS structure, it still serves to beg a number of crucial moral questions. As noted above, it attempts to side-step the disturbing, and indeed politically sensitive, issue of rationing through the rhetoric of 'need'. To ration is, it is claimed, to ignore need. To recognise and act efficiently on need, as is expected of the PCGs, is the key to overcoming the apparent shortfall in resourcing, and to overcome this shortfall fairly. 'Need' is thus credited with a certain objectivity, in the sense that the incidence and severity of disease within a given population can be assessed, and seemingly contentious and morally loaded problems of allocation or prioritisation can be resolved through reference to such assessment. The appeal to need therefore appears to resolve a moral problem (of 'rationing') into a relatively straightforward empirical one (of needs assessment).

It may, however, be argued that the concept of 'need' is not as transparent as *The New NHS* supposes, or more precisely that the concept of 'need' in 'clinical needs assessment' does not map unproblematically on to the use of need as a criterion of resource allocation. Specifically, allocation according to need may be seen to be justified in terms of a framework of moral values and not scientific objectivity, and second that needs claims may collapse into claims about medical outcomes.

It may readily be acknowledged that the rhetoric of need performs an important negative role in allowing for the identification and elimination of certain factors that would be morally irrelevant to resource allocation. Thus 'need' is typically distinguished from mere 'want' or 'preference'. To need something implies that the consequences of not being supplied with that need are dire. The satisfaction of a want or preference may give us greater happiness or pleasure than we might otherwise enjoy, but our very existence is not threatened by having the want disappointed. Similarly, need is distinguished from 'demand', where 'demand' is given the economic definition of the 'willingness and ability to pay'. To stress need as the criterion of healthcare allocation is thus to assert, at the very least, that healthcare resources should not be allocated according to the mere whim of the patient (as, perhaps, is the case of certain instances of cosmetic surgery) or according to the patient's economic circumstances.

Yet the appeal to need as the criterion of healthcare allocation is still a moral appeal and should be defended as such. This can be illustrated by recognising that there exists a substantial literature devoted to defending (whether well or ill is not the issue) the patient's economic circumstances as the principal moral criterion of healthcare resource allocation.[2] Put bluntly, the claim here is that to advocate the allocation of resources according to need is to assert, not a straightforward empirical criterion for assessment, but a moral value, and that alternative moral values exist that would lead to different and yet still morally defensible allocations. Some of these alternative values will be discussed below.

The analysis of need may be taken further by recognising the contestability of any claim based on need. To claim that I need X, is to assert that X is necessary in order for me to do something else. I do not need, for example, healthcare for its own sake. I need it, rather, because it will allow me to go on living, to live without pain or physical impairment, or whatever. It may thus be readily accepted that there are degrees of need. A claim on resources in order to avoid death is more pressing than a claim merely in order to eliminate pain. If need is a matter of degree, and therefore if all needs claims are not of the same urgency or weight, then, as Wiggins has argued, in making the claim 'I need X', I am implicitly inviting others to challenge that claim and to do so according to a number of criteria.[3] I may be asked, for example, if I really need X, i.e. will the consequences actually be as dire as I anticipate? Would Y act as an adequate substitute for X? Do I need X now or could I postpone receiving X for some time without any further worsening of my condition? Crucially, in the context of scarce resources, I can be challenged as to whether the consequences of my not receiving X will be as dire as they would be for another claimant, if they were the person to be denied X. This analysis does much to clarify what is actually entailed in the assertion that healthcare should be allocated 'according to need and only need'. In the context of scarce resources, a patient will be prioritised according to the severity of the consequences of not receiving treatment relative to others, the time period over which treatment can be delayed, the availability of alternative treatments and so on. To treat according to need is therefore not to treat immediately, but to prioritise on relevant medical criteria. Thus, the simple fact that I need healthcare may not be sufficient to justify my receiving it now, or perhaps ever.

An economist's response to this analysis may be to assert the redundancy of the concept of 'need' altogether. In practice, allocation according to need reduces to allocation according to the patient's ability to benefit from treatment. Thus, if I need treatment 'X' to prevent me from suffering chronic migraines and you need X to prevent intermittent headaches, then I have priority for I will benefit more. There will be a greater health gain from giving X to me than to you. Similarly, if treatment 'Y' will not simply save my life but keep me alive for ten years, but would keep you alive for only five, then again my needs claim appears to be the more pressing one.

The outcome of a medical intervention, as the above simple examples may indicate, are diverse. Just as a patient's need for healthcare does not have to be confined to urgent life-saving treatments, so the outcome of healthcare does not have to be measured purely in terms of the number of lives saved, or indeed the number of years by which life has been prolonged. The bulk of healthcare provision is concerned with the improvement of quality of life, rather than with life saving. Healthcare, as the World Health Organization (WHO) famously observed, adds life to years as well as years to life. The problem of fair allocation of resources, on this account, is not then a matter simply of assessing severity or urgency of need, but rather of comparing possible outcomes that are themselves combinations of improved longevity and quality of life.

Over the past 30 years or more, health economists and psychometricians have advocated various forms of quality of life measure as appropriate tools both to assess the efficacy of a particular treatment and, perhaps more controversially, to compare the efficacy of different medical interventions.[4] The idea behind the quality-adjusted life year (QALY) was to moderate a traditional measure of healthcare outcomes, additional years of postoperative life, by the quality of life enjoyed during those years. Three years confined to bed may well turn out to be less desirable than a single additional year of good health. The immediate problem posed by this approach is that of who determines the quality of a given health state, and thus who determines the relative desirability of possible outcomes. Different groups or individuals may well evaluate the worth of a given outcome differently. Much of the richness and interest of quality-of-life measures comes from the fact that in response to this problem, many researchers sought to derive not only evaluations, but also the very descriptions of health states, from the general pubic or from patient groups (rather than from medical professionals). Many of the more widely used quality-of-life measures, such as the Nottingham Health Profile, SIP and SF-36, thus appear with different values for different countries, precisely because the populations of different countries will compare and evaluate health states somewhat differently. This, however, suggests that 'output' is not a simple empirical measure. Rather, any suitably complex and sensitive output measure will reflect the values of the community within which it is applied.

Output measures, such as the QALY, EuroQol and the Index of Well-Being, have been developed by health economists precisely in order to offer a guide, not simply to the efficacy of a particular treatment but also to cost-efficiency. In considering output, the two concerns of the new NHS, fairness and efficiency, seemingly merge. For, boldly put, from this perspective a fair system is an efficient one. Given a scarcity of resources relative to demand, one seeks to use those resources to maximise output (for example, to maximise QALYs). Patients may still be turned away from the system, or have their claims on the system postponed, but only if the resources that could be used to treat them could be more effectively used elsewhere.

The problem with this approach is that it appears to generate counter-intuitive results. For example an expensive, life-saving treatment may appear less cost-effective than a cheaper treatment that merely alleviates pain precisely because of its expense. Similarly, treatments most likely to be used by elderly people may appear less cost-effective simply because elderly people have fewer potential years of life to be saved than do the young or middle-aged. In both these cases, needs claims seem to be saying something that is at odds with the assessment of output. Perhaps more precisely, the presence of counter-intuitive results indicates that values other than cost-efficiency are the more pressing. Health economists are not insensitive to this problem and have long argued that raw cost per QALY data can be 'weighted' to take account of other moral or clinical concerns. For example, if the raw data are suspected of adversely prejudicing the elderly, then a year of healthy life over the age of, say, 60 could be weighted to count for more than one QALY in any calculation. What this general approach indicates is that cost-per-QALY calculations cannot provide an algorithm that automatically resolves allocation problems. At best, such calculations highlight where the moral problems lie; which is to say, where a decision must be made over which moral values, including that of efficiency, are to inform the allocation of healthcare.

Something of this approach is illustrated by the 'Oregon experiment'.[5] The state of Oregon, in an attempt to respond to a perceived crisis in the provision of medicaid, approached the problem by establishing what were the priorities to which a given healthcare budget should be devoted. Cost-per-QALY league tables were established (using the Kaplan's Index of Well-Being), that served to rank some 709 condition–treatment pairs in order of cost efficiency. Given knowledge of the number and global cost of particular treatments carried out annually, a cut-off line could be drawn, purely on the grounds of cost-efficiency, between those treatments that the state could afford to supply and those it could not. Yet this concern with cost-efficiency was crucially framed by a broader concern with 'community values'. These values were elicited from community

meetings and telephone surveys, and raised such themes as the importance of preventative medicine, quality of life, cost-effectiveness, equity,
personal choice and community compassion. (It may readily be noted
that cost-efficiency is recognised as one value among others.) These
values informed the construction of 17 categories of healthcare by which
the condition–treatment pairs could be classified. Crucially these categories were ordered in terms of moral priority, insofar as they were
perceived to reflect the values of Oregonians. From this, every treatment–
condition pair within the six priority categories concerning fatal disease
would be funded, regardless of cost-efficiency. Of an intermediate seven
categories concerning non-fatal conditions, funding was restricted by the
availability of resources, according to cost-efficiency criteria. The final
category of treatments providing minimal or no improvement to length
or quality of life went unfunded. Thus, simple cost-efficiency is seen as
one value among others and is, at key points in the decision-making
process, overridden by other concerns, such as a communal commitment
to the preservation of life.

The above argument has attempted to suggest that allocation according
to need cannot be treated as either a morally neutral or morally incon-
testable response to scarcity. To advocate allocation 'according to need
and need alone' is to make a value statement that requires rational expo-
sition and defence. Similarly, any attempt to translate needs into medical
outputs or benefits results in a similar conclusion: efficiency is a value and
there are certain circumstances under which an efficient healthcare
system may be morally repugnant (for example, when it appears to
underfund life-saving treatments). The Oregon experiment (and one
could look equally well to the work of the Core Service Commission in
New Zealand, or the Dunning Committee in the Netherlands[6]) suggests
that a source of legitimacy for the systems of healthcare allocation lies in
the degree to which they reflect the moral values of the community they
serve.

Need and community

If the foregoing has suggested that the language of 'needs' and 'efficiency' in *The New NHS* is more complex than might superficially have
been expected, then the language of 'community' may also require examination. A significant literature has recently developed in the UK on the
desirability and practicality of discovering the moral values that communities hold towards healthcare,[7–9] and *The New NHS* seems to allude to
something of this in asserting that health authorities 'play a strong role in
communicating with local people and ensuring public involvement in

decision making about the local health service' (para 4.19). As noted above, an important feature of PCGs is that they can be responsive to local needs (para 2.4), and that in the new NHS primary care profession-als will, 'for the first time', be able to make 'real choices' about how they deploy their funds (para 5.18). There is thus, throughout *The New NHS*, a moral tone to the description of the local responsibility of the PCGs. It is morally preferable, as well as more efficient, to have decisions about allo-cation made locally.

Yet there is a fundamental ambiguity in the use of the term 'commu-nity', and most pointedly in the heavily rhetorical assertion that PCGs develop around 'natural communities' (para 5.16). The term 'community' might here be intended to imply a moral community. The Oregon exper-iment rested in part on the assumption that Oregonians did form a moral community, where individuals shared and collectively expressed certain, distinctive core values. The Oregonian community therefore was assumed to have a certain degree of homogeneity with respect to the values it held dear. Conversely, the New Zealand Core Services Commission looked for the diversity between the values held by such groups as the young, rural dwellers and Maoris.[10] 'Natural community', if it means anything at all, suggests a gathering together of like-minded individuals in such a homogeneous group. Such nuances may add a certain moral gravitas to the responsibilities of the PCGs, but it may be argued that the role of the PCG is not to respond to a moral community, and is certainly not that of identifying and cultivating the values that might inform healthcare allocation. It is rather that of responding to the epidemiological profile of its catchment area. The 'community' would therefore turn out to be little more than an aggregate of discrete individ-uals living within a given geographical area, and their commonality would be expressed in statistical data about the prevalence and incidence of disease within that area. 'Need' itself would also cease to be something that is obviously open to moral negotiation. The moral contestability of allocation according to need, and crucially the issue of ranking the prior-ity of competing needs claims, would thus be deferred to the scientific and value-free judgement of the medical professional.

In conclusion, the implications of this deferral may be examined in order to suggest something of the role that the concept of 'need' plays in the legitimation of healthcare allocation within the UK. *The New NHS* places PCGs under a dual pressure. On the one hand, they are expected to allocate resource according to need and need alone, for they are part of a universal health service. On the other hand, they must work within 'their population's share of the available resources for hospital and community health services' (para 5.17). This highlights a striking contrast between the issue of allocation in the NHS and in Oregon. Oregon began with a fixed budget and asked what core services could be supplied within that budget. The NHS begins with a commitment to universal access and thus eschews all talk of core services. If a patient needs a service, then it should be available. Consideration of the size of budget that would be necessary to ensure such provision seemingly does not arise. The necessary correlate of this is that, as suggested above, needs claims must be prioritised according to criteria of severity, urgency, ability to benefit and the like; and yet the use of these criteria can themselves be justified only through appeal to deeper moral values.

A more subtle account can be given of this situation. 'Need' remains the foundational value of the NHS. An assumption of *The New NHS* is that the population served by the NHS wants allocation 'according to need and need alone', and that it would reject any appeal to core services and the associated talk of rationing. Core services entail that certain individuals will be rejected by the system and this goes against the grain of inclusive communal commitment. We, as tax-payers (and thus funders of the NHS) and potential patients are morally offended by stories (for example, in the media news) of individuals being refused appropriate treatment. Yet this commitment is ultimately inarticulate, for it shies away from any more profound explication or negotiation of values and thus from any further articulation of the system of principles that might determine allocation.

The above argument has therefore sought to suggest that the concept of 'need' that lies at the core of *The New NHS*, and thus of the responsibilities of PCGs, is profoundly ambiguous. At one level, it appeals to the possibility of a value-neutral needs assessment. At a second level, it recognises that not all needs claims are of equal weight and thus crucially that the prioritisation of those claims requires the invocation of further moral values (such as a concern for saving lives, or for cost-effectiveness, or for personal responsibility in health, and so on). Finally, 'need' may indicate little more that an all-embracing communal commitment to the health service. If these nuances are not distinguished, then PCGs, precisely insofar as they are required to respond to need in its first, clinical sense, will find themselves in a moral vacuum. Faced with a limited budget, and thus with the necessity of prioritising needs claims, they will lack access to the deeper moral values that will allow such prioritisation to be carried out in a defensible form – or worse, they will contribute to the further inhibition of the recognition of prioritisation as an unavoidably moral choice and continue to present it as a matter of mere clinical judgement.

The moral crisis of the NHS may well lie in the fact that it is attempting to conceal the issue of rationing behind the rhetoric of need. Unless the communal values that are concealed within the concept of 'need' are articulated and subject to rational negotiation – and indeed, unless the communities that support the NHS are given their own distinctive voices – the NHS will be undermined by the impossibility of responding to potentially unlimited demands with a strictly limited budget.

References

1 Secretary of State for Health (1997) *The New NHS: modern, dependable.* Cm 3807. The Stationery Office, London.
2 Seedhouse D, Shand J (1998) Health care discourse: a dialogue concerning the philosophy of health care. *Health Care Analysis.* **6**: 237–60.
3 Wiggens D (1991) *Needs, Values, Truth* (2e). Blackwell, Oxford.
4 Edgar A *et al.* (1998) *The Ethical QALY: ethical issues in healthcare resource allocation.* Euromed, Haslemere.
5 Strosberg MA *et al.* (1992) *Rationing America's Medical Care: the Oregon Plan and beyond.* The Brookings Institute, Washington, DC.
6 Honigsbaum F, Richards J, Lockett T (1995) *Priority Setting in Action: purchasing dilemmas.* Radcliffe Medical Press, Oxford.
7 NHS Management Executive (1992) *Local Voices: the views of people in purchasing for health.* NHSME, London.
8 Bowling A (1996) Health care rationing: the public's debate. *BMJ.* **312**: 670–4.
9 Farrell C, Gilbert H (1996) *Health Care Partnerships.* King's Fund, London.
10 Campbell AV (1995) Defining core health services: the New Zealand experience. *Bioethics.* **9**: 252–8.

CHAPTER 2

Why public involvement must be at the heart of primary care

Donna Covey

One of the most exciting aspects of PCGs on their introduction was that they held out the possibility of developing a model of healthcare that would be genuinely responsive to local needs. If this promise can be fulfilled it will represent the greatest revolution in healthcare for a generation, from the patient's perspective. If the health service is to continue to demand public confidence over the next decade, it is essential that there is a greater sense of public ownership of the service. Public involvement is the key to achieving this. We live in an increasingly consumerist society. People have access to 24-hour shopping, telephone banking and home delivery pizza. It is also a society where our views are constantly sought by market researchers and opinion pollsters. Government health policy has, in part, acknowledged these changes in expectations through the introduction of initiatives such as NHS Direct, walk-in centres and the National Patients Survey. At local level, primary care professionals need to grasp the fact that people are increasingly ill at ease with a service where strategic decisions about service delivery are made by health professionals, whether clinicians or managers, with limited dialogue and input from local communities.

Public confidence in the health service has undoubtedly been shaken in recent times. For example, during January 2000, polls were being carried in national newspapers showing that health was the single biggest problem for the government.[1] Newspaper headlines have increasingly told of problems in the health service. The now ritual winter pressures coverage reached fever pitch in the early days of the century.

Although much of the hype and hysteria in the press around the health service has focused on the acute sector and the shortfall in appropriate hospital capacity, primary care has not escaped unscathed. The murder conviction of Hyde GP Harold Shipman has led to press stories about other problem GPs. Once the initial horror of the Shipman case subsided, a robust public debate began about the regulation of GPs. Commentators consistently noted just how little regulation there was of GPs, particularly in single-handed practices. The current limitations on the role of the General Medical Council (GMC) and the secrecy and lack of transparency around the accreditation and disciplining of poor or suspect doctors also came into the spotlight. Within three weeks of the guilty verdict, the GMC announced a series of wide-ranging reforms that would introduce an unprecedented degree of openness into the GMC's workings. In particular, the proportion of lay members on the GMC's disciplinary committees would be increased from less than a third to 50%. In unveiling this welcome recognition that increased public involvement would lead to better regulation, President Sir Donald Irvine, spoke of the 'cosy club atmosphere' of the Council and the need for it to become modern and open to allay public disquiet about the regulation of doctors.

But macro-level changes to regulation and other elements of health policy are only part of the solution. One of the key merits of the PCG model is that it moves decision making down to local level. It therefore provides a unique opportunity to win back public trust at local level, the place where services are delivered. Key to this is involving the public.

However, public involvement must be a core PCG activity from the start. Individual PCGs must not be allowed to defer its development until after all the systems are in place and the plans signed off. It must be an integral part of the process if PCGs and trusts are to fulfil their potential as standard-bearers for an effective, reformed health service fit for the 21st century. Early Department of Health guidance stressed that: 'As well as being accountable to the Health Authority, it is essential that Primary Care Groups are responsive to their stakeholders'.[2]

In theory, this should scarcely have needed saying. In reality, of course, it will need constant repeating as the new model of primary care develops. In the White Paper that kicked off the current round of reforms, the Government promised that: 'Rising public expectations should be channelled into shaping services to make them more responsive to the needs and preferences of the people who use them'. [3]

However, evidence is already starting to emerge that PCGs have travelled down the road from rhetoric to reality without fully taking on board the need for public involvement.

The Audit Commission report *The PCG Agenda*,[4] which looked at how PCGs were developing in their first six months, recommended that: 'PCGs should do more to involve the public'. This recommendation was based on survey findings, which showed that public involvement was a low priority for the majority of fledgling PCGs. For example, the report found that while over 60% of PCGs had measurable hard targets for cost-effective/clinically appropriate prescribing, fewer than 25% had hard targets for improving public involvement in the PCG. Furthermore, the report identified real problems in the way in which PCGs were engaging in dialogue with the public. For example, 70% of PCGs had consulted community health councils (CHCs) on their primary care investment plans, and 42% had asked established patient groups. However, comments were usually requested on plans already made, with only 18% of PCGs seeking fresh suggestions from patient groups on how services could be improved.

There has undoubtedly been a great deal of change in the health service since the election of the current government. However, public involvement and patient participation are the missing links in the progress of the Government's health reforms. Now that the structures are in place in primary care, this gap has to be remedied before PCGs can fulfil their true potential. If public involvement is not built into the work of all PCGs while they are still at the developmental stage, then it will never become a way of life for the health service. And without that, an NHS that is invariably juggling rising expectations that outstrip provision will find itself in an increasingly untenable position. Proper public involvement will lead to informed public debate in place of tabloid head-line hysteria. Public involvement in primary care is key in developing local services that genuinely reflect the needs of the local population, rather than just the view from the surgery window of what is best. As Health Minister Gisela Stuart says, in the introduction to *Patient and Public Involvement in the New NHS*, 'Working effectively in partnership with patients can also be of great benefit to the NHS. It delivers better results for individual patients and better health for the population'.[5]

Lay members on PCGs make a terrific contribution to the development of primary care in their area. Moves to PCT status will increase the numbers of lay members, with the potential to magnify that contribution. But the contribution of individuals alone, however effective, is no substi-tute for engaging the wider population in meaningful dialogue.

Public involvement in primary care is not an optional extra to be intro-duced once the drugs budget has been sorted out, the development plan put in place and the PCT proposals drafted. It must lie at the heart of current developments if they are to fulfil their promise. The case for public involvement is a business case as much as an ideological case. If you ask people what they want and what they think at an early stage in planning, you will get a service that better suits local needs. Furthermore, by engaging local communities in meaningful dialogue, you will get more responsible patients. This means less time and money lost through patients failing to keep appointments, patients turning up at the surgery unnecessarily and other inappropriate behaviour. For example, one of the issues addressed by Greg Dyke in his report on the NHS Charter is that of reducing did not attends (DNAs).[6] Both the examples of best practice quoted in the report involved campaigns carried out jointly with the local CHC. They were also both cases that emphasised direct communication with individual patients and the wider local community. They resulted in significant improvements in effectiveness for the local health authorities concerned.

An informed patient is more likely to be a responsible patient. Developing a more mature dialogue between health service providers and users will result in a more efficient use of resources in the health service. It will mean services that are more suited to the needs of the local population, by being delivered in the right place, at the right time and in the right way. It is also the best way to build and maintain the confidence of local people in their health service.

And that is why the rhetoric of PCGs can only be transformed into reality with proper public involvement. Without public involvement, PCGs run the risk of being just another government reform, with no resonance in the lives of the patients and communities they serve.

References

1 *See*, for example, Healthcare fears dent Blair rating. *The Times*: 27 January 2000.
2 NHS Executive (1998) *Developing Primary Care Groups*. HSC 1998/139. NHSE, London.
3 Secretary of State for Health (1997) *The New NHS: modern, dependable*. Cm 3807. The Stationery Office, London.
4 Audit Commission (2000) *The PCG Agenda: early progress of primary care groups in the new NHS*. Audit Commission, London.
5 Department of Health (1999) *Patient and Public Involvement in the New NHS*. Department of Health, London.
6 Dyke G (1998) *The New NHS Charter. A Different Approach*. Department of Health, London.

CHAPTER 3

Health economics and PCGs

David Kernick and Ruth McDonald

Healthcare professionals involved in PCGs are being asked to make judgements about the relative merits of different interventions which lead to decisions about resource allocation. Economics is concerned with the allocation of scarce resources in a world where these are finite and wants or demands are potentially infinite. Health economics is a sub-discipline of economics, which focuses on the allocation of healthcare resources within the context of scarcity.

The current shift in focus is away from decisions involving individual patients undertaken in the consulting room towards maximising health-care at a PCG level. Against a background of finite budgets the emphasis is on decisions being made in a transparent, fair and efficient manner. To date there has been little formal health economic input into decisions made at PCG level but the number of evaluations of healthcare technologies and treatment options is growing, and pharmaceutical companies are employing the tools of economic evaluation to persuade prescribers of the merits of their products. The growing pressures on health budgets make it increasingly important for decision makers to consider the relative costs and benefits of healthcare interventions.

The aim of this chapter is to offer an understanding of the basic concepts underpinning health economic theory, to explain how the subject may be useful to PCGs and explore why it has yet to have a significant impact in primary care. The chapter concludes with a consideration of future directions for health economics within the context of the evolving PCG framework.

Health, markets and health economics

Economics is the study of how individuals and society choose to employ scarce resources to produce commodities for consumption now or in the future. Not everyone can receive all the healthcare that will benefit them and three basic questions arise:

* What services should be produced?
* How should we produce them?
* Who should receive them?

Although traditionally economists have seen market solutions as producing an efficient allocation of resources, free markets in healthcare are rare. This is because the commodity of healthcare is characterised by certain features which render market solutions to the problem of supply and demand for care unsuitable. For example, unlike other commodities traded in markets, the need for healthcare is uncertain and difficult to predict. Additionally, consumers do not have perfect information to allow them to make choices about consumption. This leads to a reliance on clinicians to make choices on their behalf, but these same clinicians as suppliers of care are not impartial individuals in the process. A further complication is that one individual's consumption of healthcare with regard to immunisation, for example, impacts on the health of others in the community.

What do health economists do?

Health economists are not accountants. Although they are interested in costs, unlike accountants, economists also consider health outcomes. Additionally, the definition of costs used by economists is much broader than that which preoccupies accountants. Money does not have to change hands for costs to be relevant, though economists acknowledge the difficulties of valuing items, such as informal care, which are not traded in a market.

At a global or macro-economic level, health economists study different healthcare funding systems, derive techniques to measure and value health, analyse the demand for healthcare in relationship to its supply, and aid healthcare planning and budgeting. Cost-of-illness studies attempt to represent the burden of disease from a particular ailment or medical condition in monetary terms. However, these studies do not consider what can be done to reduce this burden, and they consider costs and not outcomes. Pharmaceutical companies undertake such studies to support marketing, but the value to NHS decision makers is dubious.

At a micro-economic level, the regulation of GPs and the incentive structures which influence their behaviour have also been the focus of health economic analysis. Within this context, the emphasis has been on considerations of asymmetry of information, financial incentives, supplier-induced demand and GP referral behaviour. The Department of Health has stated that incentives should be in place for prescribing, referral and commissioning.[1] There is some evidence that doctors are influenced by the way in which they are paid, but the number of high-quality studies is small and the available evidence does not support the strong opinions that are often expressed on the relative merits of different payment systems. However, before the behaviour of primary care practitioners can be influenced, policy makers need to know the direction in which change should occur. This major area of work for health economists is known as *economic evaluation* and will be the most important element of health economics at PCG level. Economic evaluation is a comparative analysis of alternative courses of action in terms of both their costs and consequences.[2] But before we can understand how economic evaluation can help PCGs, four key concepts that underpin health economic theory must be described.

1 *Scarcity and sacrifice*: because resources are scarce, choices have to be made about how to consume these resources. Sacrifice is inevitable.
2 *Opportunity cost*: the notion of 'opportunity cost' is central to economic analysis. When deciding to spend resources on treatment Y, this means we cannot now use those resources for other healthcare programmes or treatments. The opportunity cost of treatment Y is the value of the next best alternative use of those resources. This reflects the fact that resources are scarce and that choices have to be made about the best way of allocating them.
3 *Utility*: utility can be thought of as a measure of satisfaction that we obtain from the consumption of goods or services. Economic theory suggests that the rational individual will make consumption choices which maximise the utility obtained from their limited resources.
4 *Efficiency*: in general, efficiency refers to getting the most out of limited resources, either by achieving a given output from the minimum possible input or producing the maximum possible from a fixed resource.

Economic evaluation

An economic evaluation relates inputs (resources) to outputs (benefits and the values attached to them) of alternative interventions to facilitate decision making when resources are scarce. Economic evaluations always consider outcomes as well as costs, although they differ with regard to the valuation of consequences.

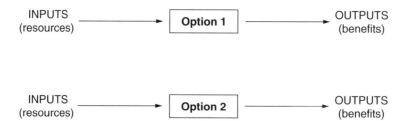

Figure 3.1   An economic analysis relates inputs (resources) to outputs (benefits and the values attached to them) of alternative interventions to facilitate decision making when resources are scarce.

This framework seeks to organise and clarify information so as to facilitate decision making. It can help to decide between innovations with different objectives with the aim of maximising health benefit. For example, should a PCG increase spending on coronary artery bypass grafts or hip replacements? Alternatively, it can look at different ways to meet a particular objective. For example, how should heart failure be treated? Should asthma care be delivered by doctors or nurses?

When undertaking economic evaluations, there are two important factors to be considered, perspective and the margin.

Perspective
Economic evaluations are undertaken from a particular perspective, which will determine which costs and benefits to quantify. This could be a societal, NHS, public sector, PCG, GP practice or other perspective. Often the perspective taken by a study is that of the NHS, but this could be much wider. The advantage of a societal perspective is that it takes account of all costs and benefits beyond the narrow NHS field. Often, NHS decision makers are concerned with NHS budgets and take an NHS viewpoint, which may not always concur with the PCG or GP practice perspectives. When reading a study, it is important to ascertain that all relevant costs and consequences have been included.

The margin
Most decisions in healthcare are concerned with the expansion or contraction of services (i.e. changes at the margin). As the relationship between costs and benefits is rarely linear, health economists stress the importance of analysing changes in terms of their marginal effects – a marginal analysis. This illustrates how increments in utility or benefit change with increments in resources invested in order to maximise additional returns from marginal increases in resource allocation.

An extreme example of the importance of marginal analysis is illustrated in Table 3.1. This example shows costs and benefits in relation to a screening test for colorectal cancer, in terms of dollars expended and cases detected, for a population of 10 000 individuals screened. The test is carried out a number of times on one specimen with cases detected increasing as number of tests increase.

For six tests the average cost is $2451 per case detected, compared with $1175 for one test. However, the marginal benefit of a sixth test (i.e. the additional benefit of moving from five to six tests) is only 0.0003 additional cases detected, while the marginal cost of an extra test for all those previously testing negative is $13 190. This gives a staggering marginal cost per case detected of over $43 million!

Table 3.1   Marginal and average costs of case detection on stool samples for carcinoma of colon (costs in dollars)

Test	No. of cases detected	Marginal gain cases detected	Total cost*	Marginal cost	Marginal cost per case detected	Average
1	65.9469	65.9469	77 511	77 511	1175	1175
2	71.4424	5.4955	107 690	30 179	5492	1507
3	71.9004	0.4580	130 199	22 509	49 146	1811
4	71.9386	0.0382	148 116	17 917	469 031	2059
5	71.9417	0.0031	163 141	15 025	4 846 774	2268
6	71.9420	0.0003	176 331	13 190	43 966 667	2451

Adapted from Neuhauser and Lewicki.[3]

Measuring benefits in an economic evaluation

Patients can benefit from both health-related and non-health-related benefits. For example, patients receive satisfaction from reassurance, choice, information and availability of medical services. The term 'process utility' is used to describe such benefits but in practice, economic evaluation has focused on more tangible health-related outcomes. There are four main methods of economic evaluation, which are characterised by the benefits that are measured as shown in Table 3.2.

Table 3.2 Types of economic evaluation

Form of evaluation	Measurement and valuation of outcomes
Cost-minimisation analysis	Outcomes are assumed to be equivalent. Focus of measurement is on costs
Cost-effectiveness analysis	Natural units (e.g. life years gained, deaths prevented)
Cost-utility analysis	Health state values based on individual preferences (e.g. quality-adjusted life years gained)
Cost-benefit analysis	All outcomes valued in monetary units (e.g. valuation of amount willing to pay to prevent a death)

Cost-minimisation analysis
In cost-minimisation analysis (CMA), the consequences of two or more interventions being compared are equivalent. The analysis therefore focuses on costs alone, although the evidence of equivalent outcomes should be established prior to consideration of costs. In practice, there are few examples of interventions which produce exactly equivalent outcomes. An example of where this type of analysis might be used would be the comparison of two drugs, which have the same treatment effects and side effects. The economic analysis would consider drug costs and any associated costs such as patient monitoring (e.g. liver function tests with statins) and GP time.

Cost-effectiveness analysis
Cost-effectiveness analysis (CEA) is used to compare drugs or programmes which have a common health outcome (e.g. reduction in blood pressure, life years saved).[4] In CEA, the results are usually presented in the form of a ratio (e.g. costs per life year gained). If two treatments, A and B, are compared and costs are lower for A and outcomes better, then treatment A is said to dominate. If, as is more commonly the case with a new drug, for example, costs are higher for one treatment, but benefits are higher too, it is necessary to calculate the *incremental* cost-effectiveness ratio of treatment A versus treatment B. This ratio compares the two interventions in terms of the extra benefits obtained for the extra cost and is calculated as:

$$\frac{(\text{Cost of A} - \text{Cost of B})}{(\text{Benefits of A} - \text{Benefits of B})}$$

Some CEAs use intermediate outcome measures, such as cases detected, however, it is important to ensure that where these intermediate measures are used, they have some clinical meaning in terms of long-term outcome for patients.

Cost-utility analysis

CEA is useful for interventions which impact on one dimension (e.g. length of life) in terms of outcomes. However, it is often the case that treatments impact both on quality and quantity of life (i.e. more than one dimension). Where this is the case, cost-utility analysis (CUA) can be used to assess costs and benefits of interventions.[5] The most frequently used measure in CUA is the QALY. Benefits are measured based on impact on length and quality of life and these changes are valued relative to one another to produce an overall index of health gain. QALYs reflect people's preferences for different health states.

Although QALYs are the most commonly used measure in CUAs, they have been criticised in a number of areas.[6] In addition to methodological debates about the extent to which QALYs adequately capture people's preferences, there are questions about whose values are to be used in the construction of QALYs. Should this be the patient who knows the condition, healthcare professionals who often claim to know what is important to patients or the members of society who actually pay for the treatment and are potential patients themselves?

QALYs have also been criticised for being ageist and for failing to adequately capture disease-specific aspects of health states. QALYs aim to provide a simple measure, but some critics take issue with the basic premise underlying QALYS: that something as complex as health-related quality of life can be reduced to a single value.

Cost-benefit analysis

In cost-benefit analysis (CBA), attempts are made to value all the costs and consequences of an intervention in monetary terms.[7] The data requirements for performing a CBA are large and methodological issues around the valuation of non-monetary benefits such as lives saved makes conducting CBA problematic. Values may be derived by asking members of the public or patients or other groups about their willingness to pay for things such as prevention, cure or screening tests. There are many problems in using willingness-to-pay (WTP) methods, including the issue of whose values should be used, how to give respondents sufficient information to enable informed choice and how to obtain values that are not related to respondents income.

Cost-consequences analysis

In some cases, studies consider multiple outcomes, and costs and outcomes are presented in a disaggregated form. This avoids the need to represent results as a crude ratio which may represent a gross oversimplification of the study. These evaluations are sometimes referred to as cost-consequence analyses.

Measuring costs in an economic evaluation

Direct costs are those costs associated directly with a healthcare intervention (e.g. physician salaries, patient transport costs). Indirect costs are costs associated with reduced productivity due to illness, disability and death. Studies which take a societal perspective usually include both direct and indirect costs. Some studies may include intangible costs which relate to the cost of pain and suffering resulting from an illness or treatment.[8] The costs to be included in any study will depend on the study perspective.

Table 3.3 Cost definitions used in health economics

Direct costs	Costs associated directly with a healthcare intervention (e.g. GP salaries, drug costs)
Indirect costs	Costs associated with reduced productivity due to illness, disability or death
Intangible costs	The cost of pain and suffering occurring as a result of illness or treatment
Marginal cost	The extra cost of one extra unit of service provided

Health economists recognise the importance of valuing a broad range of cost inputs rather than only those items for which a market price is readily available or which impact on the NHS budget. For example, indirect costs incurred by patients in terms of loss of employment or leisure time will be an important contribution to studies in primary care. However, the calculation of such costs is problematic. Intangible costs are even more difficult to quantify in monetary terms.

Acting on the results for economic evaluation

Economic evaluation facilitates rather than directs decisions in health. Nevertheless there are a number of 'decision rules' that are relevant. To undertake an economic evaluation, the alternatives to be examined must be identified. To establish whether an intervention represents good value for money it is always necessary to compare its costs and benefits with those of an alternative. The alternative may be a placebo treatment, the next best alternative, usual care or doing nothing. Guidelines have been developed which aim to maintain consistency and compatibility across economic studies, but these are of a voluntary nature.[9]

In CMA, since treatments produce equivalent outcomes, the preferred option is the lowest cost treatment. For CEA and CUA the issue is more complex. Although treatment A's incremental cost per life year or QALY gained may be £5000 more than treatment B, if it has the potential to save more lives, then society or the health policy maker might feel that £5000 is a small price to pay for a life year. In other words, CEA and CUA present incremental ratios, but unless one treatment dominates (i.e. it is superior in terms of costs and outcomes) the final decision revolves around how much we are willing to pay for extra benefits.

The advantage of CBA is that there is a clear decision rule for the process. Costs and benefits are presented in monetary terms and if costs to society are outweighed by the benefits (in monetary terms) then the programme under evaluation should be adopted.

Health economics in practice

The volume of publications reporting the results of health economic analyses has increased dramatically in recent years but little is known about the impact of health economics on local resource allocation decisions. In a recent review, Coyle found that the impact of economic evaluations in the form of directly influencing healthcare decision making was difficult to detect.[10] More recently, a retrospective assessment of the Health of the Nation policy, the first strategic approach in the NHS to direct the context for health policy making, concluded that 'there was little evidence that health economics had made any significant contribution to the way that the policy was perceived, priority areas were chosen or targets were pursued'. Concern was expressed over the 'tunnel vision of health economists'.[11] However, the criterion of clinical cost-effectiveness is used by NICE to evaluate new drugs and technologies.

Often evaluations and conclusions are reported in a way that does not facilitate their understanding or use by health professionals, let alone patients. In many areas there is disagreement among health economists about matters of principle and methodology.[12] Methodological issues aside, there are other concerns which relate to the use of simplistic rules in the complex context of NHS decision making. Health economic 'solutions' sometimes fail to consider the healthcare environment in which decisions often have to be made on the basis of incomplete information. In this environment, simple solutions do not always exist and the delivery of healthcare is complicated by considerations other than cost-effectiveness. There may be cognitive and value mismatch between political directives, technical frameworks, those who commission care, service providers and patients. Decisions in healthcare must recognise issues such as equality of access, patient and carer expectations, the need to maintain a therapeutic relationship over time, containing costs, obtaining value for money, avoiding media attention and law courts.

The decision-making context in primary care is one of uncertainty and ambiguity and economic frameworks need to reflect this complex environment.

Towards a pragmatic framework for PCG decision makers

There are signs that health economists are responding to the environment of primary care. Drummond has warned against standardising methodology of economic evaluation and emphasising the difference between cookbook and toolkit approaches.[13] The importance of effectiveness studies has been recognised where trials are undertaken in naturalistic settings that reflect the context of the environment in which an intervention is to be delivered.[14]

Pragmatic economic evaluations are being developed which can make judgements more explicit and help frame information. For example, programme budgeting and marginal analysis (PBMA) defines a pragmatic framework for resource allocation which is likely to reflect the environment in which PCGs make their decisions.[15,16]

Programme budgeting and marginal analysis
Programme budgeting (PB) and marginal analysis (MA) are two separate, but related, activities. The basic premise of PB is that it is important to understand how resources are currently spent before thinking about ways of changing this pattern of resource use. The premise underlying MA is that to have more of some services it is necessary to have less of others or, if growth monies are available, that some projects will be funded while others will not. MA asks:

1 If additional resources were allocated to this programme how best could these be deployed to ensure the greatest possible increase in benefit?

2 If resources for the programme are reduced, how best should these reductions be made to ensure the minimum loss of benefit from the programme?

PBMA is a framework which emphasises: (a) use of local cost and activity data; (b) the availability of evidence on effectiveness; and (c) that many decisions are still based on value judgements, but the important thing is to be as open as possible about such judgements. It starts from existing services and examines marginal changes in those services rather than starting with a blank piece of paper and attempting to allocate resources in some hypothetical fashion.

Box 3.1 Five stages in the programme budgeting and marginal analysis framework

1 Identification of a healthcare programme, usually disease-based (e.g. cancers, coronary heart disease), or client group (e.g. children, elderly).
2 Production of a statement of expenditure and activity by subprogrammes, i.e. the programme budget, e.g. by primary, secondary and tertiary healthcare.
3 Generation of a list of candidate services for expansion and reduction.
4 Measurement of the costs and benefits of proposed candidates for expansion and reduction, i.e. conduct marginal analysis.
5 Preparation of recommendations for purchasing.

PBMA emphasises the need to include relevant stakeholders in all stages of the process, but this does require time and commitment from participants in addition to data on costs and benefits of existing services and any alternatives. The limited evidence available suggests that this approach offers potential for use at PCG level in relation to planning and commissioning of health services.

Conclusion

By developing a basic understanding of economic principles, PCGs will be able to draw on the critical insights of economic theory, while at the same time recognising its limitations. Health economics, by providing an explicit framework for considering alternatives, can help PCGs and individual practitioners move beyond gut feeling towards a more systematic approach to decision making. Some health economists are already working more closely with those they seek to influence by developing bottom-up research and valuation techniques relevant to context. PCGs and health economists need to work together in the quest for decision-making frameworks which reflect the complexity of primary care and the wider health and social care environment. Such frameworks need to be accessible and acceptable to those who commission and deliver health-care and, importantly, to the end users of the service.

References

1 Health Service Circular 1998/228. Department of Health, London.
2 Drummond M (1994) *Economic Analysis Alongside Control Trials.* Department of Health, London.
3 Neuhauser D, Lewicki A (1975) What do we gain from the six-stool Guaic? *NEJM.* **293**(5): 226–8.
4 Robinson R (1993) Cost effective analysis. *BMJ.* **307**: 793–5.
5 Robinson R (1993) Cost utility analysis. *BMJ.* **307**: 859–62.
6 Carr-Hill RA (1991) Allocating resources to health care: is the QALY a technical solution to a political problem? *International Journal of Health Services.* **21**: 351–63.
7 Robinson R (1993) Economic evaluation and health care: cost benefit analysis. *BMJ.* **307**: 924–6.
8 Kernick D (2000) Costing principles in primary care. *Family Practice.* **17**: 1766–70.
9 Drummond MF, Jefferson TD (1996) Guidelines for authors and peer reviewers of economic submissions to the BMJ. *BMJ.* **313**: 275–83.
10 Coyle D (1993) Increasing the impact of economic evaluation on health care decision making (Discussion paper 108). Centre for Health Economics, University of York.
11 *The Health of the Nation Policy Assessed* (1998) Department of Health, London.
12 Kernick DP (1998) Has health economics lost its way? *BMJ.* **317**: 197–9.
13 Drummond M, Brandt A, Luce B *et al.* (1993) Standardising method-ologies for economic evaluation in health care. Practice problems and potential. *International Journal of Technology Assessment in Health Care.* **9**(1): 26–36.
14 Revicki D, Frank L (1999) Pharmacoeconomic evaluation in the real world: effectiveness versus effficacy studies. *Pharmacoeconomics.* **15**(5): 433–4.
15 Craig N, Donaldson C, Walker A (1995) *Programme Budgeting and Marginal Analysis: a handbook for applying economics in health care*

purchasing. Commissioned by SNAP, Scottish Forum for Public Health Medicine.

16 Scott A, Currie N, Donaldson C (1998) Evaluating innovation in general practice: a pragmatic framework using programme budgeting and marginal analysis. *Family Practice.* **15**(3): 216–22.

Further reading

General background

Donaldson C, Gerard K (1993) Markets and health care. In: *Economics of Health Care Financing: the visible hand.* Macmillan, London.

Normand C (1991) Economics, health and the economics of health. *BMJ.* **303**: 1572–7.

Williams A (1987) Health economics: the cheerful face of the dismal science? In: *Health and Economics.* MacMillan Press, London, pp 1–11.

Economic evaluation

Byford S, Raftery J (1998) Perspectives in economic evaluation. *BMJ.* **316**: 1529–30.

Jefferson T, Demicheli V, Mugford M (1996) *Elementary Economic Evaluation in Health Care.* BMJ Publishing Group, London.

CHAPTER 4

Quality indicators for primary care

Martin Marshall

A doctor working in general practice in the NHS 30 or 40 years ago would hardly recognise the demands and expectations made on today's GPs. Within the memory of some practising doctors, most GPs worked in isolation, detached from peers, loosely accountable to administrators for reimbursement purposes only, and implicitly trusted by their patients to be competent and to remain up to date. Judgements were rarely made about the quality of care provided by GPs. This was probably just as well, since there were few agreed criteria by which to judge whether the care provided was good or fell below acceptable standards.

Today's GPs operate in a very different environment – more accountable for their actions, more often judged by peers, by managers and by patients, and less likely to be trusted simply because they are professionals.[1] There are many interrelated reasons for these dramatic changes. In part, they are a consequence of the widespread deprofessionalisation of society and the high expectations resulting from consumerism. There are now greater demands for information and this feeds, and is fed by, the increasing availability of computerised data and advances in methods of measuring quality of care.[2] Politicians' demands for efficiency increase the pressure on managers to judge whether doctors are providing value for money. Alongside these changes have been some high-profile examples of poor-quality practice that have dented the public's confidence in implicit professional self-regulation.[3]

One of the consequences of these changes has been an increasing interest in the use of 'quality indicators'.[4] The term is often used loosely to describe any objective measure relating to the quality of care, but useful quality indicators should satisfy certain specific criteria (Box 4.1).[5,6]

This chapter looks at the implications of the potential use and abuse of quality indicators relevant to the emerging PCGs and PCTs. It will concentrate on the indicators relevant to general practice-based primary care, since this is where attention has been focused in recent years.

Box 4.1 Characteristics of useful quality indicators

Useful quality indicators should:

1 represent measurable aspects of care
2 be based on scientific evidence (and prioritised according to the strength of the evidence), supported by expert opinion where necessary
3 represent aspects of care that are within the control of the practitioners for which they are designed
4 be appropriate for the clinical situation in which they are used
5 be used to highlight areas for further investigation, not to make definitive judgements about performance.

Adapted from Lawrence & Olesen[6] and Baker & Fraser.[7]

Categorisation of quality indicators

The bewildering number of primary care indicators that have been developed and marketed in recent years has resulted in the need for some form of classification. Such a system might help users to compare the relative merits of indicators relating to similar areas, identify areas where measurement tools are lacking and help PCGs to select a set of indicators relevant to their needs.

At the most basic level, the classification of indicators may mirror Donabedian's quality triad of structure, process and outcome.[8] Structural indicators, such as the number of health professionals per head of population, are least likely to satisfy the criteria for effective indicators. This is because structural aspects of care are rarely within the control of health professionals and because there is little evidence that changing structures has a significant effect on quality of care. Process indicators (e.g. the examination of the feet of diabetic patients) and outcome indicators (e.g. patient satisfaction) tend to be more useful as indicators of quality. The development of valid and reliable outcome indicators would be an ideal but this presents both theoretical and practical problems, particularly in primary care.[6] Outcomes are often long delayed, easily confounded and weakly related to the current activity of health professionals. Process indicators, in contrast, are easily measured, sensitive to changes in quality of care and readily 'owned' by health professionals. Process indicators which are based on scientific evidence linking them to effective outcomes, sometimes referred to as intermediate outcomes, are generally recognised as the most useful indicators in primary care.

A more detailed classification might make use of Maxwell's dimensions of quality.[9] These reflect the diverse and sometimes conflicting aspects of quality of care and include access (e.g. waiting times for a routine appointment), availability (e.g. whether a practice has an on-site physiotherapist), acceptability (e.g. patient satisfaction), efficiency (e.g. prescribing costs), effectiveness (e.g. use of aspirin in patients at high risk of ischaemic heart disease) and equity (e.g. relative waiting times for operations between different population groups).

The classification of quality indicators in terms of modalities (prevention, screening, diagnosis, management and follow-up) or diseases (acute or chronic conditions) can be useful because it reflects the familiar medical model and highlights areas for which there are few measures of quality. For example, while chronic care is represented by many different indicators, the development of quality indicators for the care of acute problems in general practice has been largely ignored.[10]

With the launch of the National Performance Assessment Framework, the UK government has described six domains within which quality will be assessed in the NHS.[11] This classification of indicators is likely to dominate the policy agenda for the foreseeable future. The framework, together with possible examples of some basic primary care quality indicators for each domain, is described in Table 4.1. The indicator set is likely to be modified (and probably to expand) in the future as the science of quality measurement and the availability of data in primary care improves.

Uses of quality indicators in primary care

Quality indicators are viewed by some commentators as little more than proscriptive and punitive tools to be used by managers to judge health professional activity.[12] This narrow perspective is only one, somewhat negative, interpretation of their use and in reality quality indicators can be used in a wide variety of ways (Box 4.2).

Box 4.2   Potential uses of quality indicators

- Facilitate regulation
- Ensure accountability
- Assist purchasing
- Inform service users
- Influence provider behaviour
- Encourage quality improvement

Table 4.1   National Performance Assessment Framework classification of potential primary care quality indicators

Domain	Examples of quality indicators
Health improvement	Number of females under 16 registered with GP for contraceptive services
	Percentage of practices offering diabetic disease management clinics
Fair access	Number of practice nurses per weighted population
	Percentage of practices offering child health surveillance clinics
Effective delivery of appropriate healthcare	Ratio of asthma preventative drugs to bronchodilators
	Volume of benzodiazepines prescribed
Efficiency	Generic prescribing rates
Patient/carer experience	Having to wait three or more days for an appointment
	Patient complaints
Health outcomes of NHS care	Percentage of target population screened for cervival cancer
	Percentage of target population vaccinated for childhood diseases

Viewed individually, indicators do not necessarily satisfy all of these potential uses. For example, the generic prescribing rate represents a good indicator to ensure accountability for efficient use of resources but does not provide particularly useful information for the majority of users. Sometimes there is a risk that indicators are used in a frankly contradictory way – the use of proscriptive indicators to identify unacceptable practice may be at odds with the facilitation of professionally led quality improvement. For example, using acute hospital admissions for asthma as an indicator of the quality of asthma care in general practice (on the assumption that good primary care reduces acute exacerbations) might act as a perverse incentive to admitting patients with severe asthma.

The likely use of the quality indicators therefore dictates the form, data sources, necessary rigour and criteria used to evaluate the impact of the indicator.[13] In addition, the various stakeholders are likely to prioritise the use of indicators in different ways: government for regulation, professional bodies for accountability, health authorities and PCTs for resource allocation, the general public for information and to help them make choices and individual health professionals to encourage quality improvement.

The characteristics of good indicators

Few indicators will satisfy all the criteria described in Box 4.1 and inevitably the indicator sets that might be used by PCGs will represent a compromise between what is desirable and what is practically attainable. There is a danger, however, that the quality indicators advocated by health authorities and the NHS Executive in the past have been too much of a compromise to achieve any buy-in or sense of ownership by those who are most likely to benefit from their use.[14] Box 4.3 highlights the issues that clinical governance leads in PCGs might consider when choosing an indicator set which balances the requirements to promote professionally owned quality improvement, to facilitate regulation and to ensure public accountability.

Box 4.3 Factors that influence the choice of an indicator set

1 **What do you want to achieve by using quality indicators?** It is appropriate to use indicators for regulatory purposes, for accountability and for quality improvement. The choice and method of use of the indicators should be determined by their purpose.

2 **What are the priority areas for your PCG?** It is not possible or desirable to attempt to select an indicator set that addresses all areas of practice. This would be too cumbersome and resource-intensive for all the stakeholders. An indicator set should be selected for a limited number of local and national priority areas (e.g. access, mental health issues). These might be determined by the prevalence of the condition under study, the implications and cost of quality problems in this area, and the importance of the area to those who will make greatest use of the results.

3 **What are the scientific properties of the indicators?** Quality indicators should be valid (i.e. should measure what they are

---

designed to measure), reliable (i.e. produce reproducible results) and sensitive (i.e. should reflect changes in quality when they occur). It is, however, inappropriate to aim for perfection and compromises will have to be made. The rigour of indicators used to identify unacceptable performance should be greater than that required for quality improvement purposes. The scientific rigour also has to be greater if the indicators are to be used to compare performance at a low level (e.g. individual GPs), rather than at a high level (i.e. between PCGs).

4 **Is the indicator set comprehensive within the chosen subject area?** In the past there has been a tendency to focus on indicators relating to structural issues. More recently outcome indicators have become fashionable. Indicators representing all three of Donabedian's quality triad have their advantages and disadvantages and a balance should be achieved. In addition, indicators should reflect the broad range of clinical care, from prevention and screening to diagnosis, management and follow-up.

5 **What data will you use to operationalise the indicators?** Data may be collected from routine administrative databases (e.g. immunisation rates, referral rates to hospitals), extracted from patients' records or derived from specially designed surveys. Administrative data is most commonly used because it is readily available and cheap to extract but it is less likely to reflect the complexities of clinical care. Data derived from surveys or extracted from patient records are often more sensitive and meaningful but more expensive to collect.

PCGs will not be restricted to the primary care indicator set produced by the Department of Health as part of the National Performance Assessment Framework. Indeed, most of the currently proposed indicators are not directly relevant to primary care. However, it is likely that there will be a statutory requirement to contribute to the framework and it is therefore appropriate to review the extent to which some of the proposed primary care indicators (Table 4.1) satisfy the criteria for effective quality indicators.

The proposed indicators reflect the six domains of quality outlined as part of the government's policy for the NHS and therefore have a clear conceptual basis for their choice. The indicator set is largely reliant on routinely available administrative data and is therefore weak on clinical areas such as the effective delivery of appropriate care. A trade-off has therefore been made between the clinical credibility of the proposed indicators and resource constraints. The new survey of patient experiences provides useful data in areas such as access, communication and satisfaction, which builds on the administrative data.[15] The validity, reliability and sensitivity of the indicators are largely unknown and further research is required before they achieve an acceptable level of credibility among clinicians.

Development and operationalisation of quality indicators

A large number of primary care quality indicators are available to the PCGs that want to take a set of established indicators 'off the shelf'. A set of potentially useful indicators has been published recently by the National Primary Care Research and Development Centre[10] and further guidance will be published in mid-2000. Accessing these indicators has the obvious advantage of bypassing the long and expensive task of developing indicators *de novo*. Rarely would it be appropriate for a PCG to invent new quality indicators but nevertheless they should adopt an appropriately sceptical approach to the indicator sets that are currently available. Understanding where indicators come from assists this process.

The least rigorous approach is for individuals or groups to simply select an indicator because it represents an aspect of care that is easy to measure or for which data are readily available. Some of the indicators used within the NHS fall into this category and while the indicators have the advantage of being cheap to develop and use, they are rarely sensitive or meaningful in terms of measuring the quality of clinical care. For example, gathering data for an indicator that measures the number of male GPs per weighted population will be quick and easy but will have little or no impact on the care provided by practices within a PCG.

The next way of developing indicators is to utilise an evidence-based approach.[16] Such indicators are based only on high-quality scientific evidence from randomised controlled trials or meta-analyses of such trials. Examples might include the use of aspirin for the secondary prevention of coronary or ischaemic cerebrovascular events or influenza vaccination for those aged over 65 years. Such indicators have an obvious advantage in terms of their rigour and their acceptability to practitioners but restricting primary care quality assessment to only those areas that have a firm scientific base has obvious limitations.

These limitations can be overcome by adopting a third approach to the development of quality indicators. This approach combines the available scientific evidence with the opinion and experience of experts in the field. The RAND/UCLA expert panel procedure is the most systematic and rigorous method of achieving this.[17–19]

The scientific evidence, in the form of a systematic or semi-systematic review, together with a preliminary set of quality indicators derived from the literature, is presented to a panel of experts. This panel, composed of about nine members, is nominated or selected from the relevant professional body – for example, a primary care panel might be made up of Fellows by Assessment of the Royal College of General Practitioners. The panel members are individually asked to rate the indicators in terms of their validity as measures of quality in primary care and the feasibility of data collection to operationalise the indicators. This rating is based not only on the scientific evidence provided for them, but also on their expertise and practical experience. The ratings are then analysed to determine the individual scores for each indicator and the level of agreement between panel members. The scores are fed back to the panel members, who meet to discuss their individual ratings and then re-rate the indicators. The second round of ratings are therefore based on expert group discussion, as well as individual expert experience and the scientific literature.

This approach helps to fill the gaps in the literature and ensures that the scientific data are applicable to clinical practice. The final set of indicators are those that have achieved high validity and feasibility scores and a high level of agreement between panelists.

Once the quality indicator set has been selected, it needs to be operationalised or described in detailed terms that allow a data collector to extract data from the relevant source. This is not as easy or straightforward as it might appear. The prescription of aspirin to patients at high risk of ischaemic heart disease is a good example of a simple indicator that presents problems for data collectors. How do they identify patients who should be receiving aspirin? Are the data readily extracted from electronic records or do the paper records have to be examined? What criteria would they accept for patients for whom aspirin is contraindicated? How do they take over-the-counter prescriptions into account? Who should extract the data? What training do the data extractors need? How do they gain access to individual patient records? Who's permission do they ask? What data collection tools do the extractors use? Who will analyse the data and how will it be done? How will the results be presented and who to? Will the results be published? How can they be used to improve the quality of care? This list of questions is by no means exhaustive but it does demonstrate the complexity of operationalising quality indicators in primary care.

Public reporting of quality indicators

One of the inevitable consequences of producing information about the quality of care in general practice is a demand to make that information available to the public.[1] Such disclosure of objective performance data allows comparisons to be made among providers (GPs, practices or PCGs), over time or against defined standards of care. This will require a significant culture change that might in the future be appropriately led by the PCGs and PCTs.

Public disclosure has both potential risks and potential benefits for GPs, patients and the NHS. It could help to focus attention on specific problem areas by highlighting both absolute levels of quality of care and the degree of variation among practitioners, practices or PCGs. Making performance information public could serve to heighten the sensitivity of members of the primary healthcare team to the results and increase the chances of remedial action being taken where necessary.[14] In addition, public disclosure of performance data can help patients to make informed choices and to have an informed discussion with their GP.[20] Making performance information public may also help to highlight significant underperformance of individuals or resource problems resulting in poor quality of care.

There are also some significant risks associated with publishing quality indicators. GPs might feel threatened as they move from a predominantly data-deficient style of practice to one characterised by explicit account-ability based on their own and their colleagues' measured performance. Public recognition of deficiencies in the quality of care may result in patients losing trust in their GP and misleading information may damage a GP's reputation. Technical issues pertaining to public reporting, such as reporting levels, risk adjustment and sampling methods, are beyond the scope of this chapter but there is little doubt that the information contained in public reports can easily be misinterpreted by the public, the media, health managers and health professionals themselves.

At present there are few examples of public reporting of comparative performance data in UK general practice but the Labour Government has made it clear that this is a central plank of their health policy in the future. This policy is unlikely to change, despite the evidence from the USA that at present the various stakeholders make little use of compar-ative information.[14, 21–24] Already in the UK, the media is showing interest in the performance of hospitals, with comparative mortality rates for specific conditions published in 1999 for Wales and England.[25] Before too long it is highly likely that local newspapers will start to publish information about, for example, the relative performance of neighbouring practices or PCGs in terms of patient satisfaction with access to appointments or the percentage of hypertensive patients with well-controlled blood pressure.

   Public reporting of quality indicators in general practice is an inevitable consequence of the societal trend to greater openness and greater accountability. PCGs are in a prime position to ensure that this is conducted in such a way that the benefits are maximised and the risks are reduced.

Disadvantages of using quality indicators in general practice

The fact that the increasing use of explicit quality indicators in general practice is inevitable and has several potential benefits does not mean that their use is without risk. Potential problems and unintended consequences have been well-described by a number of commentators and are summarised in Box 4.4.[10, 26, 27]

Box 4.4   Disadvantages of using quality indicators

- Quality indicators measure only easily measured aspects of care and fail to encompass the more subjective aspects of general practice.
- They encourage a 'piecemeal' approach to a holist and integrated discipline.
- It can be difficult to interpret apparent differences between providers.
- They are expensive and time-consuming to produce and at present there is little evidence that they are an effective way of spending limited resources.
- They can encourage a 'blame' culture and discourage internal professional motivation to improve.
- They can lead to 'tunnel vision', i.e. an inappropriate focus on what is being measured.
- They can lead to short-termism rather than long-term strategic planning and might highlight differences in the objectives of the various primary care stakeholders.
- Clinical data required for quality indicators can be difficult to access and are of questionable quality in many general practices.

- Demonstration of deficiencies might lead to an erosion of trust and morale in the health service.
- They can offer perverse incentives and lead to manipulation or massaging of the data.

Most of these problems are predictable and their impact can be minimised if quality indicators are used carefully.

Quality indicators in the context of primary care health policy in the UK

Health policy decisions relating to the quality of care provided in general practice are being made at a bewilderingly rapid rate. What some see as a coherent and structured approach to quality improvement, others perceive to be threatening and confused. Primary healthcare professionals could justifiably be mystified by the large number of initiatives that have been launched since 1997 and which directly effect their daily practice. Where do quality indicators fit into this picture? The final section in this chapter places quality indicators in the context of the following initiatives.

The National Institute for Clinical Excellence (NICE)

NICE is responsible for identifying new and existing health technologies that would benefit from appraisal and for collecting evidence to assess the clinical and cost-effectiveness of the interventions. In addition, it will produce and disseminate guidelines and co-ordinate a national strategy to ensure equitable and effective health interventions across the NHS. The production and dissemination of explicit quality indicators (or audit criteria) will be an integral part of the guideline development.

National Service Frameworks (NSFs)

The NSFs set national standards and define service models for specific diseases, services or care groups. In addition, they are responsible for ensuring that the models are implemented in a co-ordinated fashion across the different sections of the NHS and for establishing performance measures against which progress can be measured. The Calman–Hine NSF for cancer services is already established and an NSF for mental health services was published recently. Service frameworks for coronary heart disease and diabetes will be published in the near future. Again, the use of explicit quality indicators to assess the rate of implementation of the frameworks will be a key part of the exercise.

Clinical governance

Clinical governance is a framework through which healthcare organisations are accountable for continuously improving the quality of their services and safeguarding high standards of care. The aim is to create an environment in which excellence can flourish. The process is led in the main by health professionals but includes all relevant stakeholders. A variety of mechanisms will be used to implement and monitor clinical governance. Some of these will already be familiar to many primary care professionals, for example peer review, audit and educational initiatives. In addition to these 'softer' monitoring and improvement mechanisms it is likely that explicit quality indicators will play an increasingly important part.

The Commission for Health Improvement (CHI)

CHI is an independent 'watchdog', which will be used to monitor the performance of healthcare provider organisations. It is proposed that it will combine the roles of inspection and regulation with consultation and guidance. It will ensure that clinical governance processes are in place, carry out a rolling programme of inspections of NHS organisations and intervene if local quality assurance mechanisms have not been effective. It is likely that hospital and community trusts will be inspected first, then PCTs and finally PCGs. CHI will use public performance data, alongside other types of evidence, to make judgements about performance and quality of care.

The National Performance Assessment Framework

The framework includes six domains for performance measurement, as described earlier in this chapter. It will include data from the patient/carer experience survey. It is proposed that for any designated clinical topic all six domains will be utilised for performance assessment. Standards for each of the specific indicators within these areas will be agreed on between the NHS Executive Regional Offices and health authorities, between health authorities and PCGs, and between PCGs and PCTs. Local HImPs will have to take them into consideration.

Revalidation and appraisal

Starting within the next couple of years, all doctors on the general medical register will have to go through a process of periodic revalidation, in order to be allowed to continue practising. In addition to or alongside revalidation, the government would like to introduce a system of annual appraisal for all doctors, focusing on underperformance. The details have yet to be decided on, but again it is likely that the government and the general public will expect at some stage in the future to see the results of explicit quality indicators as part of this process.

Conclusion

Quality indicators represent one of the tools that will be used by PCGs, PCTs and health authorities to manage healthcare, to ensure that health professionals are accountable for their actions and to promote improvements in the quality of primary care. In an increasingly 'performance-managed' environment, their greater use is inevitable despite the justifiable criticisms that are levelled against them. Rapid advances in our ability to produce valid and reliable measures of quality of care will ensure that quality indicators play an important role in primary care in the future.

References

1 Marshall M (1999) Time to go public on performance? *British Journal of General Practice.* **49**: 691–2.
2 Brook R, McGlynn E, Cleary P (1996) Measuring Quality of Care. *New England Journal of Medicine.* **335**: 966–70.
3 Smith R (1998) All changed, changed utterly. [Editorial]. *BMJ.* **316**: 1917–18.
4 Thomson R, Lally J (1998) Clinical indicators: do we know what we are doing? *Quality in Health Care.* **7**: 122.

5 Baker S (1996) Use of performance indicators for general practice. *BMJ.* **312**: 58.

6 Lawrence M, Olesen F (1997) Indicators of quality in health care. *European Journal of General Practice.* **3**: 103–8.

7 Baker R, Fraser R (1995) Development of review criteria: linking guidelines and assessment of quality. *BMJ.* **311**: 370–3.

8 Donabedian A (1980) *Explorations in Quality Assessment and Monitoring 1. The definition of quality and approaches to its assessment.* Health Administration Press, Ann Arbor.

9 Maxwell R (1992) Dimensions of quality revisited: from thought to action. *Quality in Health Care.* **1**: 171–7.

10 Roland M, Holden J, Campbell S (1998) *Quality Assessment for General Practice: supporting clinical governance in primary care groups.* National Primary Care Research and Development Centre, University of Manchester.

11 NHS Executive (1999) *The NHS Performance Assessment Framework.* NHSE, Leeds.

12 Davies H, Crombie I, Mannion R (1999) Performance indicators in health care: guiding lights or wreckers' lanterns? In: H Davies, M Malek, A Neilson, M Tavakoli (eds) *Managing Quality and Controlling Cost: strategic issues in health care management.* Ashgate, Aldershot.

13 Marshall M, Shekelle P, Leatherman S, Brook R (2000) What do we expect to gain from the public release of performance data? A review of the evidence. *JAMA.* **283**: 1866–74.

14 Marshall M, Shekelle P, Leatherman S, Brook R (2000) *The Public Disclosure of Performance Data in Health Care: learning from the US experience.* Nuffield Trust, London.

15 Department of Health (1998) *A First Class Service: quality in the NHS.* Department of Health, London.

16 McColl A, Roderick P, Gabbay J, Smith H, Moore M (1998) Performance indicators for primary care groups: an evidence based approach. *BMJ.* **317**: 1354–60.

17 Brook RH, Chassin MR, Fink A *et al.* (1986) A method for the detailed assessment of the appropriateness of medical technologies. *International Journal of Technology Assessment in Health Care.* **2**: 53–63.

18 Hicks N (1994) Some observations on attempts to measure appropriateness of care. *BMJ.* **309**: 730–3.

19 Shekelle P, Kahan JP, Bernstein S, Leape L, Kamberg C, Park R (1998) The reproducibility of a method to identify the overuse and underuse of medical procedures. *New England Journal of Medicine.* **338**: 1888–95.

20 Lansky D (1998) Measuring what matters to the public. *Health Affairs.* **17**: 40–1.

21 Schneider E, Epstein A (1996) Influence of cardiac-surgery perfor-

mance reports on referral practices and access to care. A survey of cardiovascular specialists. *New England Journal of Medicine.* **335**: 251–6.

22 Hibbard J, Jewett J, Legnini M, Tusler M (1997) Choosing a health plan: do large employers use the data? *Health Affairs.* **16**: 172–80.

23 Hibbard J, Jewett J (1997) Will quality report cards help consumers? *Health Affairs.* **16**: 218–28.

24 Schneider E, Epstein A (1998) Use of public performance reports. *JAMA.* **279**: 1638–42.

25 NHS Executive (1999) *Quality and Performance in the NHS: high level performance indicators and clinical indicators.* NHSE, Leeds.

26 Smith P (1995) On the unintended consequences of publishing performance data in the public sector. *International Journal of Public Administration.* **18**: 277–310.

27 Davies H, Lampel J (1998) Trust in performance indicators? *Quality in Health Care.* **7**: 159–62.

PART 2

Functions

CHAPTER 5

Improving health: making health improvement programmes work

John Bewick

This chapter proposes that health improvement programmes (HImPs) and PCGs are central to each others' success. It also asks the question 'What should PCGs look for in a HImP to help them do their job?'.

By way of specific, local experiences, we try and cast some light on the general issues to be addressed, hopefully assisting the reader to move from rhetoric to reality.

The main part of this chapter is in effect a check list of some of the qualities a PCG may need in a HImP, but before that list is brought together, we need to set the scene by staking out some basic assumptions about what HImPs are and what PCGs/Ts are trying to do.

Setting the scene

HImPs lie at the heart of the changes taking place in the NHS. They mark a move away from the competitive philosophy of the internal market and a move towards collegiate working within one local, shared strategy for health improvement and service modernisation. Some have seen the HImP as simply another planning document – but this is to miss its real significance. HImPs are far more importantly an ongoing set of partnerships working across the NHS and beyond into local government, the voluntary sector and local communities. Indeed, the HImP document can be meaningless without the processes of engagement behind it. In this way of working the challenge is to ensure that each organisation is making its full contribution – that the right people in the right place are making the right decisions at the right time.

Within the overall system of a local health and social care community, each organisation's capabilities to contribute needs acknowledgement, respect and the opportunity to flourish. The HImP is not then the arena for a wrestling match between competing organisations, it is about achieving coherent action across agencies on a shared set of priorities.

In asking why this drive for coherence is so important we reach ideas at the heart of government policy which can easily be forgotten when focusing on the immediate structural changes in the New NHS or producing a HImP document. The first idea is about the state of public services. The government's agenda for public service is set to make it more responsive to changes in society, such as demography, public expectations and the way we live our lives; and able to take advantage of the new opportunities available to it, such as advances in IT. Central to ensuring that the public sector can respond is the idea of breaking down barriers between organisations, e.g. those which sustain inflexibility, prevent integration and reflect the needs of institutions not users.

For the NHS, this interprets into a simple message – if we are to tackle the complex problems behind inequalities in health and take advantage of new opportunities to modernise service delivery, we all need to focus on the same priority needs of local people and move away from any other motivations our existing organisations may have had. Further, we need to review our organisations and how they work together, and change them if necessary. Public sector organisations that fail to do this risk becoming an unresponsive, 'dark force of conservatism'. This may be what HImPs address above anything else.

Applying this review of existing organisations to the overall functioning of the NHS brought forward an obvious omission from our ability to tackle inequality and modernise – namely that while primary care had a pivotal role to play, it was largely blocked from fulfilling that role by the way the NHS was organised. The major focus of decision making lay between the health authorities and trusts (and fundholding was not designed to address this omission at a whole-system level).

Primary care sits at one of the most influential positions in the underlying function of the health and social care system:

- It knows a great deal about the needs of individuals and the local communities they live in – as a basis to shape services as a commissioner.
- It is based in local communities alongside local government and the voluntary sector where many decisions and actions to tackle the determinants of ill health need to be taken – it can therefore drive the health improvement agenda.
- It is based alongside much of the social care and community-based care, the integration of which is essential to promote independent living and avoid unnecessary use of hospital services.

- Its actions determine a large part of the overall demands made on acute services.

Enabling these qualities of primary care to be introduced into the management of health and social care systems is one of the underlying reasons for creating PCGs (and remains a bench mark against which the further benefits of the move to PCTs can be assessed).

So in this brief analysis we can construct a model in which HImPs and PCGs are seen as inseparable parts of the same picture. HImPs are creating the opportunity for the NHS to be responsive and improve. PCGs have a great and largely untapped potential to take that opportunity. They are mutually dependent on each other for success.

PCGs depend on HImPs to create the opportunities for them to influence every aspect of the overall health and social care system where they can add value. They will be frustrated and isolated without a supportive HImP which breaks down barriers and makes the whole system amenable to their influence.

HImPs depend on PCG/Ts to bring their new capabilities to the overall system. Without them there will be far less change to many of the key priorities for health improvement and service modernisation. Together they can drive the change agenda in a responsive, proactive way. Separately, neither will control the change agenda and will be reactive to the actions of the other.

Local experiences

In North & East Devon we are trying to make this mutual dependency model a successful reality. Our first local HImP was reviewed by the Health Services Management Centre (HSMC) in 1999. Their overall conclusions included:

> ... a strong and shared view that the HImP is a framework, a process, a system and a way of working which builds on the present. It is different from previous plans because it is based on health improvement as well as service delivery and it covers the local health economy: it is, therefore, a system plan rather than a series of plans of separate organisations.
>
> Much effort was given to creating a process for longer term involvement and to encourage ownership by NHS trusts, local authorities, PCGs, the voluntary sector and CHC. Steering groups at member and officer level were created with benefit, and relationships are constructive and positive.

So what is a system plan? What are the building blocks of this approach? The answer is presented as a series of questions which PCG/Ts could usefully ask in their own local circumstances.

In North & East Devon we have learned a great deal from hearing other people's solutions to problems, which although not entirely applicable to us, helped us with our own thinking. The practical examples in this paper are offered in that spirit. To make them a little more real, here is a thumbnail sketch of North & East Devon.

North & East Devon Health Authority has a budget of £330 million and covers a population of 480 000. The boundary of the health authority is not coterminous with Devon County Council and there are five district councils in their entirety and part of two other district councils. North & East Devon covers a large geographical area and is characterised by having two main population centres in Exeter and Barnstaple, together with a large, sparsely populated, rural area. North & East Devon has a very small ethnic minority community. While the overall population is generally healthy by national comparison, there are significant areas of deprivation which clearly affect the health of those communities. Exeter has relatively high levels of homelessness and deprivation while East Devon has a high elderly population. Mid-Devon and North Devon have rurally isolated communities and market towns with some deprivation from the low incomes associated with farming and tourism.

Four PCGs have been established around natural communities, with populations from 100 000 to 150 000. They cover the geographical areas of East Devon, Exeter, Mid-Devon and North Devon. PCGs have a good fit with District Council boundaries. There are two acute hospitals in Exeter and Barnstaple, about 50 miles apart, and a relatively high number of community hospitals outside the Exeter conurbation.

What should PCGs look for in a HImP?

- **Does the HImP provide a view of the whole health and social care system within which PCG/Ts and other organisations can see and develop their contribution?**

North & East Devon's HImP brings every aspect of the health and social care system together into one story which relates many of the activities which can often seem separate. We include the whole health story – both health improvement and health and social care – because we are striving to orchestrate the whole system (not just the preventative health agenda as many early HImPs have). Table 5.1 is taken from

Table 5.1 Our HImP is structured to bring the vast array of local health and social care issues together within one story

National policy direction	Within the overall guidance of national policy ...
Local partnerships for health improvement	... we are committed to working together ...
Health needs assessment overview	... to tackle our greatest inequalities and health needs ...
Resource mapping	... within the resources allocated nationally to the people of North & East Devon
A strategic framework	We share an understanding of the unique circumstance of North & East Devon and the people who live here ...
Priorities across the district	... and develop services accordingly
Continuous improvement	We also strive to improve everything we do, all the time, pursuing best practice and best value
Fit for the future	We ensure that our organisations serve the changing needs of local people ...
Supporting strategies	... and align our workforce, technology and capital investments to those priorities

the foreword to North & East Devon's 2000/2002 HImP. The left-hand column is in fact the contents of the HImP.

The story is focused around tackling our greatest inequalities and health needs, not around organisations. Each element of the HImP is addressed by an appropriate partnership group which develops its approach on an ongoing basis. PCGs are involved in every element and take a lead wherever that is appropriate. It is then a simple step for PCGs to be able to influence any part of the system where that is beneficial and in turn extract their actions coherently with other partners.

- **Is there a clear HImP planning cycle which allows PCGs to effectively bring about change?**

Managing change across several organisations requires clarity about when plans need to be made. Often the most worthwhile changes come from influencing the use of mainstream existing resources over the medium term, not the use of incremental growth available in the short term each year.

In North & East Devon we are working to move away from the annual Service and Financial Framework (SAFF) as the opportunity to lever change and focus on longer-term service quality programmes which may take two or three years to achieve or even ten years in the health improvement agenda (Figure 5.1). PCGs lead many of these programmes.

During the spring and summer, the first PCG accountability agreements and primary care investment plans were produced. These were derived from the HImP and ensured that specific actions at a local level were coherent with the shared vision across North & East Devon.

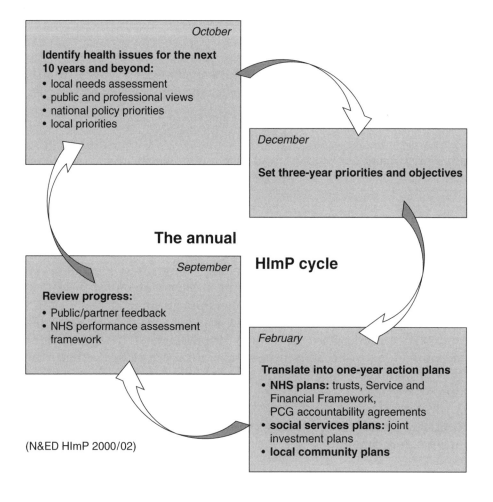

Figure 5.1 The annual HImP cycle.

In the same process all four PCGs led the prioritisation of local plans, greatly strengthening engagement of local government and working directly with the public. PCGs also lead formal discussions with each local trust to establish their proposals for service improvement and build them into the overall process.

- **Does the HImP have ways to achieve consensus when 'top-down' policies meet 'bottom-up' policies?**

The balancing of the national agenda with local PCG priorities can be a difficult challenge in a HImP.

Our approach to date has been to be very clear about the national policy framework within which we all work and the 'must do' agenda which drops out of it.

It is probably fair to say that in PCGs, GPs find this a challenging reality to handle. The health authority continues to hold ultimate responsibility for maintaining financial balance in the local healthcare economy and delivering the 'must dos' and in some GPs' eyes the 'us and them' relationship lingers on around this debate with the health authority being a proxy for government policy. As PCGs take full responsibility for their allocations, and certainly as PCTs, this dynamic will change as the debate about priorities moves to be played out more within the new responsible organisation. However, even PCTs will need to take the rest of the healthcare community with them and may find the HImP the best vehicle to do so.

Locally we have favoured having as many 'open and honest' discussions between all partners as possible. However difficult the decisions, there is a level of trust which keeps everyone at the table and gains commitment once the decision is made. We devote considerable effort to ensuring people are as engaged in decision making as possible and the reasons for decisions are transparent. We have standing groups for directors of finance and those involved in commissioning but a far wider set of discussions across the NHS and local government are scheduled in good time within the planning year. The implications of the annual allocation on priorities are interpreted together and resolved as a whole system. Having one part of the system in balance while another is in deficit is considered a failure. We are one system before we are separate parts. However, the process remains a difficult one.

HSMC commented:

> ... *concerns centred on the tight resource constraints, the inflexibility of earmarked allocations of the Modernisation Fund, the need to create early wins for all, to balance national and local priorities and*

> *to create the capacity for change to deliver a growing national and local agenda.*

- **Are local partnerships in place in the HImP which allow PCGs to work effectively with agencies they want to influence?**

Developing effective partnerships is at the heart of North & East Devon's approach to improving health and social care. PCGs have been involved in three major examples of innovative partnership which have changed how services develop.

Community planning fora

PCGs recognised the significant challenge of delivery on the wider health agenda and gave much thought to the needs of local authorities in the HImP process as their concentration is almost exclusively on that agenda. They invested considerable effort in forming devolved Joint Consultative Councils with each of the seven local authorities, recognising that this is the level at which many of the decisions which influence the determinants of health (e.g. employment, education, housing, leisure services and access to services) are taken. These have moved on during 1999 and in April 2000 become community planning fora, involving a wider range of agencies in producing single, local community plans. One PCG, to the delight of its rural community, is taking a strong interest in the improvement of rural transport co-ordination. Our GPs are beginning to realise their long-held dream to be able to prescribe good housing as easily as tablets.

The development of community planning fora has also clarified a long-standing debate about respective responsibilities between local government and the NHS. The working arrangement is that where an action is primarily concerned with health and wellbeing at a community level, this is led by local government, recognising the responsibility of local government for community leadership. Where an action is primarily concerned with health and social care services received by individuals, this will be led by health and social services (PCGs and district social services). These arrangements are summarised in Figure 5.2.

Health forum

A mixture of elected members and officers from many local organisations are partners in the North & East Devon Health Forum. The forum is the major vehicle by which the HImP drives action on the health improvement agenda. The forum supports the work of PCGs at a local level in community planning fora by:

- commissioning profiles of health status locally and interpreting national targets to make them real locally
- bringing together best advice on which interventions are effective in addressing local problems
- gaining the commitment of senior members of organisations so that their local teams have support in forming partnerships on the ground.

Early issues tackled have been smoking, accidental injury and physical activity.

It remains the responsibility of PCGs to make their commitments to the specific local work which they feel is most appropriate, but they have a supportive framework around them which makes influencing other agencies easier.

HImP management board
PCG chairs now meet monthly with the chief executives of local trusts and social services in the HImP management board. This ensures that every aspect of the HImP for which there is an NHS/social services responsibility is implemented in a co-ordinated, effective way. The board commissions all the partnership groups which contribute to the HImP. In this way we are enabling each of the various parts of the NHS

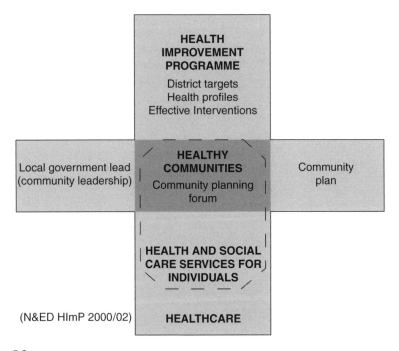

Figure 5.2

to take their decision through their boards while being assured that the necessary links have been made through 'joined-up thinking' with other parts of the system.

- **Does the HImP promote and rely on an understanding of health status and health needs assessment?**

As PCGs have ventured into the world of priority setting they have had to face an array of competing voices across the NHS, local government and local communities. They now face the same challenge health authorities have had in not being just another voice, but needing to lift themselves above the crowd to make judgements against criteria which all will recognise as reasonable.

The PCGs have found the use of health profiles and meeting health needs a powerful basis for priority setting. Its introduction into local government via local joint consultative committees has been particularly effective in providing a common ground on which different agencies can meet. The consistent use of health profiles and health needs assessment has reduced the amount of unproductive debate on priorities and also promoted consistency into the future as health status changes slowly.

The public health function of the health authority was commissioned by the HImP management board to lead a health needs assessment group which includes PCG, trust and local government representatives.

- **Does the HImP provide clear resource mapping and financial planning?**

Even with helpful moves towards unified budgets, the complexities of the annual NHS financial round and its influence on behaviour of the NHS remain a daunting mystery to many non-financial people, including clinicians taking on board wider responsibilities for the first time.

PCGs have generally not had their own director of finance, which understandably contributes to feeling disadvantaged within the local NHS community, however good the support from the health authority.

However, a more difficult issue for PCGs has been the realisation that they are commissioning within a finite system. Changes they may wish to make, say, to remove a service from secondary care, which are beyond the capacity of a trust to respond within the desired timescale, simply leaves an unfunded cost which still ultimately has to be met from somewhere in the public funds allocated to the PCG (local population) as their fair share of the national cake. The arrival of a director of finance with PCT status will not in itself resolve this problem.

In North & East Devon we use the HImP to share an open, ongoing assessment of the financial position of all parts of the NHS community. Directors of finance meet monthly and PCT directors of finance would join this group. A key success has been the agreeing of pace of change and risk pool policies which acknowledge the realities of the financial frameworks we all operate within. They give certainty to both PCGs and trusts in planning ahead and have helped the SAFF discussions considerably.

- **Does the HImP have a clear vision of the unique characteristics of the local area and population which shapes local services?**

PCGs deliver and commission services locally, but need to work with other local PCGs and the health authority to effectively commission larger, population-based services, such as renal or some mental health services. This is important for equity, efficiency and risk sharing.

To do this, PCGs need to be able to agree with all other parts of the system what is appropriately commissioned at what level. This will vary according to local circumstance. Service delivery by a local hospital in a dense urban area, may be more appropriately delivered by outreach community services in a sparsely populated rural area. To support this understanding, North & East Devon's HImP contains a 'strategic framework', which identifies the defining features of the local area and how they impact on the shape of services at each level. An example is the effect of geographical isolation on the small specialties in a general hospital, balancing access against safety.

PCGs have found the framework provides a language with which to hold often robust but clear discussion about service configuration options.

- **Does the HImP state priorities clearly and manage their delivery?**

Having been through the priority setting processes, PCGs need to know that priorities are clear to everyone who has to take action and that they will be delivered.

In North & East Devon priorities are presented in a progressive order from prevention to treatment:
- healthy communities
- keeping well (individual action)
- vulnerable groups
- diseases and conditions
- treating emergencies (and reducing waiting).

There are many priorities beyond those which attract additional funding. This flows from a philosophy of 'change not more' in working on existing services within existing resources. It also acknowledges that across the healthcare system, many priorities do not actually compete with each other because they will be implemented by different organisations. In this way the HImP allows PCGs to be part of far more change than when change is linked to growth or attempted separately.

PCGs take leads on particular issues (NSFs) on behalf of each other, rolling out new services after piloting in one PCG. This has increased the efficiency of PCGs in making change happen. The HImP and the HImP management board are used by PCGs to manage the process.

- **Does the HImP promote continuous improvement?**

Beyond priorities for improvement, many people are striving to improve everything they do, all the time, through clinical governance (best practice) and efficiency bench marking (best value).

Both these issues are addressed by standing groups across the healthcare community. Benefits for PCGs include:
- improved links with secondary care clinicians in the District Clinical Governance Group, which is achieving a strong reputation for its work across organisational boundaries on care pathways and interface audits
- certainty that the services it commissions from trusts are bench marked as being efficient and representing value for money, and where they are not, remedial action plans are in place.

In both best practice and best value, PCG/Ts would find it difficult to deliver alone without the HImP frameworks to engage other parts of the system.

Locally, improving quality within the healthy environment created by the District Clinical Governance Group is held as one of the most important long-term activities within the HImP. Taking advantage of the opportunities offered to focus on changing clinical practices is undoubtedly where primary and secondary care clinicians will make their greatest contribution to improving the health experience of the population they serve. (This far outweighs effort put in via commissioning around the cost/price of existing clinical practice whatever its quality.)

- **Does the HImP align supporting strategies, workforce/information technology/capital investment, with service priorities?**

Whatever priorities PCGs may wish to pursue the whole system needs to be working to ensure that the workforce, IT and capital investments respond and support those priorities. Without them change will be delayed if not prevented.

PCGs have made a major contribution in each of these areas, as both a provider of services and as a partner in issues where systems must cross boundaries, for example electronic patient records. PCGs are sharing resources to undertake their own organisational development and participate in shared learning events with other parts of the NHS and local government workforce.

Conclusion

If the questions in this chapter can be answered positively, PCG/Ts have some of the essential supports they will need to fulfil their potential role in the new NHS. This will not come about unless PCGs themselves proactively work closely with their local health authority and trusts to make it happen.

Many of the activities described may well be going on locally in some shape or form. However, they may not be readily accessible or clearly related to the functioning of PCGs. Those links need to be made by PCGs. The HImP is an excellent vehicle for making those links.

HImPs are primarily a means of managing local healthcare communities within consensus frameworks. This is at the heart of the health authorities' new role of strategic leadership.

HImPs depend on mutual support and are not a forum for competing organisations to fight over priorities. PCGs need to help change the culture towards this approach.

As PCGs move to PCTs there will be an inevitable inclination to want to build new walls around new organisations. The new NHS is based on keeping those walls down and being constantly responsive to the changing needs of local populations and new opportunities for improving service delivery. HImPs are a means of keeping these walls down and keeping responsive. PCG/Ts bring a powerful set of new qualities to the management of health and social care communities. HImPs can harness those qualities. PCG/Ts need to show leadership as the NHS's newest organisations by using HImPs effectively, at the heart of the new NHS.

CHAPTER 6

PCGs commissioning services within the new culture of co-operation and care pathways: the role of long-term service agreements

Chris James

The White Paper *The New NHS: modern, dependable* left many in primary care believing that finally we would see a system of healthcare management that would redress inequalities that had evolved over many years, allow primary care to be fairly developed and deliver effective healthcare to the communities we know so much about. PCGs are charged with three key objectives:

- improving the health and addressing health inequalities of their communities
- developing primary care and community services
- commissioning a range of hospital services which meets their patients' needs.

This chapter is concerned with the final of these objectives, commissioning services.

Prior to April 1999, the language was not of commissioning, but of purchasing. Secondary care services were purchased in one of two ways to be available to referral from primary care. The majority of services were purchased by health authorities, and within health authorities some practices were able to purchase a specified list of procedures and activities for their patients. The fundholding scheme was successful in allowing a practice to look at the needs of its particular patients and buy services for them. It allowed many developments that brought services closer to the patients. It seemed able to secure preferential waiting times in many areas. Unfortunately there was little regard for the effect of fundholding on the rest of the system of healthcare in a given area, as the concentration of work and incentives to manage contracts and activity was held in a very small pocket of care in the health economy. The fundholding scheme often pitted practices against each other. Unless there was a total purchasing pilot or multifund that brought some practices together, fundholding could at best benefit a practice, but could not deliver the best use of resources for a community.

Before April 1999, activity was purchased, rather than services being commissioned. That is a very important distinction. Activity was largely measured by a 'finished consultant episode' – the FCE. This of course meant that payment from either a fundholder or health authority was made once a patient had been seen in a hospital. There was little incentive for the quality of that contact, or even the appropriateness of the contact. As long as the patients were seen, the money would follow. The incentive for the hospital was to get patients through the door, irrespective of clinical need. The incentive to even do that was reduced when there was a move to make contracts as simple as possible, and block contracts guaranteed monthly payments with little regard for volume of activity.

The FCE was a hospital-based currency, creating the incentive to keep services at the hospital. Well-demarcated budgets and contracts meant that the attention of hospital and community services were on how to keep their own activity up, not on how they could work together for the benefit of the patient.

The picture I am trying to build is not one that is anti-fundholding – I was a fundholder myself. What it illustrates, however, is some of the issues that must be addressed if commissioning in the future is not only different, but can be called an improvement – a success. Commissioning for PCGs must be based on primary care professionals working together with, and for, a community of patients. This community of patients should be analysed, with their needs assessed. Services must be commissioned that allow patients to have appropriate, timely care that is convenient to them and involves them in their definition. PCGs must be advocates to those excluded from society, and work together to identify and tackle the inequalities that are found in the system.

Services must be delivered in a variety of ways which aim to reduce the impact illness may have on patients' normal lives. This will require healthcare to be delivered in many varied and often new settings that deliver care closer to the patient's home, allowing patients to maintain the maximum level of independence.

What is commissioning?

Commissioning is the identification and definition of content, agreement and monitoring of service agreements that implement the HImP. The commissioning process must give due regard to the long-term relationship between the partners involved, and an agreed strategic direction that will best serve a local community. It is intended that new ways of commissioning will allow more effective arrangements for commissioning specialist services, replace extra-contractual referrals (ECRs) with out-of-area treatments (OATs) and introduce a programme of long-term service agreements (LTSAs).

Commissioning services has never been a straightforward process, but it is now more complicated than ever. There are a number of principles that must be applied to the commissioning process that impact on the resultant agreements.

- **Partnership** – there must be a partnership approach that involves all local health organisations, local authority, social services, voluntary services and many other partners.
- **Openness** – there must be a sharing of information that allows all involved to assess relative risks of options discussed, with transparent financial information.
- **Joint assumptions** – key assumptions relating to local activity must be agreed (e.g. inflation and GP referrals). Where these variables are allowed between individual organisations, they must be agreed.
- **Key deliverables** – all involved must recognise and agree national targets expected by the NHS Executive. These will include activity and financial targets.
- **NHS trust break-even** – there is a duty to draft financial plans that facilitate a break-even position, and support financial recovery plans that have been agreed with regional offices.

The PCG must embark on commissioning services with local providers while working within these principles. There is little wonder that many PCGs have scant confidence in being able to balance all these given principles and deliver changes to services that represent an enhancement responding to local need. Their appears to be just too many 'givens' to attend to on the way.

PCGs are, however, best placed to understand and determine local responses to need, and it is a challenge to the local health economy as a whole to create flexibilities within local negotiations that allow some local determination of services.

Commissioning for service changes

There are a number of practicalities that must be recognised when proposing a service shift. A PCG must discuss the proposed change with the relevant party at the earliest practical opportunity. This will need to be followed by formal notice once proposals have been finalised. The relevant trust must be given at least six months' notice prior to the proposed date of implementation and copies of the notification should be sent to the regional office.

A significant service shift is one that involves an annual revenue cost of £100 000 or more. This figure relates to the impact of a single service shift, but also relates to a single trust, should an aggregate of different service changes amount to a change of £100 000 or more.

The NHS Performance Assessment Framework (PAF) will be used to judge if the service shift is worthwhile. A high-level impact assessment will be required for such a service shift, and should be set out under the six headings of the NHS PAF. These are:

- health improvement
- fair access
- effective delivery
- efficiency
- patient/user experience
- health outcomes.

Commissioning appropriate services in appropriate settings

The vast majority of health economies are struggling with dismantling the contracts and currencies of healthcare that have evolved over the years. A patient with back pain is not best served by a simple contract between a health authority or PCG and a hospital trust. That patient may be better served by a contract between the commissioner and the orthopaedic directorate of the trust – a contract that can be monitored, not only by volumes of service, but also with clinical outcomes agreed. Even this can only be a contract, and we are still not serving this patient, because what the patient needs is a *service* for his back pain, not a contract with an orthopaedic surgeon. A true service agreement working for this patient is one that provides for a service to respond to that patient's back pain, and may involve a rheumatologist, a neurologist, a neurosurgeon, physiotherapist, psychologist and so on.

The point I make is that in the near future, commissioners of services will do just that, commission a service that relates to the illnesses that present and require a response, not one that is at the convenience of the organisation that provides that care.

Bringing services to the community

Where appropriate, hospital services can be brought into the community. As an example, many commissioners of care will be exploring the possibility of investing in community rehabilitation teams, finding ways of promoting independence after suffering a variety of medical problems. This may not only mean new styles of services for our elderly, vulnerable population, but for all members of our society, children and adults alike. The successful early promotion of independence in the community will facilitate movement of patients out of acute wards, freeing capacity where it is needed. Increasing independence will combat the spiralling costs to social services of long-stay residential care. Most importantly, a person may be able to achieve a greater quality of life. Greater community care will have implications for those of us in primary care. We are all aware of the inability of previous shifts from secondary to primary care to attract the shift of funding. The unified budget, if applied correctly, gives us the responsibility and the tools to manage future transitions.

There are some broad aims that many PCGs will be working towards. To help understand some of the objectives I would like to reproduce (with permission from Southampton Community Health Services NHS Trust) an example that both brings together the notion of multiprofessional care and shows an aim to place services as close to the patient as possible (*see* Table 6.1). It is an example of a managed care network for a person with rheumatoid arthritis. As you can see, a whole host of agencies will have a part to play. I believe the aim of PCGs will be to commission services that encompasses all or most of the elements in this scenario *in a single service agreement*.

Information for commissioning

Assessing needs

Commissioning services is the means to implementing the HImP. If the HImP is to be locally sensitive, a great deal of information is required to allow PCGs to understand the needs of the locality. PCGs will need data

Table 6.1 A managed care network for a person with rheumatoid arthritis

	Intervention
Wellness	• Lifestyle • Exercise • Self-help information • Support group
Primary care	• Drug management • Monitoring condition • Physiotherapy • Joint protection techniques
Community care	• Environmental assessment • Home adaptation • Support for carer
Intermediate care	• Community hospital admission • Drug review • Biochemical assay
Acute care	• Orthopaedic admission (knee replacement) • Intensive post-surgical rehabilitation + hydrotherapy
Specialist/tertiary care	• Consultant outpatient session at regional RA centre for drug management review

on local prevalence and incidence of diseases, conditions and problems. They will also need information on inequalities of health or access to services. This information will be needed while assessing the impact of primary care developments and integration.

Assessing activity and contract monitoring

There are two basic information sets that should be flowing from NHS trusts to health authorities relating to secondary care provided to individual patients. These are the clinical correspondences sent to GPs and the commissioning data sets sent to the responsible HAs. While primary care is slowly bringing clinical systems to a state where information is consistent and useful to them, PCGs must rely on having access to, and ability to analyse, commissioning data sets.

NHS trusts and health authorities should have:

- the completeness and accuracy of recording the details of the GP who has referred the patient, and the GP (and practice) with whom the patient is registered
- the completeness, accuracy and consistency of clinical coding in commissioning data sets including consistency with details included in clinical correspondence sent to GPs
- the timeliness of information flows
- the consistent use of NHS numbers.

Health authorities must by now be able to provide PCGs with access to these patient-specific, commissioning data sets, if this is requested by PCGs.

It is now a minimum requirement that PCGs receive, on a monthly basis:

- total number of FCEs for ordinary admissions and day cases by specialty
- emergency and elective episodes reported separately for admissions and discharges
- levels of activity for comparable time periods in previous years.

There should also be regular reports at specialty level within individual NHS trusts covering:

- length-of-stay distributions
- comparisons of actual lengths of stay to those in previous years.

Commissioning for patient-sensitive services

While PCGs and PCTs are driven by clinicians, there is a real opportunity for services to be commissioned that are sensitive to the clinical needs of the patient. While a GP still retains a responsibility to an individual patient, a PCG/T has a responsibility to a collection of patients. It may be a dream that sometime in the future, waiting lists no longer exist, but certainly the reality of today is that they do very much exist. Given that we must work with waiting lists, PCGs will attempt, through commissioning, to create mechanisms that ensure the waiting list is managed and sensitive to clinical need.

There are a number of models in action around the country, most based on a scoring system. Commonly the score is the basis of the referral form to secondary care. The advantage of this is that the order that patients are listed to be seen in outpatient departments may be based on the severity of their symptoms relative to others on the list. Scoring has also been used by secondary care clinicians in determining the relative order of a waiting list for an operative procedure.

There are now many scoring systems that can be adopted, but one of the benefits of agreeing the process locally is the contact it requires between primary and secondary care clinicians. The process of agreeing a scoring system will expose the pressures that each service experiences, and that understanding will be shared. It will also expose misconceptions about each others' views. Many secondary care clinicians are amazed when GPs request that if their referral is deemed to be inappropriate, they are simply returned without being processed but accompanied by an explanation as to why. Most consultants think that GPs would be offended, but many GPs feel that this sort of information is essential if we are to really make the best use of resources.

Commissioning to do things differently

I have mentioned that a drawback of having contracting for FCEs is that the main objective of the service provider is to get patients through the door rather than to ensure the quality of that contact. The other main drawback of the FCE is that payment to a provider demands that a patient sits across the desk from a consultant in a hospital. The FCE as a currency of healthcare is going, and will be replaced by LTSAs. We must now think how we can commission services that achieve the same outcomes as the historical way of referring patients, but use our resources (including ourselves as a resource) in new, more efficient ways.

It is worthwhile looking at the many reasons we refer patients to a consultant. They include:

- diagnosis
- investigation
- advice on treatment
- specialist treatment
- second opinion
- reassurance for the patient
- sharing the load, or risk, of treating a difficult or demanding patient
- deterioration in GP–patient relationship (desire to involve someone else)
- fear of litigation
- direct requests by patients or relatives.

We must question whether it is necessary for the patient to be physically present in front of a consultant to fulfil these objectives. When commissioning services for our patients, we have a long way to go in using technology, other professions allied to medicine and our GP colleagues in managing this demand that has traditionally been placed at the door of the secondary care hospital.

Commissioning long-term service agreements

There is an expectation that year on year, there will be a growing number of services commissioned under LTSAs. The services where this will be a priority will be for mental health, coronary heart disease and cancer services. LTSAs will offer the health economy a degree of stability. They will facilitate three-year plans for commissioners and providers that hopefully create an environment that allows change in service provision to be planned. It will help financial recovery plans to be more feasible.

They are not intended to represent an elongation of the traditional way of contracting and commissioning with a hospital trust, but be part of a new emphasis on care and care pathways. LTSAs will be based on integrated care pathways, focusing on conditions or client groups rather than organisations.

Integrated care pathways must surely be within the grasp of PCGs more than any previous system of healthcare management in Britain. A fully functioning PCG will be working closely with social services and hospital colleagues as well as community staff. Such integration could ensure that discharge and rehabilitation plans are made and understood by the team as a whole *prior to admission* for a whole number of elective and emergency procedures. If successful, then patients are dealt with effectively and seamlessly across the agencies involved, and flow through acute hospital beds will be maintained as intermediate care (discussed elsewhere in this book) is fully utilised.

Commissioning in partnership

Partnership is a key word in the New NHS. There will be many services that will require PCGs to commission jointly. There may well be some services that PCGs commission from a local PCT. The health authority has a tradition of commissioning services in consultation with social services and local authorities, but that process needs to be both simplified and strengthened.

Health authorities will have joint investment plans (JIPs) for older people, and PCGs should have played a part in their formation. These plans were expected to roll forward from April 2000. There is now an expectation that JIPs for adults of working age who have mental health problems will be developed. By April 2001, authorities are required to complete a JIP for people with learning disabilities, and welfare to work for disabled people. As PCGs become more functional across involved agencies, they are the natural home for much of this work. They will certainly be the main vehicle for their effective implementation.

Apart from JIPs, there are new flexibilities described towards the end of 1999 that give potential for formalising joint planning into true joint commissioning. There are three new proposals that allow health and social services to work together in new ways.

Pooled budgets

Organisations would agree a range of health and local government services that could be purchased from a pooled budget. It would provide an opportunity to bring money together to give a truly co-ordinated package of care not previously available because of disputes between health services and local authorities about financial responsibilities.

Lead commissioning

This again brings together local authority, health authority and PCTs, and agrees one agency taking on the function of commissioning services on behalf of the other. The responsibility for fulfilling the commissioning will be taken on by the lead agency, but the liability ultimately remains with the originating body. It is an extension of joint commissioning already used by many health authorities.

Integrated provision

This offers an opportunity to allow different professionals to work within one management structure. It is hoped it will avoid duplication of services such as: patients having to go to two buildings for different parts of the same service; or visit different agencies for similar services; or several people from different agencies coming to see them. The ability to join up services will be enhanced and in some cases it may be possible for one member of staff to perform several tasks, providing a seamless service for the user.

Commissioning to create incentives

Through many activities that change the way we work, PCGs will want to:

- save money to invest in existing hospital services
- show greater clinical effectiveness for clinical governance agenda
- create resources to purchase new services and implement the HImP
- enable GPs within a PCG to work corporately towards common goals
- bring hospital consultants and GPs together to discuss and agree aspects of patient care
- provide leeway within budgets to help implement NSFs.

If PCGs are successful in approaching these aims, then there is a huge corporate incentive to continue to work to those ends. It is likely that many PCGs will need to create further incentives at a practice level that may reward control of the demand side of the service agreement. These incentives will take a variety of forms, ranging from equipment and practice premises enhancement to new training, career and research opportunities.

Incentives will also be needed when considering the supply of services from providers. LTSAs will in themselves be welcomed as an incentive for services due to their stabilising nature. Commissioning will continue to require further financial incentives, ideally in the form of performance rewards rather than penalties, to encourage performance of activity against service agreements. As well as clinical activity, clinical liaison between primary and secondary care is essential for the success of many new developments. This requires incentivisation and realistic resourcing.

Incentives are important to maintain not only activity, but also quality of service. The advent of clinical governance and PAFs has made quality a key objective when commissioning services. Primary and secondary care will want to continue to develop and enhance services, and this invariably requires the investment or shifting of resources. One of the criteria that can be key to the decision as to whether a service, such as one provided by a hospital directorate, is worthy of investment is its ability to demonstrate a quality service. This would be a strong incentive that puts quality at the forefront of service plans.

The effect of the desire to provide a high level of service by the dedicated people working within the NHS should not be underestimated. For many who work in the caring professions, the knowledge that they are successful in improving the health of the population they serve is the most powerful incentive they could experience.

Health professionals are charged with the task of finding new ways of commissioning care. They must engage both primary and secondary care, address inequalities and inadequate service, and produce outcomes that fulfil each criteria in the performance framework.

This is a huge task, but when addressing these issues, we must act in ways that allow us to learn the principles of assessing current activity and need. With careful thought and preparation, I believe we can source information and develop techniques that can be applied to a number of care areas and commission services in a way that is more effective than previously possible. We can use a range of mechanisms, techniques and partnerships that were not previously available. I believe that if these new opportunities are used to the full, we will actually make an impact on the health of our population.

Source documents

Health Act 1999, section 31 (pooled budgets).

NHS Executive (1998) *Commissioning in the New NHS*. HSC 1998/198. NHSE, London.

NHS Executive (1999) *Primary Care Groups: taking the next steps*. HSC 1999/246. NHSE, London.

NHS Executive (1999) *Planning for Health and Health Care*. HSC 1999/244. NHSE, London.

NHS Executive (1999) *Governance in the New NHS*. HSC 1999/123. NHSE, London.

CHAPTER 7

Primary care 1: clinical governance in primary care

Stephen Gillam and Nick Bradley

Every round of reforms generates new catch phrases – concepts that are supposed to hold solutions to the system's ills, particularly in the field of quality assurance. When historians look back at this phase of the NHS's evolution, it is likely that clinical governance and its implementation will provide the touchstone for judging this government's stewardship of the NHS. Where has clinical governance come from, what is it and how can it be implemented by PCGs?

Policy drivers

Many public sector bodies have sought over the past ten years to import the organisation-wide quality improvement strategies perceived as successful in manufacturing and service industries. The advent of clinical governance heralds the latest of many attempts in the NHS to exercise greater managerial control over clinical activities. Concern over variations in the quality of primary care, particularly in inner cities, has been a prominent concern of policy makers since the inception of the NHS. Previous attempts to address these variations have met with limited success.

The 1989 White Paper *Working for Patients* extolled the virtues of audit.[1] In some disciplines, 'the critical analysis of the quality of health care' was already established as best practice. What was new was an attempt to generalise audit activity. Over £500 million has been spent on audit in the hospital and community sectors to mixed effect. The audit movement fell short of expectations in various ways.[2] First, audit topics have reflected the priorities of doctors with little non-medical involvement (*pace* the shift from medical to clinical audit). Second, it has proved difficult to routinise audit activity. *Working for Patients* did not free resources for health professionals to dedicate time to audit. Finally, involvement remained patchy. Clinical audit has not engaged the traditionally 'hard-to-reach'. Participation was voluntary and not previously a contractual obligation on GPs.

The unfolding events at Bristol Royal Infirmary and widespread public concern over the management of poorly performing doctors have given further momentum to clinical governance.

What is it?

> *A system through which NHS organisations are accountable for continuously improving the quality of their services and safeguarding high standards of care by creating an environment in which clinical excellence will flourish.*[3]

Three aspects of this much-quoted definition are usefully underlined. First, clinical governance is a system of drawing together elements of quality assurance that are often ill co-ordinated. Second, managerial involvement stresses the corporate nature of this new responsibility. Third, this requires, in the overused phrase, major 'cultural change'. For PCGs, this implies sharing intelligence about quality across professional and practice boundaries and health professionals seeing themselves as collectively accountable for the clinical and cost-effectiveness of their colleagues' work. In short, it implies a new understanding about the nature of professional accountability.

Clinical governance is the glue that binds together a national frame-work in which two new bodies have central roles. NICE will be helping to set standards and guide the development of NSFs. The CHI will be responsible for monitoring implementation and will, in time, be under-taking regular visits to assess the performance of PCTs. Clinical governance links critically to the processes of continuous professional development and is supposed to involve users. The centrality of clinical governance in this scheme highlights two particular challenges for PCGs. First, in setting their own clinical governance priorities they will have to reconcile national 'givens' with local concerns if the priorities they iden-tify are to be 'owned' by their constituents. Second, they need to link forward planning and implementation of clinical governance with primary care investment and the implementation of their local HImP. Box 7.1 illustrates the scope of clinical governance in primary care. Risk management refers to a systematic programme of clinical and adminis-trative activities undertaken to identify, evaluate and prevent the risk of injury to patients, staff and the wider organisation. Otherwise, this is a familiar list of activities.

Progress to date

Leadership

PCGs were given four tasks in their first year in relation to clinical governance (*see* Box 7.1). Reporting mechanisms may be in place and lines of accountability clarified but the extent to which these have been internalised by clinical governance leads is more debatable. Many are scrabbling up steep learning curves and only now beginning to understand the complexity of their jobs. They are learning to manage at least three sets of accountability. Their relationships to the chief officer and board will be tested in the first round of appraisals. They are accountable to peers within practices who they are just beginning to get to know. Third, they may be placing strain on relations within their own practice teams both as absentees and as the new 'arbiters of quality'. The role can therefore be a lonely one; hence the importance attached within most PCGs to identifying clinical governance leads within practice teams and fostering networks at this level.

Most PCGs have appointed a doctor and nurse to share the brief.[4] Most PCGs have set up a clinical governance subcommittee. In over three-quarters of PCGs, most practices have appointed their own clinical

---

Box 7.1   The scope of clinical governance in primary care

- Clear lines of responsibility and accountability for the overall quality of clinical care.
- A comprehensive programme of quality improvement activities:
  - evidence-based practice
  - National Service Frameworks/NICE
  - workforce planning and development
  - continuing professional development
  - safeguarding patient confidentiality
  - clinical audit and outcomes
  - quality assurance
  - research and development.
- Risk management.
- Identification and remedy of poor performance.

governance lead. However, levels of support from other agencies such as public health departments, academic bodies or education networks vary considerably. Few clinical governance leads have dedicated input from information or finance managers.[5] While cross links with clinical governance structures and community trusts are developing swiftly, particularly among those planning an early transition to PCT status, links with the acute sector are largely invisible.

Resources

The Audit Commission found wide differences between the amount that PCGs planned to spend on clinical governance this year (ranging from £5000 to £128 000 but averaging £1667 per practice). This in turn has ensured variable levels of local support in the form of new staff. The emphasis this year is on setting the right cultural tone as much as on concrete achievements. PCGs are rightly trying to adopt a non-threatening, facilitative and developmental approach to clinical governance. The threats both to independent contractor status and professional self-regulation may make their task harder. For the time being, PCGs may be limited to the exercise of peer pressure and advice. But most health professionals are starting to understand that PCTs in collaboration with new bodies like the CHI, using new assessment processes – presaged in *Supporting Doctors, Protecting Patients*[6] – will have rather sharper teeth. Whether this increases willingness to share data and conduct audits is not easy to predict.

Mapping

Most baseline assessment of capacity has been 'light touch', based on practice visits or simple questionnaires. They contain little detailed information with which to compare the quality of clinical process across practices. Few PCGs are in a position to establish the databases they will need to refine resource allocation in future. Many forward plans are necessarily tentative where agreement is still to be reached on key priorities and leads are still marshalling resources in support of clinical governance.

Priorities

Clinical governance activity should be part of an integrated package focused on HImP priorities. Seven out of ten PCGs confirm that their clinical governance programme would include inter-practice audit of treatment/referral for conditions mentioned in the HImP.[4] Most commonly these were heart disease, hypertension and diabetes. Improving data quality, for example through the agreement of common diagnostic classifications, is a high priority as is adverse event monitoring. However, only one in three PCGs are trying to agree evidence-based protocols for community or practice nursing interventions. It is important that clinical audit is not confined to medical issues and the treatment of specific conditions but examines the total package of care available to patient groups.

Infrastructure

A typical PCG has a clinical governance subcommittee comprising the lead doctor(s), nurse, support worker and perhaps the PCG chief executive. These teams are formulating action plans based on rudimentary assessments of local capacity assessment, local HImPs, national priorities, and on the style, preferences and resources of each PCG. Their briefs are extensive (*see* Figure 7.1).

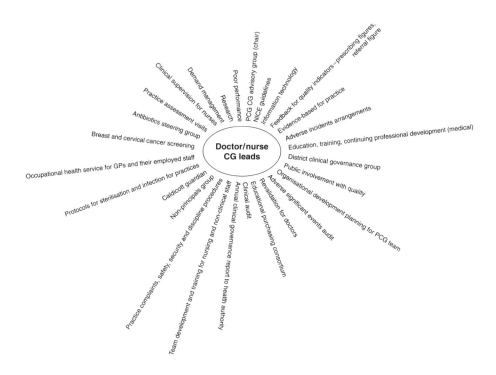

Figure 7.1   A plethora of portfolios.

Many PCGs have set up a multidisciplinary clinical governance task group, comprising leaders from pharmacy, dentistry, optometry, professions allied to medicine, social services, patient groups, IM&T and secondary care, as well as general practice clinicians. Their strength lies in bringing breadth and a positive outlook to discussions which might become over-medicalised and negative under the current spotlight of doctors' poor performance. Yet their diversity can be their weakness: a lack of genuinely shared experience.

While PCGs remain subcommittees of health authorities, communication between the clinical governance leads in a given health authority is easily promoted. This makes good operational sense. Part-time leads cannot cover the range of tasks, even in their own teams. If the leads co-operate by agreeing to major in particular areas, duplication can be avoided. One lead may have skills in education and professional development, another in audit and significant event analysis, another may major on poor performance arrangements and risk management. When PCTs emerge in competition with one another, a history of local collaboration will limit the tendency to disengage from colleagues in neighbouring PCTs. There are anyway big questions over the dis-economies of scale implied in the establishment of hundreds of small 'primary care development units'. Other bodies that can contribute in support are listed in Box 7.2.

Box 7.2   Existing resources

- Audit groups
- Postgraduate educational networks
- Clinical effectiveness initiatives
- Educational consortia
- Health authorities (the old 'FHSA')
- R&D networks
- Academic departments
- Community trusts

Engaging practice teams

Baseline mapping using available data or surveys will have highlighted gaps in the quality profile of local practices. Designing projects, educational events or commissioning services to fill these gaps makes good sense. An initial orientation visit to each practice by the lead doctor and nurse may provide insights into a practice's approach to development. How do they respond to this visit? Are they welcoming? How do they deal with a struggling team member? What audits can they show? How do they organise continuing professional development? Many practice teams think clinical governance is something to be done *to* rather than *by* them. The PCG leads are charged with ensuring that systems are in place, not putting them in place. However, practice visits from a large team might be very intimidating, particularly for small or underdeveloped practices for whom all this is new. Bringing practice clinical governance leads together in their own group for educational and policy-forming meetings is a central part of the work. Practices have not traditionally met as organisations before, only as individual people and friends.

Concentrating on a project which is achievable quickly and affordably is energising. Early examples have involved significant event audits, shared chronic disease registers, nurse supervision, an occupational health service for general practice and receptionist training schemes. Early projects have not always gone well. Wrong data on practice staff hours in a primary care investment plan caused anger, extra work and some loss of trust in the PCG board among constituent practices. Trying to tackle demand for hospital services under the quality banner is a mistake so early on, since data on referrals are notoriously difficult to interpret.

Key challenges

National versus local priorities

The smaller population of a PCG, around 100 000, naturally defines cherished local issues, e.g. a community hospital, homeless rough sleepers, underinvestment in practice premises, the quality of nursing homes. National priorities come with a service framework, a list of imperatives and operatic lyrics. They could stimulate work which saves lives but tend to belong to no one. An effective PCG will balance the effort – and money – spent on each.

Health improvement programmes

HImPs expose the tension between the utilitarianism of public health and the individualism of primary healthcare. With mortality from cervical cancer falling, why is the public so concerned with screening programme failures? The answer is postmodern. How can an individual woman or her family experience fewer deaths from cervical cancer? Experience beats knowledge in the public's mind; knowledge beats experience in public health thinking.

HImPs need to include the experience of healthcare in their measures of health gain. This will mean concentrating on items of process such as access, availability, level of respect shown at reception, hospital food, communication skills, measures of trust and understanding, and length of consultations. More sophisticated ways of assessing patients' views are being developed. The GPASS questionnaire is one such currently being validated.[7] Measures of greater 'enablement' following the clinical encounter appear to be associated with longer consultation lengths and closer doctor–patient relationships.[8]

Rivalries

Tensions exist between the controlling parent of the health authority and the rebellious child of the PCG. PCGs' contribution to district HImPs has so far been limited. PCGs will want to spend money on services to which the health authority does not accord priority. PCGs in the same health authority will compete with each other as siblings – for parental recognition, kudos and money. Rivalries need acknowledging, not denying. They will act as spurs to innovation. The dominant policy issue to cause tension is the move to PCTs. PCGs threaten to consume the health authority, which currently controls and protects them. Community trusts may be dismantled by PCTs, and neighbouring PCGs could enhance or damage each other's positions by the speed or scope of their move to trust status.

Identifying and managing poor performance

One source of pressure may be the illusory search for a package of performance indicators to help identify substandard performance. The problem for clinical governance leads is that the easily measurable is rarely useful, and technical obstacles such as the difficulties of controlling for case-mix are hard to resolve. Because healthcare is the public's main preoccupation, measures of process will continue to be more important than measures of outcome. The former can be truly 'evidence-based'. Many patients blur the distinction between their healthcare and their health: the two often represent one and the same thing. The quality of the doctor–patient relationship is measurable[9] and will, if it has not already, become an endpoint in its own right; and the use of informed choice will become an outcome in its own right.

The consultation paper *Supporting Doctors, Protecting Patients*[6] proposes compulsory annual audit and appraisal for all doctors, with assessment and support centres for failing doctors. It is not yet clear where the centres would be or how they would operate. For the moment, complaints, colleagues' expressed concerns and contractual audit visits by the health authority are the main means of detection, although practice assessments and revalidation for doctors will provide new ones.[7,10]

Support and development

Best practice is also reflective practice. Learning organisations need space to bench mark with others, to ponder on mistakes, and to dissect adverse events. Individual and organisational self-confidence are required to share their experience. The 'learning network' is a welcome sign that this is understood centrally but the concern must be that time for self-directed learning is squeezed under the pressure of 'must dos'.[11]

The establishment of new systems to identify and manage poor performance will be delayed to take account of responses to the government's latest proposals. Postgraduate deaneries lack the capacity to support individual PCGs. Nor is it clear how clinical tutors and others are to foment the construction of practice-based development plans. Clinical governance may be hardest to advance in the neediest areas where general practices are least developed with little track record of working together. This 'inverse care' phenomenon is not restricted to clinical governance but will test health authorities' capacity to target support.

Boosting educational links with universities, co-ordinating and attracting funding for all primary care team members' development, and persuading doctors, nurses and other clinical staff to organise mentoring or supervision: these are the next hurdles.

Organisational development

PCGs are complex organisations. They will develop, and have style, character and weaknesses. Most will soon change into trusts, may merge with neighbours and may reinvent themselves. Leaders with long sight, hooked on change and who anticipate the unexpected will prevail. Discontinuous change will be the rule, if not the plan.[12]

Public involvement

While some lay members of some PCG boards share the clinical governance brief, evidence of patient involvement in these new mechanisms is, as yet, limited. PCGs offer a chance for health, social, educational and civic organisations to co-operate. Indeed, cross-boundary working is a defining feature of primary care. Patients and colleagues will contribute by giving feedback on individual clinicians and on services; and public exposure, through publication of performance measures, will become a normal fact of professional life.

Postmodernism

Suspicion of science lies at the heart of postmodernism, and we live in a postmodern society.[13] Fear of prions in meat and altered genes in plants are signals of reduced public trust in science and, by association, in medicine and healthcare. Patients are shifting their gaze from benefits towards risk. When no children in your city get polio any more, why risk polio in your own child from the immunisation? It seems a lot safer at home than in the doctor's surgery. People with hypertension will dwell on the risk of stroke and the side effects of their tablets, rather than a modest chance of health gain.

GPs are comfortable seasoning evidence with a pinch of values to reach a human, patient-centred opinion. Postmodernism moves on from doctor-centred decisions made on evidence, *in vacuo*, to decisions balanced by preferences and beliefs – the patient's – informed by evidence. Because professional insider knowledge has lost its power, the closed 'head without a world' of the library mollusc will have to open or perish.[14] A confident, educated patient can learn more about their condition from electronic knowledge banks than ever their doctor will. It is recognition of the multiple realities which exist in the different worlds of patients who clinicians often see as homogeneous that will inform future clinical decision making lies at the heart of the called for cultural revolution.

Future prospects

In 1984, Julian Tudor Hart made a characteristically radical proposal: to make GP groups responsible for the general public health of their neighbourhoods as well as for personal care. The primary healthcare team would be involved in an active search for unmet need, in planning the continuing care of chronic disease and in both collecting local morbidity, mortality and risk factor data and making them available in intelligible form to the local populations on an annual basis. In many ways, he was prefiguring PCGs. Yet we still have a way to go to reach his vision.

What would count as progress on clinical governance in three years' time? First, a regular flow of data from local hospitals, practices and health authorities to aid decision making. Second, evidence of close involvement of public health specialists with practice teams and clinical governance leads, each coming to understand the parallel world of the other – flat and vertical systems, patient and disease-centred methods. Third, some specific projects identified in the 2000 clinical governance plans yielding measurable improvements. Fourth, the use of patient-centred indices (of informed choice or the next generation of enablement scores) as outcome measures rather than crude uptakes of immunisation, cervical cytology or mammography screening. Fifth, longer mean GP consultation times could be achieved by a mixture of fewer, more effective consultations and greater involvement of nurses. Finally, that every GP and his or her team has received formal feedback from patients on the quality of service offered and interpersonal communication achieved.

Enthusiasm for clinical governance remains high but will it 'work'? Expectations are rising and the nature of practice is changing too fast for any systemic readjustments to keep pace. Politicians hoping to avert health scandals may be disappointed, because scandal sells newspapers. The Internet and escalating access to all manner of information – good or bad – will fuel that interest.

The impact of NICE will be closely observed. A major determinant as ever will be the availability of resources. Will the implementation of early NSFs be properly funded? Or will clinical governance leads in PCTs find themselves defending painful local rationing decisions? Will clinical governance itself be properly funded?

Clinical governance is essentially about changing the nature of professional accountability. Health professionals are starting to see themselves as collectively responsible for quality – particularly the cost-effectiveness of what they do – as their siblings' keepers. That alone is progress.

References

1 Secretary of State for Health (1989) *Working for Patients*. Cm 555.78. HMSO, London.
2 Spencer J (1993) Audit in general practice: where do we go from here? *Quality in Health Care*. **2**: 183–8.

3 Department of Health (1998) *A First Class Service: quality in the new NHS*. The Stationery Office, London.
4 Audit Commission (2000) *The PCG Agenda: early progress*. Audit Commission, London (in press).
5 Hayward J, Rosen R, Dewar S (1999) Thin on the ground. *HSJ*. **26 August**: 26–7.
6 Department of Health (1999) *Supporting Doctors, Protecting Patients*. The Stationery Office, London.
7 Roland M, Holden J, Campbell S (1998) *Quality Assessment for General Practice: supporting clinical governance in primary care groups*. National Primary Care Research & Development Centre, Manchester.
8 Howie J (1999) Quality at general practice consultations. *BMJ*. **319**: 738–43.
9 Marshall M (2000) An instrument for measuring the therapeutic relationship (submitted to the *BJGP*).
10 Royal College of General Practitioners (1999) *Practical Advice on Clinical Governance for Primary Care Groups*. RCGP, London.
11 Department of Health (1999) *The Learning Network*. The Stationery Office, London.
12 Handy C (1989) *The Age of Unreason*. Arrow, London.
13 Gray JAM (1999) Postmodern medicine. *The Lancet* **354**: 1550–3.
14 Canetti E (1946) *Auro da Fe* (translated by CV Wedgewood). Jonathan Cape, London.

CHAPTER 8

Primary care 2: primary care investment plans

Helen Tanner

If you are reading this chapter of the book, then almost certainly this is because you have some responsibility for the production of your PCG's primary care investment plan (PCIP). The information provided here is therefore of a practical nature, based on real experiences in Mid-Devon. It is designed to help you produce a plan that will be an effective, strategic planning tool, which represents the interests of all those involved in the provision of primary healthcare services.

So what is a PCIP?

One of the three main functions of a PCG is to develop primary and community health services. The PCIP is the mechanism by which the PCG defines its strategy for this development and how and where investments will be made. It must also demonstrate how current expenditure in general medical services (GMS) is to be maintained. The government intends that PCGs should address issues of equity of access to, and improvements in, the quality of primary care services through a programme of investment that builds on and extends current services.

Put simply, the PCIP is a business plan for the development of primary care services. PCGs are required to prepare an annual costed PCIP covering a three-year investment cycle, the first plan covering the period 1999/2000 to 2001/2002, and forms part of the annual accountability agreement with their health authority. The PCIP will enable the PCG board to begin to identify some of the inequalities in resourcing, but it should be remembered that the board is concerned with inequalities in the health of, and healthcare provision for, patients in the PCG area and not necessarily achieving apparently equal distribution of resources to GPs. This is a vital consideration and one which will invariably lead to some difficult decisions!

What goes in a PCIP?

There are ten key elements that must be included in the PCIP but these should serve as a guide to collecting data and planning rather than a prescription for the contents page. Later in the chapter, we will outline the approach to overall presentation that we took in Mid-Devon and how we linked it other key work for the PCG.

Baseline requirement for GMS infrastructure support

This is the sum of money that covers existing commitments to recurrent GMS staff reimbursements or IT maintenance costs that formerly came out of the GMS cash-limited budget. This sounds as though it might be quite straightforward but the reality is that it is here that there is big potential for problems, particularly with staff budgets.

The overall approach taken by our health authority was to develop 'fair-share' target GMS staff budgets by progressively weighting practice list sizes for age and need characteristics. Further adjustments for branch surgeries, temporary residents and economies of scale were then made, the objective being to produce a weighted list size for each practice. This is then used to determine a figure for the relative share of available resources currently invested by the health authority in GMS staff to produce a 'fair-share' target for each practice. Inevitably, on applying this formula, some practices are going to be under target and some over target – you will have to determine a pace of change for moving practices to their targets and engage in some major thinking about how you are going to support those practices who may find themselves having to face a situation where they receive no growth in their reimbursement levels.

Plans for additional GMS investment

Strange as this may seem, this section includes existing commitments to premises such as cost rent, or IT capital investment or leasing – even if funding is managed by the health authority. You can include aspirations, but only agreed commitments for the first year of the plan. You should consider investment in practice staff, IM&T and premises, as well as developments related to the HImP.

Proposals for new investment in GMS infrastructure

This should include plans for new investment in GMS infrastructure to be financed from the health authority's out-of-hours development fund or the national GMS non-cash-limited budget. Items under this heading are the responsibility of the health authority.

Stocktake of existing practice-based services

You will need to define what services are currently provided by the practices – this section should include details of existing PMS pilots and local development schemes provided under Section 36.

Plans for new practice-based services

Here is where the PCIP starts to get exciting – here is the opportunity to present plans for new services, including new personal medical services (PMS) pilot applications. You will need to consider how to encourage practices to develop services that support national and local HImP priorities or specific local health needs.

Review of the local primary care workforce

This covers the numbers and types of doctor, nurse and professions allied to medicine (PAMs), and also management and support staff. Problems with recruitment, retention and skill-mix should be identified, along with training needs. It should also consider other community services such as pharmacists, dentists and optometrists.

Community nursing

In the longer term, PCGs will wish to consider developing nursing capacity and capability to support their increasing role in the move of care from the secondary sector to the primary sector. This might include the development of specialist nurses, integrated care pathways and addressing the training needs of existing nurses. This should be closely linked to the HImP and to partnership working, for example with social services.

Proposals for deployment of former fundholder savings

The PCIP should include the plans agreed by the PCG and former fund-holders for the use of any savings.

Details of the practice incentive scheme

The plan should summarise the incentives which the PCG plans to operate and the planned use of resultant savings from previous schemes.

Plans for continuous professional development

This section should give details of the plans for developing a multidisci-plinary approach to continuous professional development and how individual and practice professional development plans link with PCG aims.

Collecting the data

This is where co-operation from practices is vital. You will need to collect a wide range of data about practice staff, premises and IT, and also the services they currently provide. In addition, you will need to know their development plans in these areas and details of their training needs and practice priorities.

In Mid-Devon we developed a detailed questionnaire and worked with the practice managers' group to ensure that everyone had a clear under-standing of our requirements. There is nothing worse than 20 people answering the same questions in 20 different ways, and this helped to avoid this problem. It also got the practice managers 'on board' with the PCIP and we found this to be very helpful.

You will also need information from other stakeholders, such as details of community nursing hours from the local community trust and any plans they have for service developments. This will help other parties to feel committed to the PCIP and is an excellent opportunity to begin to build a successful working relationship with these groups, something that will be essential to the success of partnership working in the PCG.

How can you bring all this together?

So far, all we have is a list of data that are needed. If it is presented like this, PCIP will be dull and uninteresting and will not seem like a business plan for investing in and developing local primary care services. What you need to do is to plan your structure, and take into account who is going to be reading and using PCIP, and the other key aspects of PCG activity – such as local health improvement in an enhanced partnership working.

In Mid-Devon, we took the following chapter headings:

- Executive summary.
- Introduction – what is a PCIP, defining some terms, introducing the HImP and partnership working.
- Mid-Devon health needs – some basic health needs data, limited by what was available, including standardised mortality ratios (SMRs) of key conditions and deprivation indices highlighting future needs.
- Mid-Devon primary care financial framework – summary of the financial resources available to the PCG, including sources and applications of funds, and the actual proposals for investment in primary care services.
- Resource allocation – GMS staff budgets; current baselines and development plans for staff, premises and IT; PCG prescribing plans and incentive schemes; use of former fundholder savings and plans for existing fundholder contracts.
- Community-based care – community nursing strategy; community nursing staff allocations and plans for changes (including professions allied to medicine); details of partnership links, such as social services, community pharmacists and optometrists.
- Developing the quality of care – clinical governance stocktake and action plan; details of the plans for continuous professional development and practices' identified training needs.
- Our partners in health improvement – plans for prevention of ill health and details of current projects; how we involve patients in PCG work; other partnership matters.
- Primary care investment – future developments – future service development plans from practices and how they match health needs assessment and priorities; next steps.
- Appendices – tables and graphs with resources data. It is a good idea not to clutter the main document with supporting data, hence we put all this at the back of the report.

Throughout the document, we introduced 'PCG Action' boxes, giving details of the actions proposed by the PCG in that specific area, for example establishing a task group to undertake a piece of work. This gives the casual reader a quick way of seeing what is planned and aids future development work.

Consultation

It is important that the PCIP is circulated to all stakeholders for consultation prior to the final document being agreed. You will probably need to ask for two kinds of feedback – corrections to factual data and more general comments on the proposals in the document. Make sure that you have a mechanism for dealing with the feedback and for responding to individuals where appropriate. This is one of the key areas where you can help people to feel involved with and committed to the PCIP, so it is worth spending time on. You may want to consider these groups:

- all practices in the PCG
- local medical committee
- community trusts
- health authority
- acute trusts
- social services
- community pharmacists – Local Pharmaceutical Committee (LPC)
- dentists – Local Dental Committee (LDC)
- opticians – Local Opticians Committee (LOC)
- district councils
- community health council
- local user forum.

What will we do differently next time?

Our experience of preparing the first PCIP in Mid-Devon was on the whole a successful one and we have received some good feedback from various groups. However, there are some key things that we will be doing differently in the next PCIP.

- **Greater involvement of the community trust** – we need to work much more closely with the community trust, both in terms of the data we publish and, more importantly, in developing primary care services in the area, where integrated care pathways offer huge opportunities.
- **Encouraging practices to have 'plans on the shelf'** – short timescales for the first PCIP meant that investment proposals were rushed and this

did not allow practices to develop ideas that were not already under way. There is much scope for innovative work here.

- **Thinner and more strategic** – the first PCIP was a weighty document, containing large amounts of baseline data, and considerable explanation of process and terms. It was also quite light on strategy as the PCG itself was still finding its feet and information on the health needs of our population was not published in time for the deadline for the PCIP. Knowing that many people have difficulty finding the time or the inclination to read this type of document, we would hope that next time the PCIP will be able to concentrate more on the strategic planning and linking in with other plans, such as the HImP, and less on graphs and tables.

After the PCIP is published

A final word of caution! Writing the PCIP is just the beginning, because what this does is set a huge agenda for development work that will need to be undertaken by the PCG. You cannot just write the PCIP then put it away in a cupboard – your stakeholders will be looking to you for action not empty promises!

CHAPTER 9

Managing human resources in PCGs

Alex Trompetas

As PCGs around the country developed as distinct organisations, human resources became one of the most important issues in determining their success. A 'helicopter view' of their development reveals different stages of progress, but also evolution to widely differing models. Some PCGs have a close relationship with their health authorities, sharing resources including human resources, while others have taken a more independent developmental route.

Size is one of the determining factors in human resources, with some of the larger PCGs (100 000+ population) having to deal with human resources earlier in their business agenda. A further reminder of the importance of human resources to PCGs is the latest guidance regarding applications for PCT status.[1] In the guidance, it is made clear that a robust and acceptable human resources business plan would be a prerequisite for a successful PCT application. As for many PCGs their current position is just a transient developmental step on the road to becoming a PCT, the importance and urgency of the task becomes clear.

In this chapter we examine the different models developed by PCGs and how they relate to human resource management. We also give an overview of the different facets of human resources within a PCG organisation including general practice development and allied organisations.

Finally we show how human resource management theory can explain some of the practical developments in the first year of PCGs and how it can provide the basis for the key themes for future development and successful transformation to PCTs.

Different PCG models

PCGs and health authorities

In human resources terms there is a range of PCG development in relation to the PCG integration with the health authority. This can be expressed as a continuum from fully integrated to fully independent (Figure 9.1).

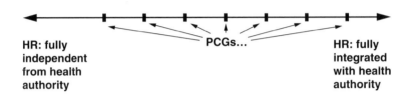

Figure 9.1   Range of PCG integration with the health authority. It is rare to find a PCG at either extreme, i.e. fully integrated or fully independent.

Integration can be measured in terms of basic PCG identifiers, such as premises, management allowance, origin of PCG staff (ex-health authority or external staff) and corporate identity.

A recent Audit Commission report of PCG management allowances, for example, showed a range of between £1.80 and £4.50 per capita. It also showed that in many areas, what was measured as management costs was a mixture of cash and staff transferred from the health authority to the PCG on secondment. Where staff were transferred from the health authority to the PCG this would have been a major influence in human resources terms.

In many PCGs, health authority personnel have filled the positions of chief executive and other senior management, either as a permanent career move from the health authority or as a secondment. The relation of a PCG with their health authority is therefore, in many cases, more complex than just 'integrated or not integrated'. A simple linear presentation would not have taken into account the different factors that may have influenced human resources development. A multiaxial mapping can more accurately and graphically demonstrate PCG variation around the country (Figure 9.2).

PCGs sharing premises with the health authority are more likely to share human resources, and PCGs with a higher per capita management allowance are more likely to have health authority staff transferred from health authority functions to PCG functions, contributing to the higher management allowance.[2]

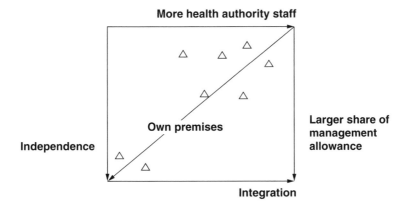

Figure 9.2 A multidimensional map of integration with the health authority, with PCGs (∆) positioned according to management allowance, premises and staff.

Different aspects of the PCG organisation

Mapping the organisation

In terms of human resources needs, we can define here:

- the role of the health authority
- the core PCG management structure
- the PCG practices
- the PCG sister organisations.

Clearly there is a delicate balance here. The PCG management structure and the PCG practices are core parts of the PCG, and their human resources planning can be directly influenced by the PCG itself. The PCG sister organisations, however, which include the local community trust, the social services and many extended primary care services such as therapists, community psychiatric nurses (CPNs), midwives, etc., have their own human resources agenda.

The challenge here is to integrate these diverse agendas building for a future where the PCG transforms successfully into a new primary care organisation, the PCT.

The role of the health authority

The PCG is a subcommittee of the health authority. Often, PCG management staff are appointed by the health authority and comply with health authority personnel rules. In fact, in many cases workforce planning will have taken place looking at the combined PCG and health authority staff. This means analysing the functions required in order to decide the staffing needs.

The PCG core management staff

Human resource policies here would, in the majority of PCGs around the country, mirror those of the health authority. As reflected earlier PCGs are health authority subcommittees and developmentally have evolved from the health authority stable.

The PCG core management staff are the chief executive and other PCG office staff. For descriptive purposes we can list some of the personnel positions, although there are wide local variations depending on the local PCG functions. An example of an analysis of functions required and relevant personnel is given in Table 9.1. There is a characteristic similarity with health authority functions.

Table 9.1   Example of PCG functions and relevant personnel

PCG function	PCG staff
Overall management	Chief executive
Office support	PA/administrators
Office support/secretarial	Office secretaries
Primary care development	Primary care facilitators, nurse development facilitators
Prescribing	Lead pharmacist/ prescribing advisors
Commissioning	Commissioning leads
Commissioning	Data analysts
Epidemiology/public health duties	Attached public health personnel
Finance	Finance lead
Communications/IT	Communications analyst/ IT support
Corporate affairs	Attached corporate lead
Human resources	Attached human resources

If PCG core functions were assumed to be similar around the country, a similar table of human resource requirements would be found in various PCGs. It is an interesting fact that management costs in the first year of PCGs have a wide range (£1.89–£4.50 per capita).

The PCG practices

There are human resources issues in individual practices. These concern the professional and the support staff. The main categories of practice staff are:

- doctors and nurses
- ancillary clinical staff
- practice management staff
- receptionists
- secretarial/administrative staff
- IT support staff
- attached staff.

In dealing with practice human resources there are specific issues arising from the fact that practices are individual organisations within the umbrella of the PCG organisation:

- Do individual practices have a human resources policy?
- If a practice has a human resources policy is this in line with:
  - other practices within the PCG?
  - the PCG's human resources policy?

The first issue is an equity issue, while the second is a corporate development issue. PCGs have tried to deal with this issue through primary care development and in some areas through clinical governance. PCIPs have looked at the issues of human resource provision within the PCG corporate body but also at individual practice level.

In many PCGs, detailed work has taken place at practice level, including practice visits. This has started as a 'stocktaking' exercise of the existing practice workforce. It has progressed to a 'mapping' of the different competencies matched to the performed functions in the constituent practices. This new knowledge of the human resource stock is now used in many PCGs for the next developmental phase.

PCG sister organisations

Community trusts around the country have a well-developed human resources department and human resources policies. The issues arise here from the relation between community health trusts (CHTs) and:

- the PCG itself
- the individual constituent practices
- the future development of a joint organisation, the PCT.

Arguably, the essential elements of HR policy should also be very similar around the country. CHTs are similar organisations offering primary care and community health services within the overall NHS umbrella. It is again an interesting observation that management costs can vary so widely around the country (11–17% staff 'on costs').[3]

CHTs may have an extremely important human resources role to play in the future of primary care organisations. As health authorities are 'slimming down' community trust human resources departments may become the only source of human resource expertise in primary care in a local health economy.

Social services departments will also have human resources policies, however, these will have more to do with the overall local government policy and less with the health community. Nevertheless in a joint primary care future with organisations providing the entire extended range of primary care services, human resources policies in social services will have to reflect this new integrated working.

Clearly then, there is a new shape of things in human resources terms in local health economies. The initial core human resource function is now extending outwards to encompass GP practices and the sister organisations in a single new organisation. The different layers of human resources within primary care and the move to become one organisation is depicted diagrammatically as a bullet moving from PCG to PCT in Figure 9.3.

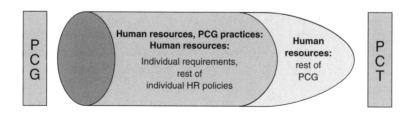

Figure 9.3 Human resource management as a force for change, 'moving like a bullet'.

Key human resource themes for the future

We have already seen how PCGs went through a period of intense organisational development. From fledgling, almost virtual, organisations, many PCGs have now reached a new stage of maturity. Below, I examine four major themes in human resource development:

- human resource processes as a force for change
- recruiting and developing a high commitment workforce
- managing for high quality and balancing a professional organisation
- managing careers.

In examining each one, I will compare the new agenda and how it has been applied in practice so far.

Human resource processes as a force for change

The new agenda
One of the biggest challenges for PCGs has been to link people with the vision and the organisation's strategic needs. A survey of the first national commissioning pilots showed a high level of enthusiasm and involvement among some of the primary care professionals in the PCGs.[4] The rhetoric of many PCG mission statements referred to 'Creating an organisation which will provide high quality, equitable and inclusive health services, aiming to improve the health of their populations'. The overall agenda set for all PCGs is to:[5]

- improve the health of the community
- develop primary and community health services
- commission secondary care services.

What has happened so far?
The first challenge faced by the PCGs in workforce planning was that the new 'agenda' was in contrast to the earlier health reforms and the 'internal market'. In particular changes had to take into account:

- the abolition of the fundholding scheme and absorbing fundholding staff
- the restructuring of the health authorities and the consequences for their staff
- the reorientation of CHTs away from the internal market to reflect the new PCGs

- the creation of new organisations with a new corporate identity (PCGs).

To achieve the above, PCGs went through a period of organisational change. This is still continuing for many PCGs. Many workforce planning issues are still evolving and particularly issues such as:

- requirements of employment legislation
- staff training and development
- staff numbers, skills and diversity to deliver the new objectives
- developing the organisation while delivering the agenda.

The tremendous pace of change and the need for parallel development of human resource strategies while delivering the first HImPs and implementing clinical governance has resulted in great diversity in the human resource progress of PCGs.[6]

Recruiting and developing a high commitment workforce

The new agenda
The recently published NHS human resource strategy made clear the need for developing a quality workforce, which will encompass primary care.[7] This meant designing and implementing a human resource strategy that will meet the national human resource standards as part of a long-term objective, while at the same time dealing with short- and medium-term organisational needs.

The first challenges faced by the new organisations were:

- understanding the context
- achieving vertical and horizontal integration
- delivering short-term organisation goals
- preparing for long-term success.

What has happened so far?
The introduction of the *The New NHS: modern, dependable* in 1997 ushered an era of intense change.[8] The 'old contract' for primary care was challenged and at the same time the psychological deal for many of the employees in primary care changed. Paul Kotter described as early as the 1970s how the change of what he called the 'psychological contract' can have a profound effect in the relationship between people and their organisations.[9]

The contrast of the old and the new were epitomised around fund-holding with its workforce and employment implications. This change of psychological contract may have created a vacuum of commitment in some PCGs or among some of the workforce. Monitoring primary care organisations' surveys and website discussions reveals a variety of anecdotal stories of low involvement and commitment.[10] Dr Denise Rousseau described the four stages of changing the psychological contract as described in Table 9.2:[11]

Table 9.2   Changing the psychological contract

Stage	Intervention
Challenging the old contract	Communication, information
Preparation for change	Staff involvement, Ownership of changes Acknowledge good features of old contract Create transitional structures
Contract generation	Active involvement in new contract creation Make people sign up
Living the new contract	Consistency in new terms Following through Reinforce and refresh

Source: Rousseau (1996).[11]

Examples of PCG staff affected were:

• previous health authority staff now working for PCGs
• current health authority staff who have not yet adjusted to the changes
• GPs and particularly ex-fundholders and their staff
• single-handed GPs, who have yet to adjust to the new collaborative spirit
• community staff such as health visitors, community nurses and others whose line of management and orientation may have changed.

Managing for high quality and balancing the professional organisation

The new agenda

PCGs are professional services organisations or knowledge-based organisations that provide health services to their populations. To achieve this their workforce consists of three main groups (Figure 9.4):

- the professional staff including management
- the technical support staff
- the administrative staff.

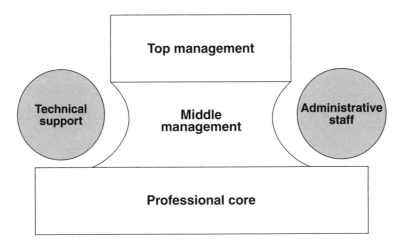

Figure 9.4 The structure of the professional services organisation. *Source*: Mintzberg (1989).[12]

Reality so far

Professional health service organisation needs technical support staff mostly for IT communications and office support functions. Technical support staff are vital to maintain the corporate structure and integrity of the organisation. However, technical support and administrative staff in a professional services organisation are smaller than in other organisations such as retailing, manufacturing, etc.[12]

As PCGs have found in their first year, creating a virtual organisation and absorbing a number of small organisations such as individual practices is an administrative challenge. Furthermore, the sheer amount of new regulation and guidance from the Department of Health and monitoring the new performance requirements for PCGs make the administrative support function essential.

The professional staff are the most populous class of the PCG. They can range from being the frontline workforce offering services to having more specialised project management duties. The professional workforce has been involved in the PCGs to different degrees, with the GPs showing some of the lowest levels of enthusiasm. Issues of communication among professionals, training and development for the professionals, and developing career paths have been employed to increase their involvement.

The management section of the workforce in a professional service organisation has normally evolved from the professional class itself. Many of the chief executives, PCG chairmen, commissioning and public health managers, prescribing managers, etc., have evolved from a more pure clinical professional role. For example, most PCG chairmen are current practising GPs, many of the management staff have come from the nursing professional ranks and management of prescribing often lies with pharmacists.

Management staff in many PCGs has devolved from health authorities and are influenced by the human resource culture of the old health authorities. This may relate to pay and incentives, to professional training and development, and to employment conditions.

Managing careers

The new agenda
Working Together guidance makes clear that managing careers in the NHS is an essential part of human resources. The creation of PCG organisations as well as other developments in primary care, such as NHS Direct, 'walk-in' centres and, of course, the arrival of the first few PCTs, opens new career pathways within the organisations.

This means further periods of intense change, which will have to be managed. This includes professionals and management making difficult decisions either voluntarily or reacting to organisational changes around them. The new PCGs around the country are gradually developing professional development plans (PDPs) and personal learning plans (PLPs) for their workforce. Managing the careers of this workforce will become an essential part of achieving the PCG vision.

The PCG as a professional services organisation
The archetypal structure of the professional service organisation is an organisation containing three professional levels, which serve as a

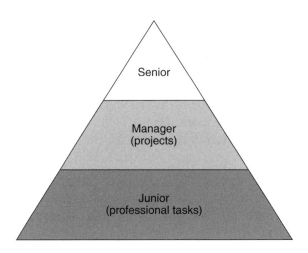

Figure 9.5 The Professional Pyramid. *Source*: Maister (1982).[13]

normal or expected career path.[13] This is seen in the Professional Pyramid (Figure 9.5).

Successful human resource management will have to manage this career pyramid when planning the workforce of the future. People with management potential, and ambition will need to be identified early on and nurtured and developed. Professionals without management ambitions will also have to be offered personal development opportunities to retain commitment.

Issues for the future

Looking ahead

Having reached with a degree of success the first stages of organisational development PCGs have ensured their early survival as new organisations. PCGs will now have to face the new challenge of the future, becoming mature organisations as PCGs, or progressing to PCTs. This challenge will need a robust and coherent human resource policy. This may in practice have very similar requirements whether they choose to remain as PCGs or develop to PCTs.

Those that decide to progress to PCTs will have to time their human resource implementation much earlier so that they can meet the requirements for PCT status application. Human resources guidance by the NHS

Executive has outlined the requirements for PCTs and highlighted several important areas:

- securing a quality workforce for the NHS
- working time regulations implementation of the NHS
- modernising the NHS pay system
- improving working lives in the NHS
- tackling racial harassment in the NHS
- campaign to stop violence against staff working in the NHS
- management of health, safety and welfare issues for NHS staff.

Conclusions

Delivering the current agenda is still in progress. Addressing the future and the new guidance for workforce, as well as other new developments such as PMS pilots, new requirements for equal opportunities, and a constant requirement for training and development of the workforce, will present the new challenges for the young PCG organisations and those moving to PCTs.

Where PCTs are planned, there will be the further upheaval of possible merging with other sister NHS organisations such as community trusts and social services. Many PCGs will find that despite their earlier steep learning curve, there is little human resource expertise in their ranks. Utilising the human resources expertise of some of the new partner organisations may be one of their best options. This will allow them to make the best use of the workforce and meet the requirements for a successful PCT application.

References

1 NHS Executive (1999) *Working Together: human resource guidance and requirements for primary care trusts.* NHSE, London.
2 *NHS Alliance PCG survey* (1999) www.nhsalliance.org.uk
3 Audit Commission (1999) *First Assessment: a review of district nursing services in England and Wales.* Audit Commission, London.
4 Smith JA, Regan EL, Goodwin N *et al.* (2000) *Getting Into Their Stride: report of a national evaluation of primary care groups.* Health Services Management Centre, Birmingham.
5 NHS Executive (1998) *Developing Primary Care Groups.* HSC 1998/139. NHSE, London.
6 Audit Commission (2000) *The PCG Agenda: early progress of primary care*

groups in 'The New NHS'. Audit Commission, London.

7 Department of Health (1998) *Working Together: securing a quality work-force for the NHS*. The Stationery Office, London.

8 Secretary of State for Health (1997) *The New NHS: modern, dependable.* The Stationery Office, London.

9 Kotter JP (1973) *The Psychological Contract: managing the joining-up process*. California Management Review, University of California.

10 www.nhsalliance.org.uk

11 Rousseau DM (1996) Changing the deal while keeping the people. *Academy of Management Executive*. **10**(1): 50–8.

12 Mintzberg H (1989) *Inside Our Strange World of Organisations*. Free Press, New York, Chapter 6.

13 Maister DH (1982) Balancing the professional services firm. *Sloan Management Review*. **24**(1).

Further reading

Audit Commission (1999) *PCGs: an early view*. Audit Commission, London.

Audit Commission (2000) *The PCG Agenda: early progress of primary care groups in 'The New NHS'*. Audit Commission, London.

Daft RL (1995) *Organisation Theory and Design* (5e). West Publishing Company, St Paul, MN, Chapter 6.

Moscovici S, Doise W (1994) *Conflict and Consensus: a general theory of collective decisions*. Sage, Thousand Oaks, CA.

NHS Executive (1998) *Developing Primary Care Groups*. HSC 1998/139. NHSE, London.

Prahalad CK, Hamel G (1990) The Core Competencies of the Corporation, Harvard Business Review.

Secretary of State for Health (1997) *The New NHS: modern, dependable*. The Stationery Office, London.

Useful websites

www.audit-commission.gov.uk
www.doh.gov.uk
www.msf.org.uk
www.nhsalliance.org.uk
www.nhsp.org.uk
www.rcn.org.uk
www.unison.org.uk

PART 3

People

CHAPTER 10

The PCG chair: roles and responsibilities

John Wood

The PCG chair is accountable to the chief executive of the health authority. The PCG board is accountable to the health authority for its decisions, and to the stakeholders in the PCG and to the patients. The chief executive/general manager of the PCG is responsible for the daily business of the PCG and is accountable, in turn, to the PCG board chair.

As a committee of a statutory body, PCG boards must operate in an open and transparent way. The PCG board chair must ensure that the board abides by the standing orders and standing financial instructions adopted by the health authority. These protect the health authority's, and the PCG's, interests. The PCG board chair needs to have a working knowledge of these documents and to seek advice and clarification from the appropriate health authority staff when necessary.

Relationship with the health authority

While the chief executive of the health authority is ultimately the 'accountable officer' for ensuring that the work of the health authority and any of its committees (e.g. PCG boards) is carried out within the available finance, the PCG board chair acts as 'responsible officer' in support. A close relationship with the health authority is vital to ensure propriety and value for money in the use of public funds.

The chair has responsibility for ensuring that the PCG is able to take on specific delegated financial responsibilities, and to ensure that the PCG works with the health authority and individual practices to agree and to take forward risk management and incentive schemes which contribute to sound financial management across the health authority.

The PCG board chair acts as a conduit for information and opinion from the PCG to the health authority and needs to be aware of the issues and discussions within the PCG to accurately reflect the current situation.

Provide leadership

The PCG board chair must provide leadership and encouragement to the other board members, particularly in the way they carry out their lead roles on the board, and help to resolve any difficulties that may arise. All stakeholders must feel that they are involved in providing an input towards decisions on policy, the HImP and the PCIP. This involves seeking opinions and comments from all the primary healthcare teams, and representatives from the public and voluntary organisations – perhaps by holding open meetings within the PCG. The chair must ensure that there are adequate arrangements in place to provide feedback to all the individuals in the PCG.

Liaison with other PCGs is important so that common issues and problems can be discussed and a common policy developed, if this is in line with the strategic direction of the health authority. This could be achieved by a meeting of all the PCG board chairs, or the chairs of a small local group of PCGs (e.g. from a city area). This is particularly important when it has been demonstrated that some PCGs have been relatively underfunded compared to other PCGs in the health authority. The chair represents the views of the board and, on behalf of the board, can agree the pace of change to address the question of budget allocation.

PCG board chair and PCG staff

One of the most important factors affecting whether a PCG board is successful or not is the working relationship between the chair and the chief executive/general manager. It is crucial that there is an adequate flow of information between them, and regular meetings are required to discuss local issues and any tensions within the board which might lead to a destabilisation of the board dynamics and have a harmful effect on the ability of the board to carry out its duties.

A number of key functions are devolved down to PCG level and the PCG board chair is responsible for the delivery of these functions, with the support of the PCG Staff – finance manager, development manager and quality co-ordinator. Again, adequate communication between the PCG board chair and the staff is essential to promote the smooth running of the board.

PCG board meetings

The meetings of the PCG board held in public (as opposed to public meetings of the board) require the PCG board chair to ensure a corporate approach to PCG business and that the Nolan Principles of Public Life are upheld.

Nolan Principles of Public Life

1 Selflessness – holders of public office should take decisions solely in terms of the public interest. They should not do so in order to gain financial or other material benefits for themselves, their family or their friends.
2 Integrity – holders of public office should not place themselves under any financial or other obligation to outside individuals or organisations that might influence them in the performance of their official duties.
3 Objectivity – in carrying out public business, including making public appointments, awarding contracts or recommending individuals for rewards and benefits, holders of public office should make choices on merit.
4 Accountability – holders of public office are accountable for their decisions and actions to the public and must submit themselves to whatever scrutiny is appropriate to their office.
5 Openness – holders of public office should be as open as possible about all the decisions and actions they take. They should give reasons for their decisions and restrict information only when the wider public interest clearly demands.
6 Honesty – holders of public office have a duty to declare any private interests relating to their public duties and to take steps to resolve any conflicts arising in a way that protects the public interest.
7 Leadership – holders of public office should promote and support these principles by leadership and example.

These principles are echoed in the standing orders and standing financial instructions of the health authority.

The meetings themselves must be conducted in a business-like manner and it is the responsibility of the PCG board chair to ensure that there is adequate time for all the items on the agenda to be discussed and that all members of the board have an opportunity to make comments. Every effort must be taken to make sure that all board members are fully informed about the items under discussion and time allowed to explain terminology or developments since the last meeting. The chair will need to summarise the main points of the discussion and arrange for the consensus view to be recorded in the minutes of the meeting.

There must be an opportunity for the public to ask questions, and the

PCG board chair must decide, in consultation with others, how best to manage that session; how the questions will be dealt with, and by whom.

The chair has a pivotal role within the PCG. Various people will seek the comments and opinions of the chair. A full knowledge of the local issues and health needs of the local population is necessary.

The ability to demonstrate a sense of partnership and co-operation between the various stakeholders and to work with the health authority to achieve a measurable health gain will go a long way to ensuring the success of the PCG.

CHAPTER 11

The PCG chair:
a personal experience

David Jenner

With the advent of PCGs came a new role, that of the PCG chair. This was to be a local professional leading in the organisation and commissioning of local healthcare yet remaining accountable to the chief executive of the local health authority. In the majority of cases this role has been taken by GPs, some of whom had emerged from previous locality commissioning groups and total purchasing pilots. But for some it was a new exposure to the intricacies of health service management and commissioning. These people had to be elected (or very commonly not actively opposed) by their local peers to take on these new responsibilities.

After nine months it appears that the major function of the role is to act as 'rubber band man or woman' absorbing stresses and strains and radial accountability lines. More cynical people liken this to being placed on a medieval torture rack with each limb tied to the different priorities of the NHS which demands more improvements and more efficiency while the government slowly cranks the wheel. The key tensions are between the health authority and the PCG, and between the PCG and local practices. Different professional groups, patients, users and other agencies hang on to the remaining limbs. The trick of the job is to balance the tensions so that nothing gives way (especially yourself) and that everyone's interests are represented in the ensuing policy.

Becoming a PCG chair is also a leap into the unknown, for as you take on the responsibility, you become slightly distanced from what used to be your peers. That is because you not only represent them on the PCG but also the interests of the patients served by the PCG community and the other professionals involved within it. Most people are considerate but the cries of 'Judas' are never far away, especially from general practice with little history of corporate working or accountability. For the large part though people are supportive and respectful and fully understanding of the difficulties and intricacies of the role and will quickly point out when there seems likely to be a conflict of interest (as there will always be for professionals who are both commissioning and providing services).

Personal development in these roles has often followed the time-honoured medical principle of 'see one, do one, teach one' with varying degrees of support from local health authorities and regional offices. The real challenge for these PCG chairs, however, is that just over a year into their existence and still in a larval stage of development, they are now faced with the proposition of a future metamorphosis into a new role within a new organisation – that of the PCT. Should one develop as fully as possible in one form in order to prepare for this change or go for a quick pupation and reincarnation in a new role? Caution should favour the brave as the new roles of executive chair are subtly different from those of the PCG chair but clinical leadership and local strategy remains the core brief.

PCG chairs are accountable to their chief executive of the health authority and the PCG chief executive is accountable to them. Yet the model varies widely – in some areas it is implemented to the full, while in others only lip service is paid and the real driving force in the PCG is the PCG chief executive and not the chair. Does this matter? Yes, it probably does, and where clinical leadership is not strong there is a risk that the underlying principles of the new NHS reform will not be truly realised and we could even reinvent the old district health authority structure.

So a PCG chair needs to be a leader and yet clearly seen as an honest broker and somebody who is not partisan to their own professional or practice background. The role requires a commitment to working along-side and valuing the distinct skills that healthcare managers can bring rather than trying to impose the clinician's agenda over theirs. A strong sense of political awareness is also helpful – it is important to understand which of the plethora of priorities are the 'hanging offences' that really must be delivered and which are the 'nice to haves'. This is a balancing act that most NHS managers will recognise, but most primary care professionals have hitherto been insulated from the pragmatism and demands of national political priorities.

In summary then, the role is evolutionary and probably transitory, yet will be crucial in helping local communities deliver the key aims of the new NHS.

CHAPTER 12

The role of the PCG clinical governance lead

Graham Archard

Clinical governance is the inevitable consequence of the government's ambition to 'shift the focus on to quality of care so that excellence is guaranteed to all patients and quality becomes the driving force for decision-making at every level of the service'.[1] It is defined as 'a framework through which NHS organisations are accountable for continuously improving the quality of their services and safeguarding high standards of care by creating an environment in which excellence in clinical care will flourish'.[2]

To achieve these aims it is proposed that clear national quality standards will be produced through the NSFs and NICE, and clinical governance will be established to ensure local delivery of these standards through systems of dissemination and monitoring.

So, all you have to do to be a successful primary care clinical governance lead (CGL) is to identify that every doctor, nurse and professional allied to medicine is delivering high-quality clinical practice in accordance with national and local criteria and standards, thus complying with government strategy! If they do not, you quite simply have to develop an action plan to rectify the situation with their full support and respect and to ensure that at a later date the action plan has produced the results the government expects. All this in a disparate and sometimes unwilling and suspicious workforce who may hardly know you or understand what you are trying to do.

One of the challenges facing the successful CGL is to maintain the respect of colleagues against a tide of increasing demands set both by the government and the health authorities. The government advises that CGLs are to be respected colleagues within the PCG. They also need to be miracle makers and magicians and have accomplished communication and political skills. Despite this, there seems to be a large number of people who are prepared to undertake this role and, indeed, to be very successful in it.

Why clinical governance?

In 1991, the government intended to introduce clinical audit into every facet of clinical practise through the introduction of Medical Audit Advisory Groups (MAAGs). Some of these groups still very actively contribute to the quality agenda, cohabitating in a synergistic and mutually supporting way with clinical governance; others have disappeared along with much of the good work they produced. Although encouraging clinical audit at practice level, most MAAGs, including my own, concentrated on standards, audits and quality criteria across the whole geographic area for which they had responsibility. Clinical governance largely agrees quality criteria at a very local level responding to individual practitioners and practices in a way that the audit groups could rarely do.

As a result, policies and agendas agreed with individual practices will be less likely to appear 'ivory towered' and the clinical governance lead agreeing the agenda will be less distant being conversant with local circumstances and difficulties.

Job description – length and breadth

Success in clinical governance relies on the establishment of a good rapport between colleagues and CGLs. They must identify the strengths and weaknesses of colleagues and agree how best to support and assist them effectively to deliver consistent, high-quality care in accordance with agreed standards and procedures. There is the opportunity to genuinely involve everybody in the area, professionals and public alike, identifying health needs and agreeing a mechanism for the delivery and improvement of healthcare. For the first time, people can make a real difference to the outcome of the health of their community.

One of the weaknesses of the system is that clinical governance leads are expected to police colleagues as well as to support them. It will not be long before the CGL will have to address a complaint, which has been made against a senior colleague. This has to be resolved with sensitivity and understanding for the professional, while ensuring the public are protected from poor practice and that their concerns are fairly and properly addressed. If mishandled, the relationship between the CGL and colleagues can be irreparably damaged. It is important that established relationships with colleagues are preserved at all costs.

The other major weakness of the system is the ridiculously inadequate amount of time resourced to implement the agenda. There are endless documents to read and invitations to conferences to be considered. One has to learn to be selective and only spend time on those items which will give maximum benefit. It is unlikely, though, that the time spent will be adequately resourced.

Do not underestimate the additional work that colleagues will have to undertake to cover you, giving you time to become a CGL. You will not be the only one in your practice under pressure, so it is important to agree the amount of time you are likely to be away from the practice – and don't forget this time needs to be flexible. If you do not have the support of your colleagues it is unlikely you can be an effective CGL.

Locum fees to cover time out of practice are reimbursable. However, if you choose to go part time to allow you time for your clinical governance commitments you will be unable to claim locum allowances for this time. As a part-timer you will only earn the clinical governance allowance rather than the clinical governance allowance *plus* the usual pay of the full-timer. This will represent a significant reduction in earnings and is, of course, contrary to the intentions of the government. This anomaly needs urgent attention.

Where will primary care be in ten years' time? You should consider this question carefully if you are tempted to give up full-time employment. You may find yourself out of a job if the government agenda changes or if you are not as successful as you would like to be.

Baseline assessment and practice agreements

Most CGLs have now established a baseline audit to identify where the PCG is and how it can move towards the ideal. This involves making agreements with practices and individuals and monitoring progress towards agreed goals. It is made easier by each general practice appointing its own clinical governance lead (CGL), who can mediate with the CGL for the PCG as a whole. This involves a great deal of work producing the initial agreement and also interpreting what constitutes 'progress'. The political skills of the CGL are rarely more evident than in the review of these agreements!

Education and personal development plans, etc.

Within the remit of clinical governance is helping to produce personal and practice development plans and lifelong learning. Many CGLs will have little experience of education and must work closely with educators to ensure that what they suggest is sensible and in line with current policy.

Critical incident reporting

Those experienced in medical audit are probably also experienced in critical incident reporting. There are those who find the concept frightening and threatening. Critical incident reporting is not only hair-shirt wearing, it is also the opportunity to celebrate success. It is important to encourage primary healthcare teams to identify good points as well as disappointments as critical incidents. It must be practised in a blame-free culture, preferably crossing professional boundaries, and must strictly adhere to the principles of confidentiality.

Surgeries (and later professions allied to medicine for which the CGL has a responsibility) must develop a mechanism for reporting critical incidents to the CGL so that any emerging patterns can be identified and addressed. These can be discussed with the practice CGLs and, where necessary, action points identified. If you want to maintain credibility and respect from your team this must be handled with care. The problem is that the concept of critical incident reporting has been confused with whistle-blowing but this is very much at one end of the spectrum.

Problems

Pressures from health authorities

Some PCGs have the luxury of agreeing their own agendas and priorities within the confines of the HImP. This is, of course, what the government planned. There are those who are less fortunate and are subject to a strict top-down approach. Before even national standards are adopted some health authorities are insistent on imposing more rigorous and difficult local standards without the support or agreement of the PCGs and without any identified additional resources. These criteria can also lack any evidence base. There is often little that can be done in these circumstances, which demeans and devalues the professional skills and abilities of those appointed to their positions within PCGs.

Targets? – whose targets?

There is a potential problem with clinical targets. It is perfectly easy to achieve the national cervical cytology targets in the leafy suburbs of Dorset. It might be very much more difficult in an inner-city practice. The variability of age, ethnicity and social make-up between different geographic areas can adversely affect the achievement of targets, unfairly stigmatising those working in the most deprived areas of the country. Measurement of the quality of care requires a number of tools if it is to be meaningful.

Targets are one such tool. They must be used as such and not chanted like a mantra at every opportunity. The setting and delivery of targets by CGLs should take existing service provision, local health problems, culture and variations into account, ensuring local interpretation of the national agenda. There is the risk that achievement of targets rather than improvement in healthcare can become the objective. Targets must be realistic and must be locally owned. Quality must not simply be measured against absolute standards but by movement towards agreed goals relative to past performance using measures that are relevant to context.

Involving those who do not want to play

There will always be those who do not want to play. General practice in particular has been subject to numerous changes over the years. Clinical governance is seen by many as merely the latest hurdle put in the way of hard working primary healthcare teams who feel that this may be a temporary project which will be taken over by another idea as soon as this one is implemented.

Comparing the performance of the unwilling with that of their peers is an effective way of introducing change. Professionals do not like performing less well and comparisons can unsettle the poorer performers. If the unwilling are already performing well then there is not so much of a problem. Performance incentives are not the only way to encourage the unwilling – involving them in producing or monitoring the quality agenda can turn poacher into gamekeeper. Confrontation is counterproductive and will merely lead to further problems. The trick is to prevent entrenchment of colleagues into a particular attitude.

How will the job evolve?

Involvement of others

Clinical governance has rightly concentrated its initial efforts on the immediate PCG. As time moves on, the involvement of others will become more and more important. Greater public involvement in all aspects of clinical governance will be the norm. There will be greater input into other community professionals, such as opticians, dentists and community pharmacists, and closer liaison with secondary care. Each specialty will be represented by its own CGLs who will have to liaise with the PCG CGL. If the new NHS is to be primary care-led, quality standards must be agreed with these disciplines and monitored by the CGL. This will inevitably lead to a greater workload but potentially even greater job satisfaction.

Revalidation and accreditation

Clinical governance is a mere stone's throw from revalidation. There will be numerous models for revalidation both of the individual and the team. These may involve the quality initiatives of the Royal College of General Practice or PDPs. There is little doubt that the CGL will have to play an important part in the certification of professionals in the future to ensure that practise falls within the minimum standards required by the government.

Recognition of good practice is also the responsibility of the CGL. Recognition of achievement, even in a letter, will help to maintain morale. It is important, though, not to miss potential decline in performance of those with a previous record of good performance. Those with personal or health problems, depression, alcohol and drug abuse are entitled to the support of the CGL for help through a crisis, and to find assistance from whatever human resources are available in their PCG. The CGL has a moral responsibility to ensure the setting up of human resource facilities locally. There must be a move away from punitive solutions for poor performance towards genuine efforts to identify the causes of poor performance.

Achievements

How would the CGL recognise if he or she has been successful? First, there must be measurable improvement in the health and care of the community served by the PCG. There must be genuine teamworking within the PCG, the professions allied to medicine and the interface between primary and secondary care. Clinical governance provides the opportunity to ensure seamless care between all professionals, so long as a culture of genuine teamworking has been established.

Probably the most important yardstick for determining if a CGL has achieved is whether colleagues and the public still speak to him or her.

Conclusion

Clinical governance was introduced by the government to implement the quality agenda. To be a CGL is an exciting prospect but one which should be considered carefully before making a commitment. At the moment the position is poorly resourced and financed and the pressures on CGLs are increasing all the time.

Clinical governance can present the opportunity to make a genuine contribution towards the improvement of healthcare in a community. It also provides an opportunity to develop an alternative career as well as to offer help and advice to local colleagues. It is important to be politically correct as well as empathetic with colleagues who might find these times difficult and confusing. The rewards, though, can be enormous, so for those who choose to go down this pathway – good luck!

References

1 NHS Executive (1998) *A First Class Service: quality in the new NHS.* NHSE, London.
2 Secretary of State for Health (1997) *The New NHS: modern, dependable.* The Stationery Office, London.

CHAPTER 13

The role of a GP member of a PCG board

Mike North

Why did we do it? More to the point, why are we still doing it? Why did large numbers of intelligent doctors with more than enough on their plates volunteer to do yet another job, which, at the time, was largely undefined, potentially underfunded and decried by the large majority of our profession?

I guess the majority of us had very personal and individual reasons for taking part. Fundholders may have joined to try and ensure that their privileges were protected, non-fundholders may have joined to ensure that they weren't, or perhaps to try and share in the perceived benefits which they had seen others receiving. Others, such as single-handed or dispensing practitioners, may have wished to protect their personal situations and others may have been in imminent need of staff or premises development. Against the odds, most PCGs were able to look to the great and the good to fill the GP places on their board and I suppose it is always possible that some of us are there with no personal agenda.

I do not recall ever having to have an election among my peers and this presented us with one of our earliest problems – how to arrange the voting so that we achieved a representative spread of all areas and all types of practice. One of my sons kindly offered to design a mathematical voting scheme which would maximise the likelihood of attaining the result we wished to achieve! We eventually settled for having four 'local elections', with each of our four geographically distinct areas electing one of their members to the board, and a subsequent PCG-wide election to choose the three remaining GPs from anybody from any of the four areas who wished to stand. This worked well and gave us a wide range of GPs, including two single-handed GPs, dispensing GPs, ex-fundholding and non-fundholding GPs, with only one practice having two representatives. Nurse representation was decided in an even more rigorous and expensive way with manifestos, campaign speeches, the Electoral Reform Society and a slight hiccup when they realised they hadn't offered all nurses a vote. Selection of the lay representative was flawed by several potential applicants not standing as at the time they were led to believe there was to be no reimbursement – subsequently amended to £4000 of course, as for other board members.

One of our biggest problems at that time was that we were continually being asked to make decisions before information on which to base our decisions was issued by the Department of Health. I had the opportunity at the NHS Alliance Conference in November 1998 in Blackpool to ask Alan Milburn, the then Minister of Health, whether this represented a deliberate policy on their part or simply that they were trying to progress at a rate that was too fast even for themselves to think ahead!

Interviewing for a chief executive was another new experience to us all and the work involved in rigorously screening over 30 applications has to be experienced to be believed. The health authority led us firmly on this and we had to score a whole host of attributes in order to be seen to be fair. There appeared to be no scope for selecting somebody simply because we liked them or were impressed by them. In the final event, we did select somebody we liked who had impressed us, but only once both had been mathematically proven!

Deciding who else we should invite on to our board presented another series of problems. Other PCGs varied considerably in whom they invited to sit on their board in addition to the minimum requirement. We opted for a minimalist board for various reasons, including the potential expense of having to reimburse locum fees to people such as pharmacists. We were also mindful that there might be an element of 'me too' if we decided to allow some groups representation and that the board could easily become too large and unwieldy.

What reservations did we have, and were they justified? There was much concern in the press at the time over the need for a majority of GPs on the board to ensure we could outvote the non-GPs if need be. In our case this concern turned out to be completely unfounded. We have had relatively few matters which have come to a vote, and on clinical matters the lay members have always shown themselves to be very happy to go along with the views of the clinicians.

Potential remuneration and workload was, and remains, a major concern. The hours to be worked for our £4000 were never accurately defined and different PCGs have addressed this in different ways. Our PCG expects 15 hours of work each month (£22 per hour – hardly the BMA-approved rate) before paying £60 per hour 'overtime' (nearer the BMA rate). This system of 15 hours basic work has the advantage of at least rewarding those who work a large number of hours, but is a disincentive to anybody to work a few additional hours over their board meeting attendances. Should non-doctors also receive £60 per hour or are they worth less, even if doing the same job? Should we expect everybody to log their hours to ensure fairness, or should we agree a 'salary' for the post, regardless of how many hours are spent on it?

Workload presents similar problems. Many posts overlap with each other and the skills needed for one are often similar to those needed for another. I soon became CGL, IM&T lead, Caldicott guardian and primary care tutor, but have happily seen the light and resigned several of these, albeit with a sense of guilt. It is indeed sensible that the Caldicott guardian should be somebody who is involved in clinical governance and understands IM&T, but most boards do not have sufficient numbers with the necessary skills. 'Sharing out the jobs' may be equitable as far as board members' workload is concerned, but the consequence is that we do not necessarily end up with the most appropriate person for some posts, simply the most willing, the least busy or the one with the weakest excuse not to take it.

The locum allowance has been another area which was never clearly defined and is handled differently in different PCGs. As a single-handed GP it would simply not be possible for me to take any part in the PCG were it not for my good fortune in having the ready services of a superb locum. I suspect that I will exceed my locum allowance for the year but hope that there will be money in the pot from others who do not claim the full amount. We never satisfactorily resolved the issue around what happens when others do not actually employ a locum but argue that they will work harder the next day, or that their partners worked harder in their absence and are hence entitled to claim the allowance.

How do we handle outside organisations who ask for the full locum allowance to be paid directly to them, when their representative on the board is well aware that no locum will be employed and that they would simply have to catch up on their missed work at another time with no personal reimbursement? Should we claim the locum allowance if a meeting falls on our half-day, or should we change our half-day to make meeting days a working day, employ a locum or pay the practice and have the half-day at another time when it can be enjoyed as such? Should board members from outside organisations be paid directly for attending meetings in their own time, such as evenings?

Performing in public is very new to most of us used to closed meetings. The need to be circumspect in what we say may have an inhibiting effect on some of us – this may of course not necessarily be a bad thing. I would hope that the need to say what the public wants to hear does not always override what we really want to say. Moving the board meetings from village to village each month is also a new experience which has not proved a success. It has resulted in a large number of miles travelled and many experiences of waiting for somebody with the keys to turn up and varying degrees of heating and tea (or not). The reason for doing this of course is to increase our accessibility to the public. In fact it has had the opposite effect. Our 'public' are the same small faithful handful who follow us wherever we go and, like us, would rather we had a single, fixed meeting place with adequate parking, heating and tea. It is relatively unusual for a true 'local' to turn up, especially one who could only attend because it was local to them.

Commissioning is another process which is alien to us ex-non-fundholders. The hoped-for freedom to choose what is best for our patients has not come about. Though we are keen to switch some specialties to adjacent hospitals with dramatically better performance, we are told that the problem is not that simple. The local trust tells us that if we do this, they will have to close departments and be unable to employ the promised new consultants. The ex-fundholders tell us that they have been saying this for years.

Do our colleagues appreciate what we are doing on their behalf? Frankly, I doubt it. They are certainly very happy that somebody else is doing it on their behalf, but I feel that we will be quickly held responsible if anything goes wrong.

One of my major personal reservations, particularly when I took on the role of CGL, was that it had the potential for making me unpopular with my colleagues and I have tried very hard to ensure that my relationship with them remains as very much on their side. I have avoided sending them reams of paper and have always fed back information to them promptly. My clinical governance baseline assessment for example (a single A4 side) was faxed to all practices before sending it to the health authority. (Although the health authority commented that it was 'rather slim' compared with others, they did at least acknowledge that they had read every word of it.)

In a similar vein, a thinly veiled clinical governance audit which I carried out recently on the contents of doctors' emergency bags was made more appealing by the offer that all participants would receive a regularly updated set of emergency drugs at no cost to themselves. When we repeat the audit in future, all GPs will have appropriate, in-date drugs in their bags (in contrast to the current situation). This audit will have been of obvious benefit to patients, practices and GPs' pockets and at little cost to the PCG. Clinical governance made appealing – I never thought I'd achieve that.

Our relationship with the health authority is often uncomfortable and the shedding of posts within their organisation has perhaps had a lot to do with this. On several occasions we have felt that we are not really 'in the driving seat' or 'progressing at a rate with which we are comfortable' as we were once promised, and our view and theirs frequently differ.

When we started in our various posts, we were promised that training would be forthcoming. This has not come to pass and I am currently organising a course ('Selling the unsellable') for the CGLs across the health authority. We will be using the skills of a drug company (renowned experts in selling the unsellable to GPs) and while the health authority are not happy about our taking this route, they have failed to come up with any alternative. Our local CGL meetings, which were initially a small group of eight of us, have been taken over by the health authority and expanded to include ever-more people to the extent that we PCG CGLs are now in the minority.

What of the future? We are already being pressured into applying for trust status when we have only just begun to find our feet as a PCG. The majority of board members seem to feel that 'resistance is futile' so why bother resisting, but I have major concerns at the pace of change. How will we, as a group of part-time amateurs, cope with the enormous responsibility that this will bring, in addition to continuing to function in general practice, which is itself becoming even more pressurised? Should we continue to strive for what is best for us and our patients, or should we bow out gracefully and leave it to others? I suspect that most of us will simply continue to do it to others, lest others do it to us.

CHAPTER 14

The role of the nurse representative

Liz Titheridge

I think it was the late Harold Wilson who said a week is a long time in politics and maybe it is, but in primary care a year is definitely a very short time. Although PCGs celebrated their first birthday in April 2000, they are still at the start of their long journey of change.

It has been an exciting and exhausting time for everyone involved in the development of PCGs and particularly so for the nurse members of the board. The good news is that I am yet to identify a PCG with fewer than two nurses on the board. The early days were very confusing for most primary healthcare people and at first many thought that the sole responsibility of the PCG nurse members was to represent their community nursing colleagues and, through their nursing knowledge and expertise, advise the board of nursing issues. However, since April 1999 many of the PCGs have developed at a cracking pace and the nurses' remit has expanded to take on the broad voice of the other community disciplines, such as the physiotherapist, occupational therapists and specialist nurses. It is true to say that some of these groups have felt a sense of exclusion, of not truly belonging to the tidal wave of primary healthcare reform. It is therefore crucial for PCG nurse members to be the strategic voice of nursing and health and not focus on her specific discipline. It is the knowledge and experience of the community network and working that makes nurses so valuable to the work of the PCG.

The nurse is not on the board as a member of a GP practice or as a trust representative, and this has often proved to be quite difficult to comprehend. More important is that all PCG members are equal partners and are there to confront community health, not professional or tribal interest. Board members are important, not because of their title or status but on account of their particular field of expertise and knowledge. Many people have long argued that the historical and traditional relationship between doctors and nurses has been one of subservience. This is unacceptable and can no longer be sustained. My experience is that this is simply not the case within the PCG. Nurses elected to the board need to demonstrate the significance and value of good nursing on peoples' lives and their health and wellbeing. The nursing discipline is about the prevention of disease, improved health, rehabilitation, independence, quality of life and having a peaceful death. The difficulty often facing nurses is that the issues discussed at board level often focus first on monetary reward and second on patient care. PCGs are about cultural change and it is often up to the nurses to influence the shift in power, control and authority.

Communication

Efficient and effective communication is paramount to the success of the PCG. To contribute to success, PCG nurses must ensure the involvement of all their nurse colleagues and PAMs. Many nurse board members have also taken on the responsibility of regular communication with their colleagues in the social service departments, who also need to be involved and take ownership of the PCG. It is important to set up a system to obtain true representation of this very large group. PCGs vary in size, but even in the smallest group of less than 50 000 population there would be approximately 100 community staff involved, and with a larger PCG this could be well over 300. This is a tall order, though not impossible for two nurses to do effectively.

The first message that needs to be got across is that we should not be obsessed with the PCG board members but rather everyone living and working within the PCG boundaries. Many PCGs have set up a clinical forum subgroup, chaired by the board nurses, with representation from each discipline. Larger PCGs have divided these into locality groups under the umbrella of the forum group, but the principle is the same. The forum meets regularly, usually monthly, and each member is required to disseminate information to and from their own particular professional group. It is important that information travels in both directions. Initially most of the information has been from the board members to the group but as the PCG develops the structure is in place for information to flow in all directions. This is a very important process because this is the way that those working in the community will be able to influence change. It has been a struggle to get continuing representation from all nurses and PAMs, particularly the midwives and CPNs, but improvements are being achieved. Maybe this is because community workers who are not directly involved find it difficult to understand the significance and relevance of the PCG to them in professional and personal terms.

An enormous amount of energy was used to set up PCGs and there were great anxieties about change to service and service reconfiguration.

So far most PCG issues have been GP-related, which has resulted in other PCG members sensing a level of disillusion. Maintaining motivation is a serious issue. It is important to keep people keen, informed and committed, because as the PCG develops there will be more health-related, public health matters to confront than the details of the Red Book. The challenge is to diminish apathy and inspire our fellow colleagues to bring their local knowledge, experience and special contribution to the work of the PCG.

Influencing change

How influential are the nurses on the PCG boards? The fact is that GPs have a far greater knowledge of general practice matters than nurses. Nurses, and I suspect all other non-GP members, have had to learn a new language and understand such issues as contracting, 'in-house' services, prescribing patterns, out-of-area referrals and items of service to name a few. Nurses are there to put an entirely different perspective on health and healthcare services. They have had to develop negotiation and assertiveness skills that often do not come very easily, especially if they are employed by GPs. There is the view that GPs will collude in order to meet their own professional needs, but in my experience this has not happened. Nurses have a great deal to offer the PCG boards and therefore the communities they work with. We are used to and, for the main part, enjoy working in teams and focusing our energy on health needs rather than following the medical model of tackling illness. PCGs have been developed to help improve the health of the local community and address the thorny issues of equality and equity of health and social care provision. Nurses are in a prime position to influence change.

PCG nurses are leading on both HImPs and clinical governance. Health visitors in particular have been completing health needs assessments on their practice populations for many years and this skill needs to be exploited by PCGs and health authorities. In recent years, nurses have also developed personal learning plans, successful models of clinical supervision and carried out an enormous level of activity on quality and standard-setting initiatives. These are topics that nurses can share with other disciplines.

Information

Whole forests have been felled in the interest of PCGs. Primary health-care is awash with government documents, board and clinical governance papers, presentations, bids and masses of other reading matter. There is a tendency to read everything and retain nothing and who is the person to decide which papers need to be retained for further reference and what can be thrown into the bin?

PCG nurses are primarily clinicians and experts on health. Many lack IT skills and even those with some IT knowledge do not have IT access at work. Many rely on using computers at home and spend personal time in the evening receiving and sending work-related e-mails. Surfing the net is also a popular hobby for PCG nurses. It is assumed that nurses have faxes, computers, mobile phones plus clerical/secretarial support. In many cases this is not so and far too many nurses still work in rather quaint offices with little modern technology to help make their lives easier. Efficiency is paramount, so traditional working practices must be urgently addressed and the necessary equipment and training provided.

Balancing the role

PCG nurses have to handle a large number of conflicting demands. They have to juggle the demands of patients, colleagues, employer, PCG board, family and community. Whose interests are PCG nurses, in fact, serving? In truth it is the needs of the community and this requires great strength and objectivity. It is not unusual for trusts, PCGs and general practice to have different interests. As PCGs move towards trust status themselves, more dilemmas might occur. It is important to be honest, acknowledge the problem, be aware of divided loyalties and have the confidence to confront them.

Many nurses are also feeling that their clinical role is suffering and that their colleagues are being asked to pick up some of their work. Others report that their work is not being done by colleagues and is there waiting for them for when they return from their PCG duties. While NHSE guidance gives level 1 PCGs a half-day per week, in reality the demands mean members are giving at least one and a half days to the board. Some PCGs have all their meetings at lunchtime and others have them in the evening, but either way work is attended to during so-called personal time. Replacement costs are available but it is often difficult to find bank nurses, particularly at the skill or grade that comfortably replaces the board nurse. True to tradition, improvements in healthcare often happen as a result of goodwill, commitment, dedication and enthusiasm.

Benefits

With few exceptions, PCG nurses report that this is a time of great opportunity. They believe, with good reason, that they are the catalysts for necessary cultural change within primary healthcare. However, nurses also know that PCGs are not a permanent fixture and that PCTs, with their different structures and responsibilities, will offer yet more challenges. Primary healthcare is going through a period of uncomfortable, but interesting transition. By the time the majority of PCGs have grown up to be adult PCTs, the make-up of the board will be very different.

Nurses have been given a wonderful opportunity to develop both professionally and personally but, most importantly, they are playing a major part in the development and improvement of primary care.

CHAPTER 15

The role of the social services representative

Tim Hinds

The establishment of PCGs brought lots of promise, not just of shifting strategic, needs-based health planning to local primary care teams, but implicitly also of greater strategic linkage, via a social services officer representative, to local social welfare systems and to the broader services delivered through local authorities. The promise of 'joined-up solutions' to joined-up local problems.

As this is a personal view it is based on the Slough PCG. I am committed to the aims and aspirations of the board of which I am a member and to the potential that it can deliver. This is the best chance there has been in a long time – perhaps ever – of giving the ownership of local health systems back to local communities, to focus specifically on local health needs and inequalities, and to address them through joint local action. We have made a start on this agenda through, for example, the development of rehabilitation services, initiatives on hospital discharge arrangements, on mental health services and carers. Partnership-in-Action flexibilities give scope through pooled budgets to look at joint equipment stores and joint registration of one of our residential homes for older people to include nursing care.

However, the assumptions on which PCGs are based are big ones and the ability to deliver the huge change agenda is disproportionately vulnerable to the idiosyncrasies of individuals, constrained resources and perhaps overambitious timescales. Not least, the assumptions have an underlay of contradictory and/or conflicting process.

The themes I would like to draw out are partly general – issues around process and accountability – with some specifics about change and vulnerabilities based on my experience, which are perhaps of general application.

Slough PCG

At the time PCGs came into being, Slough had just been established as a unitary authority following the break up of the previous Berkshire County Council. The local authority/PCG are more or less coterminous. The borough has a population of around 110 000 and has a rich ethnic mix – roughly one-third of the population being of minority ethnic communities – primarily of Asian origin with a smaller though significant African/Caribbean community. Slough is home to a large industrial estate and as a consequence has been relatively 'cushioned' through periods of recession/unemployment. There is considerable goodwill in the town that eases the ability to work across agency boundaries and with the voluntary sector. There is an acute NHS trust working primarily to three ex-Berkshire unitaries and South Buckinghamshire, a community trust and a learning disability trust, each primarily covering three East Berkshire unitaries.

The town has poor deprivation and health profiles. Slough is more comparable with a number of London boroughs and other inner-city areas than its Berkshire neighbours. The Jarman score is higher – by a considerable margin – than other Berkshire unitaries. There are significant health inequalities. Standardised mortality ratios for the borough are considerably higher than the rest of previous Berkshire and there are particularly poor profiles in respect of coronary heart disease and mental health. There is a large, and growing, population of asylum seekers.

The HImP has been developed through a broad-based public health forum. A similarly broad and consultative process has developed healthy living centre proposals. Slough is an Education Action Zone. It has recently achieved 'Associate' Health Action Zone (HAZ) status. An 'early win' is that a health walk-in centre will open shortly.

The role of the social services representative

The formal role of the social services representative on PCGs is largely undefined and potentially problematic. The guidance issued on developing PCGs was not prescriptive ('The choice of officer will depend on the configuration of primary care groups and the local circumstances in which social services are organised …') though it indicated that 'it is expected' that this would be an operational manager. However:

> *it tends to be the case that the more senior social services representation*

the greater the likelihood of links being made to other parts of the local authority, whereas more junior representatives not only cannot be expected to do this but are often only from the adult section of their own department.

A similar message came from the Social Services Inspectorate:

the extent to which the SSD representative can be effective in the longer term will in part depend on their place in the department's management structure and how that structure does or does not enable them to make the most of being on the PCG board.

The Association of Directors of Social Services commissioned the Nuffield Institute to measure activity in PCGs. They asked a series of questions of every director of social services and chief executive of PCGs. This was interesting in terms of the above and the *actual* representation on PCGs. Around one in ten PCG boards has a director of social services, one in three an assistant director and the remainder managers at third tier. There is – despite this spread – 'general agreement that the current status of social services board members is appropriate'. Although there was widespread agreement that the role of social services representatives is 'very useful', it was difficult to establish what had been achieved this early on. Examples quoted focus on specific commissioning activity in relation to older people and those with mental health and/or drug and alcohol problems, the change process, work on HImPs, PCIPs, HAZs and healthy living centres. This could mean more or less everything, or not very much.

Within these findings were a range of further perceptions. Despite the universal recognition among social service departments of the significance of their relationship with primary healthcare, structured links between operational staff across social care and primary healthcare were patchy. Difficulties were still being experienced with a number of issues, client groups and professionals – among the latter the most frequently cited were GPs.

Accountability

The role is further muddied by issues of accountability. The guidance notes that:

the local social services authority should also bear in mind that the officer will, as an employee, be accountable to the local authority, but as a member of the PCG board they will be collectively accountable ... to the health authority for the performance of the PCG.

The decision to look for nominations of social services officers for PCG boards rather than local authority-elected members is interesting in terms of the accountabilities of NHS systems generally to local communities and the ability of those systems to engage in a meaningful way with them. Local authorities work through democratic process and structures and engage with the community through consultation. At the end of the day the community has its say on the performance of the authority at the local elections. Lay representation in NHS systems – either through non-executive directors, trust boards or PCG boards – is by appointment, and NHS decision making still relies heavily on 'expert' views, in particular of senior clinicians and managers. The NHS has a poor history of public consultation. Appointment of social services officers, while it brings some expertise in public consultation and a 'report back' to local authority systems, is still a very long way from democratic process and continues 'representation by appointment'. And depending on the position the officer holds in the organisation, the accountability may be more to management than to consultative or democratic process.

Slough Borough Council has explicit policy priorities, which include social justice, equality of opportunity and community development. There is a particular emphasis on social inclusion and a corporate agenda to ensure 'joined-up' action on this priority across the various departments of the authority and with other partners in the town. As an example, this might mean addressing issues relating to the quality of housing generally and its impact on the health profile as much as the needs of particular communities for accommodation. It can mean work we are starting on enhanced housing with care schemes for older people. The ability of NHS systems to deliver on or contribute to this agenda is severely constrained, not through lack of commitment of local practitioners and/or managers, but by the fact that the local health systems are still locked in to a pan-Berkshire spend profile and that local accountability remains locked out.

Change

It goes without saying that the changes in the NHS are profound. National Priorities Guidance (NPG) applies equally to NHS and social services. The changes in social services are equally significant, including not only the Quality Protects and Promoting Independence initiatives but also changes in regulation standards in the workforce, the establishment of youth offender teams, etc. Even on their own, the joint NPG targets, the implementation of NSFs and the challenge of Partnership-in-Action initiatives would be significant.

Local government itself is being 'modernised' with, as a snapshot, new political structures being put in place and the introduction of 'best value' regimens to replace compulsory competitive tendering. It is the whole health/social welfare environment that is changing and the scale is vast.

In a local context, the ability of both new and established organisations to manage the process are severely tested. By way of example, the Berkshire Health Authority now deals not with one social services authority but with six, each developing their own agendas at the same time as the slog to get themselves established. In addition to the NHS trusts in the local family, there are now eight PCGs, a timetable to move to six PCTs and put in place a new pan-Berkshire Mental Health Trust. Add some detail – the development of HImPs, JIPs, PCIPs and the PAFs that go with each of these (not to mention the SSD PAFs) – and even mature organisations with well-developed information and systems are under pressure. When organisations are in change the introspection that goes with it can shift attention from operational necessities or the opportunities of the bigger picture.

The PCGs are not mature organisations. In the local context, the PCG has struggled through its first year with inadequate staffing. Recruitment processes have been as much about ensuring continuing employment for 'displaced' NHS colleagues – in particular from the health authority – as ensuring a suitable skill and experience match to new positions. The sharp end of change is therefore over-reliant on the goodwill, energy and commitment of individuals who are already in full-time employment. This has already produced burn-out. Slough is not the only PCG to have had turnover in the GP membership of its board or of its chair within the first year.

The understandings of the different board member representatives about purpose, direction and a vision of the future is challenged by perplexity in getting to grips with their own role and the nature, scope and professional background of other board members. Some GPs have a very limited understanding of what social services does. For my part, the understanding of the significance of GP independent contractor status and the Red Book has taken time to assimilate, both in terms of what GPs actually do and the background to some of their behaviours.

GPs are not by nature corporate beings. Whereas clinical governance seems broadly to be accepted as a 'good thing', this does not on its own deliver corporate ownership or a strategic approach to problem solving. Re-accreditation processes have the potential to reinforce the individualist nature of general practice at a time when broad strategic principles and objectives need to be developed.

The role of the chief executive and the relationship with the chair are critical, but overdependent – with a fragile infrastructure – on personalities that work well together and a shared sense of vision. The officer/officer relationship of chief executive and social services representative has potential to be supportive, but at the end of the day acceptance by GP colleagues is what counts.

While the election of chair, effectively by GP peers, is of itself maybe a good thing, the dependence on the tolerance of partners for time out of practice is a significant vulnerability. It may be a contraindicator to the best choice of a strategic leader.

CHAPTER 16

The role of the lay member

Roy Latham

To my mind the concept of the PCG probably originated in the *Alma Ata Declaration*[1] and its assertion *inter alia* that if gross inequalities between the world's 'haves' and 'have-nots' were to be overcome, then the proposed solution was via primary healthcare with true ownership by local communities, including those who were disadvantaged. The WHO concept of health of course is not limited to medical care but encompasses all aspects of human life.[2] Anderson further advanced this idea in 1984[3] and the Ottawa Charter gave this holistic approach further credence two years later.[4]

The general philosophy of PCGs would seem to be a natural progression from the above. The government's apparent intention was that teams of doctors, nurses, social workers and lay members, all of whom have local knowledge and professional skills covering all aspects of health in its widest sense, should work together to improve healthcare and share jointly in its governance.[5] The new thing about all this was that it was specifically stated that members should act *corporately* and include *all* those who have a 'legitimate interest and who wish to be directly involved in the policy and decision-making process'.[5]

Background

My work experience had been in education (I retired ten years ago as the head teacher of a large primary school) and therefore I was used to working in the public sector. However, my knowledge of the world of medicine, apart from visits to my GP or local hospital was largely theoretical and much was based on an Open University course (U205, Health and disease) I took some years ago. I had little knowledge of how the NHS was organised or of the internal language (jargon?) it used. From what I had seen in the media I felt that I could be facing a resentful board, mainly GPs, who were not used to members of the public being involved as equals in a sphere where, until now, doctors had been 'in control'. From earlier studies in management I knew that GPs were for the most part self-employed and free from interference or supervision by non-professionals concerning the standards of service they offered. Since they had acquired this status in the last century they had guarded it jealously. Hence, when I first joined my PCG board, I did so with a degree of trepidation.

According to the advert in the local paper in the autumn of 1998, the lay member would be there 'to represent the interests of the local community'. At the time I had only recently been elected to my local CHC so I did not apply for the position. However, there must have been a poor response to the advert because the CHC was asked if they could suggest the names of suitable candidates. Consequently some CHC members agreed to have their names put forward and I was selected after an interview with members of the health authority. Although it was not strictly necessary, I resigned from the CHC on my appointment to the board because I felt that there could in the future be a conflict of interest.

The lay member within the PCG

With equal status to other board members and a stated responsibility for community representation, the lay member needs to be aware of the latter whenever the interests of specific groups may need to be considered.[6] This does not necessarily mean that he or she needs to be on every subgroup of the PCG, but it does mean that he or she needs to keep his or her eye on the ball when subgroup reports are made to the board and final decisions are taken. When considering the work that the board covers and the different types of general practice which may be found in one PCG, the lay member needs to have an idea of the variance in styles between the groups and the different medical services the practices may offer. In my case, this has involved a number of visits to meet medical staff in practices where I am not a patient. Constraints of time mean that this is a lengthy process and I have much more ground to cover in this area.

Coming from outside the medical profession can have its advantages when looking at primary care. Until the advent of PCGs there was a tendency among the professionals to look at the task very much from a 'scientific' angle and to accept the existing systems and procedures as being almost sacrosanct. The doctor (or nurse) knows best! John Denham, the Health Minister, pointed out at a recent symposium[7] that such traditional approaches need to change in the New NHS, with greater openness so that the public begin to understand the health service as their own rather than something which is imposed from central government or elsewhere. He specifically pointed out, however, that while the lay member may take a lead role in this, it was the responsibility of the *whole board* to engage fully with the public.[8]

The latter point emphasises the need to see the PCG as a team, which shows mutual respect for all its members. The lay member has a crucial role in this and it can sometimes be subsumed by other important tasks. For instance during the last year, while PCGs have been evolving, not only have they been deciding whether they should become level 1, 2 or 3 in the NHS hierarchy, but they have also been laying the foundations for building relationships in the local community. It is important to remember that there are various ways of involving the public. All PCG meetings that we hold are open to the public but if we were to think of this as our only responsibility we would delude ourselves. Frequently we have had less than a handful of non-board members present at our meetings and so far we have not had a member of the press attend any of them. This is despite the fact that they are advertised widely in the local papers and we have covered some contentious issues concerning the future of a local community hospital and some general practices. We need to address this issue. Lay members also need to differentiate between the views of the *public* and those of *patients*. They are not necessarily congruent so links with the CHC, voluntary organisations and other community groups need to be established and maintained.

Pressure from outside local communities has meant that while the PCG has been addressing the latter it has also been involved in:

- setting priorities for prescribing
- drawing up HImPs
- looking into clinical governance
- examining ways of developing IT
- drawing up a PCG investment plans

to name just a few.

As I see it, many of the above aspects of our work have demanded a specialist (often medical) understanding of the subjects covered and, as such, specialists may need to draw up documents in the first place. The important thing is that before these policies/programmes are adopted the *whole board* vets them and the lay member, as a non-specialist can be in an ideal position to do just that.

Some personal comments

In terms of specifics, I have been actively involved in our work on public involvement, particularly with regard to a health panel, which we hope to have in place well before the time this book is published. I am also the editor of a practice newsletter that goes out monthly to practices and PAMs within the PCG. At the moment our PCG does not yet have a permanent home but as soon as it does I am hoping that we shall have sufficient resources to send out a newsletter to non-NHS organisations in the community. I am also involved on the IT strategy subgroup, which meets with members of other neighbouring PCGs.

I have been fortunate in the way I have been accepted by all my colleagues on the board and also by GPs and PAMs in the practices. My first anxieties were quelled almost immediately. This was largely because of their positive and open attitude and an obvious desire to be properly accountable. I am aware of lay members elsewhere who have felt marginalised by their treatment at board meetings and have been excluded from key decision-making processes.

In one instance I attended a conference where a lay member had not at that time (May 1999) received official notice of any meetings and consequently had not been able to be involved in the early stages of setting up the PCG. My advice at the time to this person was that she needed to have an earnest discussion with the board chairman, pointing out her own strengths and offering ways in which she might positively contribute to the board's dealings. Several of us have felt the need to persist in ensuring that NHS jargon is avoided at meetings, and where this has not been possible we have needed to insist that it be made understandable to non-medical people. I began by building up a little glossary of NHS terms and this was quite useful in the first few months as I was 'finding my feet'.

The board of which I am a member has organised a number of successful training days for itself and for GPs and PAMs. The board has also adopted a positive attitude to the support of members wishing to attend conferences and workshops and I have been able to take advantage of this.

Some anxieties I have about my role are, I know, shared by all my colleagues on the board (and indeed other PCG board members elsewhere). They focus on resources, particularly on the time that is *needed* as opposed to that which is *officially designated* for us to carry out our responsibilities. My nurse, GP and social services colleagues are definitely being overstretched because, quite rightly, they recognise their prime responsibility to be patient/client care. It is not always practicable to employ locums while they do PCG work and the time demands are definitely greater than any of us anticipated when we took post. If I were not semi-retired I should find it almost impossible to carry out my commitments in the way I know they ought to be.

I mentioned earlier about my lack of understanding of the jargon of the NHS and how this very large organisation functions. I think that the health authority itself could have dissipated much of my early unease if it had organised an induction day whereby newcomers to the NHS scene could have been acquainted with such items as:

- the hierarchy(ies) within the NHS and the health authority and how they are financed
- the principal acronyms to be expected when reading the myriad of documents that land on the doormat
- a general overview of
  - the principal officers of the health authority
  - how GPs are paid
  - the basis of funding for primary care.

As I see it, training of a high standard is vital, especially for newcomers to an organisation. In my case, I found that I had to spend an excessive amount of time addressing the above issues. (In fact my understanding of NHS financial systems is still sketchy.)

I am not recommending that all PCG lay members should operate in the way I have described. The whole essence of this new deal in the NHS is that local communities should *develop what they see best for primary healthcare in their areas*. However, I do feel quite strongly that a lay member should, as the sole community representative, keep a watching brief on *all* that takes place and should be prepared to ask what may seem 'awkward' questions from time to time. I also see the role of lay member, like that of the PCG itself, as a developing/evolving one. I am not a revolutionary and I accept that achieving all our ideals will take some considerable time but, adopting my personal motto 'Festina lente',[9] I look ahead with realistic optimism!

References

1 World Health Organization (1978) *Alma Ata Declaration*. WHO, Geneva.
2 Health was defined by WHO in 1946 as 'a state of physical, social and mental well-being'.
3 Anderson R (1984) Health Promotion: an overview. In: L Baric (ed) *European Monographs in Health Education Research*, No. 6. Scottish Health Education Group, Edinburgh.

4 WHO (1986) *Ottawa Charter for Health Promotion*. WHO, Geneva.
5 Department of Health (1998) *Modernising Health and Social Services: National Priorities Guidance 1999/00–2001/02*. Department of Health, London.
6 See also HSC 1998/139, para 22.
7 NHS Alliance Conference (1999) *Listening to the Public*. 9 November.
8 Quoted in *Primary Care Network* (NHS Alliance) 1999: issue 15.
9 Gaius Suetonius AD 69c–130c. Make Haste Slowly!

CHAPTER 17

The role of the pharmacist

Mark Robinson

The primary care pharmacist is responsible for managing the prescribing costs within the unified cash-limited budget and for the introduction of quality through clinical governance. A description of this sort explains the increasing need for pharmaceutical support but does not fully explain the full range of tasks and complexity that the job may contain. The PCGs develop through levels into trust status taking over many of the strategic roles of the health authority pharmaceutical advisor as well as developing the role of practice-based pharmacists. The roles can be simplified into three levels as described in Box 17.1. One task could cross into all three levels, from inception, through development to implementation or require the co-operation of a team of pharmacists employed within one PCG.

Box 17.1 The roles of practice-based pharmacists

- High-level strategic advice.
- Semi-strategic advice, plus hands-on support across PCGs.
- Direct facilitation of change management and the delivery of clinical care within the practice.

Managing the prescribing budget, developing prescribing policies, procedure and analysis

The prescribing budget needs to be set each year. The proportion of NHS spend on medicines is growing. It will grow further as new medicines are developed and the quality initiatives such as NSFs and HImPs are introduced. The prescribing budget needs to be set each year with a realistic uplift, reducing the risk to the PCG of a significant overspend but also recognising that a large underspend will delay developments in other areas. The prescribing budget now competes with all other developments within the unified budget. Once the allocation has been agreed the budget must be further divided between PCGs and then to practices, taking account of moves towards capitation share. If incentive schemes are set with regard to the prescribing budget final position, then the budget-setting process must appear fair and equitable.

The responsibility for the area prescribing committee moves from the health authority to the PCG and with it the strategic management of prescribing with the assessment and introduction of new drugs along with taking forward the recommendations of NICE. This would encourage the pharmaceutical input into the local HImPs, commissioning and service developments within the PCG annual accountability agreement and PCIPs. Each PCG will need a prescribing committee established to channel the information to and from the area committee and to set a local agenda, building close relationships with their GPs. The pharmaceutical advisor may be the recognised PCG interface with the pharmaceutical industry, backed with a system to take forward joint initiatives.

A prescribing incentive scheme must be developed. This year the incentive scheme needs to reflect other areas of the unified budget (such as referrals) and clinical governance issues. The scheme will be more complex, rewarding increased prescribing in certain areas and reduced prescribing in others.

Analysis of prescribing is fundamental to the development of policies and procedures. The description of prescribing success is essential to the performance management requirements of the PCG and the pharmacist may be asked to develop suitable prescribing indicators. The PCG must develop systems of prescribing analysis at all levels through prescribing and cost (PACT) data.

Sensible prescribing policies are necessary. The prescribing advisor needs to be able to feed in savings from the implementation of prescribing policies into the prescribing budget. Such savings may accrue from increased generic prescribing, reducing use of premium-price products and drugs of limited clinical value as well as therapeutic switches.

Prescribing and local advice linked to their developments within their accountability agreements will be required. Projects related to smoking cessation, hypertension screening and management of minor or self-limiting illnesses will build the relationships between the PCG and the local community pharmacists. These pharmacists also have a major role in helping patients to concord with their medication regimen and supporting the PCG's prescribing initiatives.

Information on medicines arrives at an alarming rate. GPs would value pharmacists sifting through this information, selecting important data and preparing it in an easy-to-read format newsletter. The information could be built into a website or downloaded regularly to GPs linked by the NHSnet. Information leaflets designed for patients or to be handed to patients as part of the consultation may be produced. Existing leaflets like those piloted by the consumers association may be distributed throughout the PCG.

Supporting prescribing issues and policy at the interface between practices, PCGs and the hospitals

Hospital-led prescribing may constitute 40% of GP repeat prescribing. The development and implementation of joint formulary areas is a key role of the primary care pharmacist. Common prescribing choices within formulary areas and local prescribing policies, for example the transition to CFC-free inhalers, are essential areas of work.

An interface prescribing policy, detailing who will prescribe and how that information is transferred across the interface, should be developed. With the development of a unified budget, money can be transferred between primary and secondary care to follow prescribing responsibility and cost-effective care. Medicines should be included in many areas of the LTSA, again, clarifying cost and responsibility.

Shared-care guidelines should naturally flow from this work. Many medicines are transferred to general practice without a clear dialogue about monitoring requirements. The GPs who sign the prescriptions are responsible for the patient's care and need to be reassured that the necessary monitoring is being undertaken. Naturally if this monitoring is over and above that which would be normally expected, then the GP may be able to claim a section 36 payment.

The communication flow is improved in Croydon, with primary care pharmacists working within the local hospital. They help with the admission medication history and the discharge medication advice, filling in some of the gaps of information. High-risk patients may need special transfer to the GP monitoring therapy and to the community pharmacist supplying their medicines.

Supporting practices

Providing adequate support to practices must be viewed as the key aim of the developing pharmaceutical team. Local prescribing analysis through PACT and the practice computer database feeds local clinical meetings. These stimulate the development of local prescribing choices or formularies, guidelines and protocols. They provide valuable information for the development of PCG policies and formularies. There is little doubt that this form of educational outreach has proved successful as described by the IMPACT (independent monitoring of prescribing analysis and trends) project.

Rapid implementation of agreed policies can be facilitated by the practice pharmacist, making changes to the computer and providing an interface between patient and practice where necessary. The ability to facilitate the change process is fundamental to the success of prescribing decisions. GPs should be supported through this process and the pharmacists may need specialist training to achieve this. The change process may also be supported by incentive schemes developed at a PCG level.

The practice repeat prescribing system should be reviewed, ensuring that there is an adequate mechanism for systematic review. Simple alignment of quantities prescribed and ensuring that two tablets are not used when one higher-strength (and usually less expensive) tablet exists may make significant savings on the prescribing budget. This links in well with the monitoring requirements of certain medicines and, with the NSFs, certain clinical conditions. The pharmacist should offer clinical audit services to ensure that the practice reaches 'best practice' standards.

The NSFs of certain clinical conditions will demand that practices within a PCG are able, not only to implement the recommended treatment, but prove that they have done so. The primary care pharmacist has an important role in developing the disease management process at practice level, installing templates and ensuring the accuracy of the data collected. This is an essential stage in the pharmacist's ability to audit therapeutic areas of drug use.

Drug selection could be improved by customising the computer system to simplify drug selection or improve treatment through the installation of disease templates. Using short cuts to bring up limited picklists on the computer could make the prescribing of certain products easier and would ensure a cost-effective choice.

Regular monitoring of medicine prices, pack sizes and patent expiry will ensure a continual review of 'best value for money'.

Clinical prescribing support

Pharmacists are able to offer many clinical support services to the practices. Polypharmacy results in an increased risk of side effects and adverse drug reactions. Pharmacists can provide detailed drug histories and review repeat medicines either in the practice or in the home. The aims of this service are to improve the quality of prescribing, improve the patients' health and reduce unnecessary expenditure on medicines. The review may be targeted to nursing and residential homes in the first instance or generally to patients over 70 or with four or more repeat medicines.

Examples of pharmacist-run disease management or therapeutic management clinics are available from around the country. Near-patient testing equipment is available for anticoagulant monitoring. A service could be developed that offers a high-quality service to patients near their own home. Pharmacists are running pain clinics, migraine clinics and dyspepsia clinics.

Conclusion

The PCGS will need to acquire pharmaceutical advice. This chapter covers briefly the main areas that may be included in the pharmacist's job description. It is essential to consider how much time is needed in each of the areas in addition to that required for the maintenance of professional standards through continued professional development. An example of a job description can be found in the National Prescribing Centre document *GP Prescribing Support: a resource document and guide for the New NHS*.

CHAPTER 18

The role of the chief officer

Jill Ashton

Exploration of job descriptions of PCG chief officers/executives and also chief executives from a range of health organisations reveals remarkable similarities. However, the realities of the role vary from situation to situation, and do not always resemble the job description given. This chapter explores the role of the chief officer from a personal viewpoint and experience.

First, a word about names. Some people in this position are referred to as 'chief officers' others are known as 'chief executives'. The latter name is the one given in the guidance papers from the NHS Executive when describing board members of a PCG. Does it matter? Personally, in relation to PCGs I think not. However, if we look towards the future and PCTs, the head of a PCT will clearly be a chief executive. Therefore, perhaps the most suitable name then is a 'chief officer' so as not to confuse the roles. To explain this school of thought further, this chapter ends with a resumé of the potential role of a PCT chief executive.

The majority of job descriptions of chief officers cover the same broad areas of responsibility, namely an operational management role, corporate and clinical governance, and strategic planning.

But what does this mean in practice? There is no doubt that the main responsibility of the chief officer alongside the chair is to ensure that the PCG brings together and delivers in three areas. Namely, primary and community care development, the commissioning of appropriate secondary care services and overall health improvement initiatives. This is not just undertaking work in these areas but integrating the areas strategically alongside partner agencies, service users and carers in a way that meets the health needs and improves the health of the local population. It is how this agenda is achieved that the role of the chief officer emerges.

The chief officer is essentially a senior manager. However, most PCGs are small organisations, which means that achievements are gained through networks, organisational and change management processes rather than traditional management systems and hierarchical structures. It entails the bringing together of people, systems and differing agendas to achieve positive change. As such, the role requires the chief officer to be a leader, facilitator, strategist, creator, guide, enabler, promoter, networker and teacher. Establishing relationships and creating owner-ship of the vision are keys to moving forward, as is the involvement of relevant stakeholders, including service users, carers and the local community, in decision making. Thus the chief officer acts as a link between initiatives and has a major role in their co-ordination.

Before I discuss the actual tasks involved in the chief officer role, it is essential to describe the many factors that impact on the role and the way in which it is executed. These appear to vary between health authorities. They include the relationship between the chief officer and chair, the style of the health authority, resources available and willingness of part-ners to work together.

For example, a health authority that doesn't relinquish health promo-tion activity or commissioning functions will influence the overall direction of work that the PCG takes and consequently the role of the chief officer. A national evaluation of PCGs by HSMC showed that PCGs have been relatively slow to become involved in service commissioning.[1] This is for several reasons, including the change involved for other stake-holders, namely local trusts and health authority staff in accepting the PCG's role in this. Agreement of role and direction for the PCG with the health authority from the onset steers the chief officer role, where tension takes time in negotiation.

Resources are important and have been shown to vary from PCG to PCG. The role of the chief officer with ten staff will be more strategic and visionary, whereas in an organisation with only one or two staff, the chief officer will be undertaking much of the action and work and may not be able to develop the networks and partnerships necessary to take the organisation forward in a strategic sense.

Another enormous influence on the role of the chief officer in develop-ing the organisation is credibility, not just personal but organisational. This can create a tension in that it is natural to be suspicious of a new organisation; the chief officer's role here is to build up trust both within and external to the organisation through networking and promotion of the tasks in hand and also through tangible benefits and gains.

The relationship between the chair of the PCG and the chief officer also affects the role. Much was written initially about the importance of this partnership and the need to work together closely. The chief officer has a role here in supporting and enabling the clinical view and needs of patients to drive the organisation. A chair needs to be able to trust that the chief officer will steer and manage the organisation in a professional and constructive way.

Working as part of a health and social care community is important. History has a part to play here – many authorities had commissioning group or pilots and these certainly paved the way for PCGs thus initially influencing the direction of the PCG and role of chief officer in taking the work agenda forward.

What then does the chief officer actually do? For ease of explanation I have divided the tasks into three main themes, which also encompass organisational development:

- developing people – the board and staff members
- key processes of the organisation – operational processes, working in partnership, HImP, clinical governance
- development and execution of the work programme within the framework of the HImP in response to local needs.

Developing a group of healthcare professionals, including GPs used to working independently, into a cohesive team capable and prepared to take responsibility for health improvement and healthcare provision is key to the role of the chief officer. It has therefore been necessary to work with the PCG board to build a clear understanding of its roles, a shared vision for health and healthcare in the community, and a shared responsibility to deliver this vision. The chief officer's role is to ensure that the board has the necessary skills and abilities to execute these responsibilities and where weaknesses are identified, development opportunities are accessible. The board needs ultimately to manage strategic issues, develop its people, quality assure and to be able to analyse available information in order to make critical decisions, which are then communicated effectively. These skills are also common to the rest of the PCG team.

The chief officer is required to ensure that processes are reliable, flexible, responsive to change and understood, that the organisation meets the required objectives, and to establish relationships with other agencies and the public in order to achieve the outcomes required. The establishment of an organisational structure with effective staff is fundamental to the role and running of the organisation.

Last but not least the role of the chief officer is not only to ensure that a robust organisation exists, but also that the work is executed. The HImP needs to be actioned locally and the chief officer is required to make sure that action is set out and delivered within this framework in order to meet the required targets. This includes financial and quality targets as well as health improvement outcomes. It includes corporate governance, engagement of the public and commissioning secondary care.

Perhaps a pertinent place to end this chapter is to quote Gill Morgan, Chief Executive of North & East Devon Health Authority, who when asked what she wanted from managers in PCGs explained, 'I suppose I want common sense, I want people with a bias towards collegiate working. I want people who can manage ambiguity and create exciting new futures rather than bureaucratic treadmills' (IHSM Annual Conference 1999). For me, this sums up what I have been trying to achieve, a sensible, flexible organisation which builds on the past and creates new ways in which to meet health need.

PCGs as emerging organisations are shortly to metamorphose into PCTs. The role of a chief executive of a PCT will be different than that of a PCG chief officer in a variety of ways. For instance, as well as taking on the commissioning, health improvement and primary care development roles of a PCG, a PCT will also be a large provider organisation. This means that the leadership will be complex and the chief executive will be involved in the day-to-day running of the organisation and ensuring that all that goes with this is sound. It will require not only the establishment of which services should be provided, but also bring with it clinical and corporate governance responsibilities in monitoring and improving services.

At present a PCG is part of a health authority, as a PCT responsibility clearly stops with the chief executive and board. The chief executive will therefore have a larger remit and once the organisation has been established will be a further step away from 'doing' than the PCG chief officer role at present. It is interesting to note that this new ground-breaking role will require a combination of skills, knowledge and experience that do not currently co-exist in the contemporary health environment. It will therefore be necessary for this new breed of chief executive to be able to draw together a team that will encompass an even greater diversity of complementary skills.

Reference

1 Smith JA, Regan EL, Goodwin N *et al.* (2000) *Getting Into Their Stride: report of a national evaluation of primary care groups.* HSMC, University of Birmingham.

PART 4

Getting it right

CHAPTER 19

How to involve patients and the local community

Debbie Freake and Ruth Chambers

Like so many other areas of a PCG's work, public involvement is a new concept to many and provokes anxieties in those unused to its complexities. What is certain is that PCGs will derive benefits in equal proportion to the degree of effort put in. The potential advantages to be realised will require far more than a token nod to public involvement, but will be well worth the investment of time and effort.

PCGs are tasked with being: 'accountable to patients, open to the public and shaped by their views'.[1] The reality of meaningful public involvement will be a challenge for most PCGs.[2] Evaluation of the GP commissioning pilots that were the forerunners of PCGs found that most had little direct patient or public involvement in their commissioning activities and operations. This chapter offers guidance on how PCGs may involve their patients and the local community.

Why involve patients and the public?

As taxpayers, citizen influence on a public service such as the NHS is a democratic right. There are many other benefits:

- direct involvement of patients (or their carers) in their own healthcare improves satisfaction and patient compliance
- involving patients in decision making about their own healthcare should encourage a culture of self-care and the taking of responsibility for seeking future care
- greater openness and accountability in the NHS will improve public confidence and can create a dialogue leading to a shared understanding between professionals and the public
- participation can provide novel solutions to seemingly intractable dilemmas

- involvement promotes service responsiveness resulting in improved access and more 'appropriate' use
- involvement engenders a sense of ownership that empowers those involved
- the public promote inter-agency working by adopting a broad social definition of health and can be powerful allies, for example in accessing alternative sources of funding.

Gone are the days when 'doctor knows best' was an acceptable attitude. The public is now better informed about health, illness and treatment options and expects to take a role in decision making, whether this be within the consulting room or on a PCG board. This can be threatening for some health professionals, challenging many of their traditional values. Some fear unleashing unrealistic demands or falsely raising expectations if resources are limited.

Experience shows that where sufficient information and support is given this is not the case. Just as the public needs information and support if they are to be meaningfully involved, so PCGs and PCTs need the skills, resources and ownership to make public involvement happen.

The lay member will be a token presence and his or her contribution will be based on personal views and experiences unless he or she has a way of linking in with a wider community. To achieve this linkage some make use of voluntary sector umbrella organisations or neighbourhood forums to canvass a variety of views, others work with community development workers to help them access existing groups. While it is impossible to ensure true 'representativeness' of the local community it is important that the lay member is able to access as wide a range of opinion and interests as possible on a regular basis.

To help the lay member optimise his or her contribution, agenda papers for board meetings should be circulated well in advance and the member be fully briefed on relevant issues. Good notice of forthcoming agenda items will allow lay members the opportunity to discuss issues with relevant people from their 'background constituency'. Papers should be as jargon-free as possible; some PCGs have formulated a glossary of terms – useful for all board members.

Beyond the PCG's board

The lay member does not carry sole responsibility for ensuring that public involvement occurs. This is the responsibility of the entire PCG. Although the lay member may take a lead, patient and public involvement should be intrinsic to all of the work of the PCG both within and beyond the board across the PCG's constituency.

Each of the PCG's working groups should consider how they plan to involve the public in fulfilling their functions and whether the group needs to include lay members to help them achieve this. Lay members should certainly be involved in determining clinical governance plans and priorities for the PCG, typically areas where health professionals may feel most vulnerable and reluctant to embrace public involvement.

You might subdivide the PCG's clinical governance plan into component areas, to consider how patient and community input may enhance this work and to address the fears of professionals directly, where they arise. For example, disability groups may be invaluable in assisting with anti-discriminatory training and advice on the accessibility of premises – quality issues frequently raised by patients. Community groups can advise on patient-friendly complaints systems, or focus groups may explore experiences of care for certain conditions. Practice- or clinician-specific data such as that about referral patterns should be used with extreme caution – such material may be influenced by so many factors that it is impossible to draw useful conclusions regarding quality issues; sharing such data may jeopardise relationships.

Methods for achieving your PCG's objectives

Your PCG's aims and objectives will help you to determine the methods of public involvement to use and the resources you must commit. Public involvement does not happen for free – the time of both skilled workers and lay people needs to be considered as well as the need for accessible information, interpreters, crèche facilities, transport costs, administrative support, etc.

Principles

Before embarking on surveys, focus groups and public meetings, PCGs should consider what it is they are trying to achieve. Truly involving patients and the local community has very different implications from listening to or consulting the public on specific issues. PCGs need to decide to what degree they are willing to share both power and the associated difficult decisions with the public.

As with other areas of their work, PCGs should develop a written strategy with specific targets for the systematic involvement of users and the public.[3] This strategy should be integral to all the other strategies and plans of the PCG as it will describe the approach to all PCG work.

PCGs should review and challenge their public involvement strategy:

- Is their approach tokenistic?
- Is community involvement an integral part of all PCG work?
- Are they involving as broad a cross-section of the PCG community as possible including disadvantaged groups?
- Are they prepared to share information and decision making?
- Can they justify decisions that are counter to the views/wishes of the community?
- Can they engage with a broader social model of health as identified by the public?
- Are they willing to change in response to issues raised by the community?

Practices should review how they are involving patients and the public in their development plans or monitoring the quality of care or services available.

PCG boards

PCG board meetings are held in public and the minutes are public documents. While this is a good principle in terms of transparency and facilitates considered discussion, few members of the public actually attend.

Some boards allow the public who do attend to ask questions and raise issues. This is an excellent way of showing commitment to an open process, although of course it does not indicate systematic involvement. Many PCGs have found that the local media is keen to follow proceedings, which provides a useful means of increasing awareness of the PCG and sharing information.

CHC members sit on many PCG boards as participant observers. They act as scrutineers, advise on aspects of quality of service delivery and help PCG boards link in with other organisations.

PCGs will need to use a variety of different methods in parallel to fit the particular purpose and circumstances of an exercise, always remembering how integration of a user or community perspective can be systematically achieved. Some of the most common approaches are described opposite.

Public meetings
Public meetings are good in principle but are of limited value. The atmosphere at specially convened meetings to address a topical issue is often defensive and discussion hostile and unhelpful, especially if the aim of the meeting is really to justify decisions already made. Any PCGs arranging public meetings should try to overcome these problems.

Public consultation documents
Public consultation documents fulfil certain accountability requirements as part of formal consultation processes but are of limited value in terms of true involvement. Response is dependent on circulation and literacy levels, and although some highly organised voluntary sector organisations may be able to respond, there are obvious difficulties caused by use of technical jargon and biased option appraisals of the issue.

Surveys and questionnaires
Although this method may seem attractive in terms of apparent simplicity and low cost, designing a good questionnaire is far from easy. Question bias, literacy levels, low response rates and unrepresentative respondent characteristics may all play a part in leading to an outcome of little or no value.

Focus groups
Focus groups explore identified issues. Groups of people may be specially brought together for the purpose, or alternatively involve an existing group, such as a user group or tenants' association. Focus groups need skilled facilitation, but are relatively low cost. They are a useful way of exploring attitudes and perceptions, but limited by the composition of the group and lack of any definitive 'answers'.

Citizens' juries
Citizens' juries result in specific recommendations on identified issues. Twelve members of the public who represent the local population in terms of age and gender are presented with detailed information from 'expert' witnesses and given time for deliberation. Their usefulness is tempered by the degree of commitment of the commissioning authorities to act on the recommendations made. They are expensive, often costing between £15 000 and £30 000 per jury.

Standing panels
Many health authorities have recruited panels of up to 3000 local residents whose views are regularly sought by post and who may meet as smaller facilitated groups. Their value is determined by the level of infor-

mation provided and the degree of consequent deliberation including the opportunity to reflect on the opinions of others.[4]

Rapid appraisal

Rapid appraisal is a 'quick and dirty' method of identifying health needs and priorities from a community perspective and can be a very useful starting point in planning to meet those needs. Information is gathered from a range of sources using key informants such as shopkeepers and community leaders as well as census material and public documents.

Accessing voluntary organisations, user and carer groups

The UK has a huge number of such organisations ranging from highly organised national bodies to small, informal support groups. Within these bodies from the largest to the smallest lies a wealth of experience and knowledge which can be tapped by PCGs. There may be several hundred voluntary groups within the geographical area of each PCG. Some voluntary sector organisations are also highly organised service providers. Many areas have umbrella groups of such organisations, or directories which can assist in accessing a broad range of user views. User and carer groups will be invaluable in contributing to PCG work at all stages of service planning, implementation and evaluation and should be involved in all relevant project work. PCGs should remember to involve and support smaller, less well-organised groups so that minority views can be heard.

Voluntary groups will have their own views on the best ways to access them, such as stakeholder conferences, user forums, buddying schemes, standing committees (e.g. Maternity Services Liaison Committees) and focus groups.

Community development

Community development is a holistic approach which draws on resources from within the community itself to promote participation, self-help and social support. The underlying principles of community development are commitment to sharing of information, knowledge and power, the reduction of health inequalities with a focus on disadvantaged and marginalised groups within society, and elimination of discrimination. It fosters working relationships between professional and lay people. Simultaneous organisational development allows the NHS and other agencies to respond positively to issues that are identified.

Community development uses a range of different techniques, including group work, building networks, lobbying and action groups, festivals and events, and advocacy. A community development approach can be used by PCGs to identify gaps in provision, influence service development and promote networking in the locality.

Some PCGs are funding community development workers to work with local community groups, or joining in with established local authority community development work. Community development ensures a bottom-up approach with a broad social definition of health and an agenda set by the local community. However, it takes time and commitment to realise the benefits and can be challenging to ways in which health services traditionally work.

Other methods that PCGs may consider include patient participation groups, health parliaments, deliberative opinion polls and consensus conferences.

Information and publicity

The usefulness of patient and public involvement in both individual clinical decisions and health planning is determined by the degree of information imparted.[4] People need information about health, illnesses, treatments, self-care, services available and how to access them. The community has a right to know how public money is being spent, how to influence services and where to turn when things go wrong. PCGs need to link into existing information systems to signpost people and provide information about the work of the PCG itself. An 'information lead' or subgroup could co-ordinate that work.

Ways of accessing and delivering information will include:

• word of mouth
• circulation of minutes of meetings
• posters and leaflets
• newsletters
• helplines (including NHS Direct)
• video and audiotapes
• touchscreen patient information systems
• PCG websites
• Internet
• the press
• local and national radio
• education: schools, further and higher educational establishments.

The local press and radio stations can be extremely effective ways of obtaining widespread publicity. It is worth providing media skills training for a few individuals in the PCG who can take responsibility for dealing with the press and anticipate difficulties.

Improving the health of the community

As PCGs evolve into PCTs they will take on more responsibility for improving the health of their communities and addressing local health inequalities. To function effectively they 'will need to engage with and involve patients, carers and local partner organisations' to develop appropriate services for the local community and share difficult decisions about allocating resources to best meet needs.[5]

Patient and public involvement should occur at all levels and settings within the PCGs. Most practices will need support and guidance from their PCG as to how to conduct activities to obtain meaningful involvement.

Useful resources

Chambers R (1999) *Involving Patients and the Public: how to do it better.* Radcliffe Medical Press, Oxford.

Department of Health (1998) *In the Public Interest: developing a strategy for public participation in the NHS.* Department of Health, Wetherby.

Department of Health (1999) *Primary Care Groups: public engagement toolkit.* Northern & Yorkshire NHS Executive Regional Office, Durham.

Ling T (1999) *Reforming Healthcare by Consent.* Radcliffe Medical Press, Oxford.

Olszewski D, Jones L (1999) *Putting People in the Picture.* Scottish Association of Health Councils, Edinburgh.

Wilson T (ed) (1999) *The PCG Development Guide.* Radcliffe Medical Press, Oxford.

References

1 Secretary of State for Health (1997) *The New NHS: modern, dependable.* Cm 3807. The Stationery Office, London.

2 Regan E, Smith J, Shapiro J (1999) *First Off the Starting Block.* Health Services Management Centre, University of Birmingham, Birmingham.

3 Department of Health (1999) *Patient and Public Involvement in the New NHS.* Department of Health, London.

4 Dolan P, Cookson R, Ferguson B (1999) Effect of discussion and deliberation on the public's views of priority setting in health care: focus group study. *BMJ.* **318**: 916–19.

5 Department of Health (1999) *Primary Care Trusts: establishment, the preparatory phase and their functions.* Department of Health, London.

CHAPTER 20

How to involve primary care professionals

Alex Trompetas and Sarah Baker

As chairman of the Central Croydon PCG and a GP trainer, Alex Trompetas was asked to prepare a test for GP registrars on their knowledge of PCGs. He prepared what he thought was a simple test. From curiosity he tried it with one of his partners. Out of 20 questions she got only one correct. This was 'PCG stands for primary care group'. This was an outcome of concern, considering that she was a seasoned GP in the practice of one of the first national PCG pilots.

Concern gave way to hilarity when these same questions where given to the GP registrars for whom they were intended. PCT was anything from 'primary care test' to 'personal care training', and HImP was 'health informers of members of parliament' in the eyes of one imaginative GP registrar.

PCGs the wider picture

The primary care environment is defined as everything that is not secondary or tertiary care. PCGs then become the wider organisations that were intended in the White Paper.[1] This introduces the future relationships and working partnerships that will embrace all the professionals working within PCGs. A board with a maximum membership of seven GPs, two nurses and a social services representative among others cannot be representative of all professional opinion within a PCG.

Who are the primary care professionals?

Any professional working in primary care is included in this definition, paving the way to achieving higher involvement. Recognising all the primary care professionals and the complex health partnerships in operation is the first step towards this elusive higher involvement:

- all doctors including GPs, community doctors, occupational doctors and other primary care doctors
- nurses, including all community nurses, practice nurses, health visitors, school nurses, nurse practitioners, midwives, CPNs and various specialist community nurses
- PAMs, including all therapists (e.g physiotherapists, speech and language therapists, chiropodists, occupational therapists, etc.)
- professionals working with the local authorities, such as social services, schools, etc.
- any other professional working with PCGs, including pharmacists, dentists, opticians, etc.

Where did we start?

Commissioning and fundholding GPs historically took a leading role in decision making in primary care. Inevitably, this evolved into the current primary care partnerships that will provide the integrated healthcare of the future.[2]

When looking at involvement and participation one needs to look beyond the primary care professionals on a PCG board. On average the board professionals are by far the most involved group of professionals, and self-selection would have ensured that they were already taking an active role in primary care.

The real challenge is how to involve the non-board GPs and nurses and also how to bring the decision-making process to all the primary care professionals outlined above for the first time.

PCGs a year down the road

So where is the main body of primary care professionals now? Are the people who were supposed to be at the helm actually involved at all?

An early report by the Audit Commission found mixed attitudes and a lack of involvement by some GPs.[3] This was consistent with earlier findings in a survey of the national commissioning pilots by the HSMC at the University of Birmingham. The survey showed that 70% of GPs spent no time or less than one hour on PCG activities in a typical week. This was in contrast to the nurses of the PCG who were significantly more enthusiastic. Nurses, however, felt that the GPs were dominating the agenda.[4]

A picture is starting to emerge of two distinct groups of primary care professionals within PCGs:

- those who remained uninvolved in any PCG business from the start
- those who did have an involvement, but are in danger of losing their motivation.

There is a need to enhance the 'promise' of the PCG in order to attract new converts, but also somehow to improve the reality for those already involved. Figure 20.1 is a schematic representation of professional involvement.

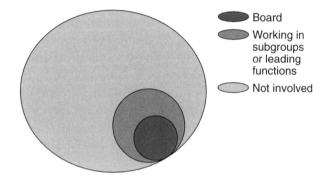

Board

Working in subgroups or leading functions

Not involved

Figure 20.1 Primary care professionals: board, involved, uninvolved.

What are the issues?

There are issues that are common to all the professional groups within PCGs and issues which are more prominent within one of the subgroups.

Workload

This is commonly identified by all the professionals within PCGs.[5] Although some form of provision has been made for the professionals serving on PCG boards, this is not the case for the wider membership. This is commonly misunderstood as the financial aspect of workload. Rewarding time, however, is dealt with in depth below.

In a health service system with too few doctors, nurses and other clinicians, and also a continuous productivity 'push', it is the sheer amount of everyday clinical work that almost inhibits any thought of involvement in the PCG structures. This may be expressed in different ways by self-employed doctors or salaried nurses but represents the same fundamental problem.

Increasing the number of primary care professionals is one possible answer, but this would be more a national planning workforce agenda item rather than just an individual PCG issue. A further way of addressing the workload issue is by looking at the balance of professional and support staff.

Mintzberg in 'the professional context' describes the 'professional services organisation' as one with a large support staff to assist the 'professional core'.[6] More support staff is a short-term solution, easier and cheaper to implement and bypasses the national question of levels of professional staff in this country. (In a limited resources environment one may be accused of scoring an own goal by advocating more support staff to address a shortage of professional staff. If more money is used for more support staff this will mean less professional staff, perpetuating the structural fault.) The extra support staff have to be seen directly to support the professionals rather than increasing the bureaucratic hierarchy. For practices, for example, this means more practice-based staff, and for nurses and PAMs, more receptionists, telephonists, typists, etc., at their work-places.

Communications

Communication was described as the 'lynchpin of effective operations' in GP fundholding consortia.[7] Such consortia were seen by many as one of the early PCG precursors. Communication in a virtual organisation, such as the PCG, where the various professionals may be isolated geographically and perform completely different daily tasks, may also be such a 'lynchpin'.

Communication will increase 'corporacy' and a sense of belonging. Anecdotal evidence showed that even among those professionals with minimum involvement regular communication was more likely to lead to some eventual participation. Lack of communication was more likely to increase isolation and even resentment of the PCGs.

> Nothing seems to be happening. **They** make all the decisions and nobody seems to be involved.
> Quote from a GP in Central Croydon made during a practice visit

We have all these meetings and discuss things, but I am not sure if they ever go to anybody else. I am sure the board never hears about our discussions.
Comment by a practice nurse in Croydon when asked about the Nurses' forum

Open meetings were identified as an important channel of communication in PCGs in the HSC 1998/139.[8] Meetings, however, are time-consuming. With workload also identified as one of the main obstacles to involvement, it is unsurprising that they are often poorly attended. PCGs are developing other communication channels to overcome this. A newsletter is a cheaper, effective and accessible way to keep primary care professionals involved. A more interactive way is electronically through intranets, including regular use of e-mail and a purpose-designed website. Such communication, however, may not be accessible by everybody and is certainly more expensive.

Remuneration

This is recurrently identified by health professionals as a major issue preventing further involvement.[5] GPs are more vocal on this issue partly because of their self-employed independent contractor status.

Financial rewards may not be the most important motivation for health professionals. There is an element of self-fulfilled truth in this statement. Career orientation at an early age will select individuals with other than just financial motivation to follow the healthcare career path.

What primary care professionals have described as remuneration is examined below as:

- direct financial benefits
- other benefits.

Direct financial benefits

The remuneration of health professionals who are board members, although considered by many as inadequate, is clearly defined in guidance about PCGs.

The payment of non-board members is, however, a grey area open to local interpretation. Health professionals may, for example, attract some payment for carrying out a specific piece of work. In PCGs around London, a sessional rate is commonly paid for commissioning work and for clinical governance development work. It is very rare, however, that there will be a reimbursement for general PCG-related tasks. PCG tasks may include, for example, turning up at locality meetings and reading carefully all the papers that come around. It can of course be debated that such tasks constitute part of a primary care professional's 'core work'.

Other benefits

For the GPs involved, indirect financial benefits would largely be those regarded as benefiting their own practice. For nurses and other primary care professionals involvement may enhance their career prospects and this may also apply to a lesser extent to GPs.

Such benefits are often more obscure and certainly more long term. They do not have an instant appeal to a large section of the professional body. Those who recognise and value such benefits would already be involved in a PCG, while those who do not intrinsically recognise these benefits will remain sceptical.

Indirect benefits may include:

- replacement costs, that do not benefit the professional involved directly, but create free protected time
- broader understanding of primary care issues. This may increase satisfaction among primary care professionals, particularly when influencing the decision-making process
- practice investment in staff and/or equipment
- improved prospects for career development.

Do incentives work?

The answer depends on what we mean by 'work'. Alfie Kohn, in his 1993 article 'Why incentive plans cannot work' in the *Harvard Business Review*, argues that they succeed at securing one thing only: temporary compliance.[9]

> *Do rewards motivate people? Absolutely. They motivate people to get rewards.*

According to numerous studies in laboratories, workplaces and other settings, incentives typically undermine the very processes they are intended to enhance.

Time and time again, findings suggest that the failure of any given incentive programme is due to the inadequacy of the psychological assumptions that ground all such plans.[10–12] Irrespective of this academic view, we have already argued above that primary care professionals may not be driven primarily by financial incentives.

This means that we should treat direct and indirect financial awards as supporting existing intrinsic behaviours rather than as attempts to modify them. This would mean in practice that we are unlikely to encourage more primary care professionals to be involved than those already involved, by offering them direct payments or replacement costs (locums, etc.). We may, however, prevent those already involved from defecting by adequate financial support for their time spent on PCG activity.

Influence

Gaining influence is one of the motivating factors for the nurse professionals in the PCG.[13,14] Anecdotal evidence would also suggest that other non-doctor professionals would become more involved if this involvement would influence the decision-making process and the delivery of health services.

> *In the first six months of our commissioning pilot the chairman and I received 24 invitations to meet with representatives of various health professionals like pharmacists, dentists, therapists, etc. This enthusiasm for involvement could be simply explained by the desire to access the perceived 'purse string' holders. But it contrasts sharply with the enthusiasm of GPs who had to be coerced to few meetings by interesting venues, good catering, PGEA and even reimbursement costs. After all these inducements, attendance was grudgingly below 40%.*
> Comment by the chief officer of one of the first national commissioning pilots and subsequent PCG

Managing influence

There is an interesting management issue here: reducing GP influence in the PCG may drive away some of the GPs already involved. Attempting to involve more GPs by increasing their influence may demoralise nurses (and PAMs) who perceive that GPs already have a disproportionate influence on the PCG (*see* Figure 20.2).

A way of avoiding this trap is by professionals having an external outlook in their involvement in the PCG.

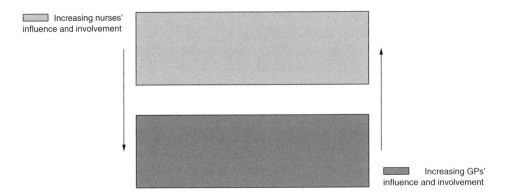

Figure 20.2 A 'zero sum' game. A direct win for one group is a direct loss for the other. An increase in the area of influence of one group will directly decrease the area of influence of the other group.

- For example, a physiotherapist is involved in negotiations with the local orthopaedic consultants in devising a new musculoskeletal service for the PCG. Competing for influence is not an internal matter anymore. Increasing the physiotherapist's influence in this example does not decrease the influence of any other group in the PCG, but in fact improves the PCG's overall standing.
- In another example, pharmacists and prescribing advisors may lead negotiations with hospital consultants on treatment protocols.

Influence therefore should not be an internal power struggle issue for the PCG, but a matter of co-operation and synergy that will further the PCG aims as an organisation. Relevant to the management of influence are structure and the decision-making process.

Structure
A highly hierarchical structure decreases involvement. A flatter, more matrix-like structure will increase involvement. A graphical observation of this is shown in Figure 20.3.

Decision-making process
Involving the professional membership of a PCG in the decision-making process is a complex task. A decision process that successfully engages includes:

- transparency of the decisions and the process
- feedback at every level of the decision making
- explaining how the decision was made and why.

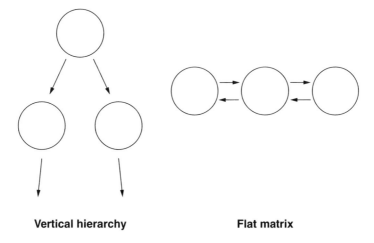

Vertical hierarchy   **Flat matrix**

Figure 20.3 Vertical versus matrix. In the former, involvement is structured and managed one way; in the latter, there is two-way interaction and greater socialisation.

There are a number of models addressing this. Commonly there is a 'funnel'-like process. Large meetings of professional groups (maybe as stakeholder meetings) collect ideas and opinion. This is fed through to a smaller group which in turn feeds to a smaller group until the process reaches the ultimate decision makers (Figure 20.4).

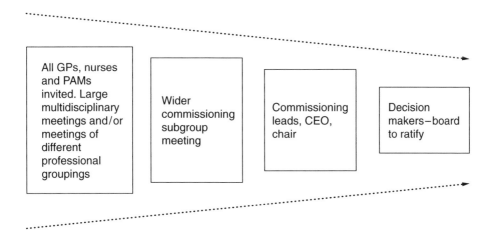

Figure 20.4 The 'funnel process'.

For example, consider the process of deciding the top priorities for next year's budget. The 'funnel' process 'hoovers up' professional views. There can be many different versions of this with different stages and different reporting mechanisms from stage to stage. Attempting to increase inclusivity will lengthen the 'funnel'. The longer the process the more difficult for those at the beginning to recognise and own the end result.

The future

Selective targeting

It is desirable to have as wide an involvement as possible by all primary care professionals. However, it is only by trying to understand and identify behaviour patterns of the PCG constituent primary care professionals that we may achieve further involvement.

While every primary care professional should be in our target list, efforts may be more effective with selective targeting. Similarly we may select how and when we involve our professionals in the PCG. Our pharmacists, for example, may want to be involved in issues of special interest to them. This is also where they are more likely to make a useful contribution.

Conclusion

The experience of the first six months has shown that although many primary care professionals, such as nurses and PAMs, have been enthusiastic and involved in numbers, many GPs remain uninvolved.

There is a need to strengthen the influence of the PCG professional body to maintain the momentum of their involvement. At the same time, addressing issues of workload, career development, communications and adequate remuneration may encourage those who have been held back.

We end this chapter with the following comment: professional involvement in the PCGs is more significant than the numbers would indicate. It is important to support those already involved as well as encouraging others.

References

1 Secretary of State for Health (1997) *The New NHS: modern, dependable.* The Stationery Office, London.

2 Singer R (1997) *GP Commissioning: an inevitable evolution.* Radcliffe Medical Press, Oxford.

3 Audit Commission (2000) *The PCG Agenda: early progress of primary care groups in 'The New NHS'.* Audit Commission, London.

4 Regan EL, Smith JA, Shapiro JA (1999) *First Off the Starting Block: lessons from GP commissioning pilots for PCGs.* Health Services Management Centre, Birmingham.

5 Smith JA, Regan EL, Goodwin N *et al.* (2000) *Getting into their Stride: report of a national evaluation of primary care groups.* Health Services Management Centre, Birmingham.

6 Mintzberg H (1989) *Inside Our Strange World of Organisations.* Free Press, New York, Chapter 6.

7 Laing A, Cotton S (1997) Partnerships in purchasing: development of consortium-based purchasing among GP fundholders. *Health Services Management Research.* **10**: 245–54.

8 NHS Executive (1998) *Developing Primary Care Groups.* HSC 1998/139. NHSE, Leeds.

9 Kohn A (1993) Why incentive plans cannot work. *Harvard Business Review.* **Sept/Oct**.

10 Rich JT, Larson JA (1987) Why some long-term incentives fail. In: HRN Totowa (ed) *Incentives, Cooperation and Risk Sharing.* Rowan & Littlefield.

11 Haegele MJ (1987) The new performance measures. In: ML Rock and LA Berger (eds) *The Compensation Handbook* (3e). McGraw-Hill, New York.

12 Deci EL, Ryan RM (1985) *Intrinsic Motivation and Self-determination in Human Behaviour.* Plenum Press, New York.

13 Young L, Poulton B (1997) Integrated nursing teams can influence locality commissioning. *Primary Health Care.* **7**(10): 8–10.

14 Hipkins L (1996) *Nurses and Commissioning: a study of skills that nurses bring to and that nurses need for commissioning.* Anglia and Oxford Regional Office.

CHAPTER 21

How to develop intermediate care

Intermediate care is the buzz word for the beginning of the millennium. Secondary care is becoming increasingly specialised, while primary care clinicians provide a much-needed generalist service. Consequently, there is now a need for a level of care somewhere in between. This has been labelled 'intermediate care' and was the prime focus of a speech by the Secretary of State for Health, Alan Milburn, who spoke at a meeting at the King's Fund in February 2000. The possibilities for intermediate care are immense. One-stop diagnostic centres, locality clinics using video conferencing and telediagnostic facilities as well as step-down inpatient care are all happening. The future may see PCTs employing generalist physicians and surgeons in their localities with clinical directorates in common specialties led by specialists, GPs or nurses. The development of intermediate care may one day be seen as a step equally as important for the NHS as the breaking down of the Berlin wall was for the wider political arena.

Intermediate care, however, is happening already and the two accounts in this chapter are by the true pioneers in this field. It is more than likely that what they are doing today, the rest of us will be doing tomorrow.

The GP specialist

Barbara Hakin

The practices in South & West Bradford have developed a network of specialist GPs who provide a variety of services to all the patients in the PCG. The concept began in the early days of fundholding when a few enterprising GPs, who had existing surgical skills, realised that they could undertake procedures previously only offered in secondary care. As practices began to work together in consortia the range of services expanded and the advent of PCGs brings new opportunities for innovative ways of working.

Range of services

Minor surgical procedures

Most of our minor surgical procedures are undertaken by GPs working in the locality. These include procedures in:

- general surgery
- orthopaedics
- plastic surgery
- ophthalmology.

Diagnostic procedures

Several GPs in South & West are accredited to provide endoscopy, cystoscopy and flexible sigmoidoscopy. They underwent a rigorous training programme and performed many procedures under supervision before they worked alone. GP specialists provide virtually all such routine procedures for South & West Bradford patients. They work in the locality setting and at the district general hospital (DGH) to cater for those patients who are less fit and require back-up facilities to be available.

Our GP specialists also offer:

- ECG clinics with interpretation
- 24-hour blood pressure monitoring
- prostate assessment clinics.

Management of chronic disorders

Working closely with specialist nurses, several GPs in South & West have developed the skills to manage complex chronic disorders. Five GPs provide the majority of care for insulin-dependent diabetics. Specialist nurses, dieticians and chiropodists support them.

Two GPs have undertaken extensive training in the management of epilepsy. They provide a peripatetic service supported by specialist nurses and local consultants. The team provides a holistic approach to the treatment of epilepsy with particular accent on emotional and social aspects.

One GP has developed a special interest in the management of Parkinson's disease. He offers a diagnostic service with the consultant neurologist and a continuing package of care for patients with established disease.

In addition, we have GPs who provide a rheumatology service for patients with chronic disease who would normally have been monitored at the DGH.

Triage of outpatient referrals

We all accept that there are areas in which we have expertise and others where our knowledge is less extensive. It is not possible for any of us to be expert in all areas. Consultants acknowledge that the standard of referrals they receive from GPs across the patch is varied. We therefore decided to identify GPs with an interest in certain specialties who would undertake further training and work alongside consultants to provide a triage system. We have, in place, such a system for dermatology, neurology, rheumatology, gynaecology and urology, and are at present undertaking a pilot study in orthopaedics. In addition we have a GP who provides a pain clinic.

All the GPs have undergone training with local consultants and often both attend the same clinic, but with the GPs now seeing their own patients to increase throughput.

These GPs are not a substitute for consultants. They are a filter so that referrals sent on to the hospital are of a high standard. Frequently these triage clinics are run alongside a consultant outreach clinic so that once the GPs have identified the more difficult cases they can be seen on the same day.

Gaining support

The triage system requires trust, co-operation and confidence between all the GPs in the PCG. We are fortunate in South & West that such a spirit is present among practitioners, who see this as the best way to keep waiting times at the DGH at an acceptable level.

Bradford has a reputation for collaborative working and none of this would have been possible without the support of both our local acute and community trusts. We have also been fortunate in the support and assistance that we have had from our consultant colleagues. They understand that the GP specialists are not a substitute for them and the idea that they would get high-quality referrals found favour with them very quickly. The clinics are all supported by our consultant colleagues who welcome this intermediate layer of care which leaves more time for patients who most need their expertise. They realise that time spent in developing GP skills now will save their time in the future. In addition it makes sense of the outreach service. Our outreach clinics can cope with the same numbers of patients as hospital clinics, since the GPs assist the consultant just as the registrars and senior house officers would have done at the DGH. Indeed, as junior doctors' hours are reduced, our clinics may become more efficient.

The patients are comfortable with the system. They understand that they are seeing a practitioner with more knowledge than their GP and that if necessary they will then be referred on to the hospital. Naturally if a patient is unhappy with this system he or she can be referred directly to the consultant.

We have taken advice from the medical defence unions, who advised us that provided practitioners only undertook roles with which they felt comfortable, there was no medico-legal concern. They say that should there be a problem, the GP's actions would be compared with those of another GP with a special interest rather than a consultant. They do not impose extra premiums on practitioners. In fact, their concern was for any delay in diagnosis that might result. Our system achieves precisely the opposite.

Training and development

All our GPs have trained alongside local consultants and for some there is a diploma or qualification relative to the specialty they have undertaken. They also attend conferences and courses.

They are all accredited to provide secondary care under HSG 96/91 and the local consultants are key to this accreditation. It is of course important that the GPs continue with their professional development and education and maintain contact with the consultants. This is ensured by joint clinics. We are confident that the training, education and accreditation of these GPs is robust and stands up to medico-legal scrutiny.

In the longer term, we would like to see an even more defined training programme and an extension of our system, which might allow a national training programme, perhaps tied in to vocational training. We envisage a situation whereby during their vocational training, young GPs could indicate a specialty to which they would devote more time and receive an extra qualification.

Development of premises

In the early days of fundholding, most of these procedures were undertaken in our surgeries. However, we soon found that we were running out of space and we were keen to ensure that care given locally was of the same high standard as we would expect in secondary care. We felt it would be even better if delivered from appropriate purpose-built premises, provided that the locality focus was not lost. We have therefore developed two intermediate care centres in South & West Bradford and there are plans for a third. These centres have outpatient suites and theatres equipped for diagnostic procedures and day-case surgery. One of the centres has been built under the Private Finance Initiative (PFI) scheme and the other is owned by the community trust and has been extensively modernised and refurbished for this purpose.

Effect on GMS

We are often asked whether the time taken to deliver these services compromises GMS provision by our GP specialists. Most of them only spend one or two half-days per week on this work and for them it is simply an alternative to the activities which GPs have traditionally undertaken outside GMS. The GP specialists all enjoy this work and indeed we believe it may help to avoid the burn-out which so many GPs experience nowadays.

Clearly the size of the practice dictates how easy it is for GPs to fit in this work and individual practice circumstances vary. Some of our practices with several GP specialists have been able to take on an extra partner or assistant using the income generated from the service.

Funding the GP specialists

Once able to undertake procedures and see patients unsupervised, most funding for GP specialists has come from secondary to primary shift as in HSG 96/91.

It is more difficult to identify finance for GP training and we have been fortunate over the past few years to have assistance from pharmaceutical companies and national disease societies. In the early days, many of the GPs invested their own time in training.

Our PCG now has a policy whereby it will pay locum and training costs for any GP undertaking training where the PCG has identified a clear need for a GP specialist. One of our main reasons for moving to PCT status is so that we can develop and provide these services ourselves and hopefully employ some salaried GPs across the area who can cover the GP specialists.

Conclusion

Each of our services has been audited showing successful outcomes. Patient satisfaction surveys clearly show their delight with the accessible user-friendly service, provided in familiar surroundings and with shorter waiting times.

We believe that using these practitioners represents a cost-effective and efficient way of delivering local services which significantly reduces our referrals to secondary providers. Our waiting times for outpatient clinics and our waiting list for procedures is consequently reduced. While we accept the initial increase in costs we are certain enough of the long-term benefits to invest from our unified budgets.

We have been encouraged recently by the interest our scheme has aroused and hope that others may follow our example.

Setting up integrated clinics

David Paynton

All PCGs have aspirations to change the way services are delivered to their patients. Intermediate care is seen as a bridge between specialist and community care and is seen as an attractive option in the reshaping of services. PCTs at level 4 will also wish to see themselves as providing some intermediate care services rather than just commissioning them.

There must be some agreed common ground rules that govern the development of intermediate care. These include the following.

- Intermediate care must integrate with wider service developments based on each specialty.
- Part of the work of clinicians providing intermediate care will be to work with primary and secondary care in developing care pathways.
- Patients with complex needs should be fast-tracked through the system.
- Service agreements with secondary care should recognise that fewer but more complex clinical problems will be seen in secondary care.
- Secondary care can only eventually restructure if all local PCG/Ts have a similar approach.
- Even if intermediate care is being provided within a PCT, secondary care has a vital role in training, monitoring and backing up clinically that service.

This requires a shared common objective and considerable mutual trust if PCG/Ts and secondary care are to sit down and start to reshape services. Legitimate clinical concerns can be used as a defence against perceived loss of control or loss of income. At present, with single block contracts with providers, there are few incentives within the system for change. The only real incentive is punitive if waiting time targets are not met.

In future, PCG/Ts will want to enter into service agreements with individual directorates as a means of stimulating a more integrated approach. Any significant change will require an understanding of the NHS planning and business cycle, a few enthusiastic product champions, good-quality information, professional management and a degree of clinical consensus.

The musculoskeletal service and Southampton East Healthcare PCG

Our musculoskeletal service at Moorgreen Hospital has been developing since 1996, when our locality was coming together as a multifund. Fundholding, in those days, made it easier to shift funds out of secondary care. Nevertheless it still required considerable discussion within the practices to get them to agree to pool the physiotherapy budget into a central pot and use this to open a disused ward in the local community hospital.

At the heart of the discussions was the understanding that the centralised physiotherapy service would see itself growing into a much wider role than just primary preventative physiotherapy. GPs, being by nature short term in decision making, wanted to see the final product before they would agree to lose the practice-based service.

The service itself is provided by the community trust and now has five whole-time equivalent physiotherapists. After a couple of years this service has now grown to include psychologists and occupational therapists. They provide a dedicated eight-week course for patients with long-term back pain. This will now extend to cover all chronic pain and will involve a clinician from the pain clinic in the acute trust.

Plans are now advanced to set up a new rheumatology clinic. A local GP, working in collaboration with the rheumatologists in the acute trust will run this. Part of the session will be to set up integrated care pathways between primary and secondary care rather than patient contact time. It is also envisaged that this clinic will attract specialist nurses, occupational therapists and physiotherapists with a specific interest in rheumatology.

Implications for a PCT

As PCTs develop, it is inevitable that this service comes under the direct management of the PCT as a provider. The creation of PCTs will set off a wider debate about the role of the acute trusts of the future. Acute trusts will need to focus on shorter inpatient stays, developing a more specialist diagnostic and treatment role, and moving patients back out into the community as soon as possible. LTSAs of the future may well be between PCTs and directorates. We will also see 'managed clinical networks' across a wider geographical area encompassing more than one acute trust.

The majority of rheumatology is long-term care, which does not require complex inpatient treatment. In this context, the bulk of services such as rheumatology might be provided by the PCT, rather than commissioned from the acute trust. Some more specialist services will, however, still need to be centred in an acute trust or hosted by a PCT on behalf of the other PCTs in the area.

How can this be achieved?

All PCG/Ts have aspirations to provide better services to patients. We are all learning, however, that achieving change in the health service of today is difficult. There is little real growth money in the system and most of this is swallowed up in cost pressures, such as pay awards and prescribing costs. This means that investment in a new service has to be offset by disinvestment elsewhere.

Most of our initial developments were in the days of collective commissioning as a multifund. Using the rules that existed then, professional management allowed us to gain maximum flexibility within the system to develop local services. The rules have now changed and while overall fundholding as it existed was not sustainable, PCGs will struggle unless they can adapt to the new mechanisms in place. PCTs will have a little more freedom as a provider, but this still has to be tested in the new environment. Understanding the planning cycle, the HImPs and SaFFs, seizing opportunities, negotiating some financial flexibility and selling the vision to one's colleagues needs a professional approach if PCG/Ts are really going to effect change in the NHS.

In today's tight financial framework there is no funding for double running costs so any funding shift will have to be incremental.

Key steps that need to be considered

- Agree within your board what you want to do. Prioritise your aspirations with other demands being made on you.
- Identify a clinical lead within your board to take this through. This role must be supported managerially by the chief executive.
- Look at the current physiotherapy budget. Is it lost in a block contract with the acute trust or is it divided up into all the practices? Is there money leaking out on private physiotherapy?
- Discuss the advantages and disadvantages of taking out practice-based

physiotherapy and repositioning it within a more centralised service. GPs will be reluctant to see any erosion of practice-based services unless they are convinced that the alternative is better and deliverable. **It is vital that there is a mechanism in your PCG/T to talk to practices as well as the Executive Board.**

- Identify potential sites. Access and costs of conversion need to be considered. Local community hospitals are the best bet but may not be available or have free space. Remember that your requirements will grow.
- Start discussions with the local physiotherapists and rheumatologist. Work with them in looking at the opportunities of working in a different way. Opportunities are a better motivator for change than threats.
- Think about the long-term developments and the need to involve other professionals, social services, local employers and other agencies.
- Involve your lay member and local special interest groups linked to arthritis.
- Talk to the other PCG/Ts in your area that might have an interest. They may want to share resources in developing a local centre supporting more than one PCG. Equally if the long-term aim is to restructure the local rheumatology service there needs to be a co-ordinated approach across a number of PCG/Ts.
- Start discussions with the health authority. It is especially important to discuss your ideas with the director of public health who is responsible for producing the HImP. Your plans can come under a number of headings, including promoting independence, promoting primary care, improving access and reducing waiting times.
- Link your plans with the NHS business cycle especially so any funding shift is incorporated into the SAFF.
- Make sure your plans include start-up costs and equipment.
- Look for any sources of money not already badged against something else. This might be the pump-priming money you need to get started. Modernisation funds or waiting list initiative money may suddenly materialise so have your plans ready to send in a bid within the usual two-week time frame. There may be residual uncommitted fundholding savings or unallocated growth. If any PCG/T has 1% of its budget unallocated it is doing well but that may be all you need to create a new service. Once started, however, it is imperative that the new service is incorporated into baseline recurrent budgets, otherwise it will always be under threat.
- Provide regular reports and feed back to your board and practices.
- Make a plan of campaign with dates and milestones.

Finally

The whole process could take 6–12 months to deliver so only embark on the journey if you feel it is in the long-term interests of developing improved services to patients. Be determined, but remember that it will still take 2–3 years for the full potential of your local centre to materialise. PCG/Ts will be judged on their ability to effect change and make a difference in both the medical and social dimension. Those that cannot, do not have a long-term future.

CHAPTER 22

How to develop a PCG communication strategy and how to involve the media

Ian Wylie and David Jenner

At the end of Shakespeare's *The Tempest*, Miranda, the daughter of Prospero, the ruler of the island, looks around in wonder at the ship-wrecked sailors, now reunited. 'Oh, brave new world', she exclaims in joy, 'that has such people in 't!'. To which her father mutters ''Tis new to thee'.

The brave new world that is the new NHS has had PCGs in it for a year. If nobody has actually greeted PCGs with the exact words of Miranda, there has nonetheless been a sense of wonder and perhaps amazement on both sides. In the old world of the established NHS, some Prosperos have doubted whether anything much is new. But within PCGs there has been a sense of discovery as local structures, previously meaningless, have become real and relevant parts of their world.

But the newness of PCGs, like a government or a new NHS, is a transitory thing. One year on and PCGs are part of the fabric of the NHS. No longer the latest thing in town, PCGs have climbed a steep learning curve to become the primary agents of delivery and commissioning of health-care services. And they have the opportunity to take radically different approaches to issues, which the more established parts of the NHS have conspicuously failed to tackle. They could, for one, get their communications right.

The failure of most parts of the NHS to invest in effective external relations over the past decade or more has cost everyone dear. Anyone remotely interested in the activities of the NHS has a story to tell about poor communications. Each year the health service commissioner publishes a selection of cases where poor communications have been contributory factors in avoidable death or suffering of patients. And there has been collective failure, as the NHS has failed to explain, engage, involve and enthuse local populations about service changes and development plans. In most cases, the individuals charged with leading the changes were articulate, effective communicators, well used to putting their views over and presenting arguments clearly and cogently. So why has the NHS been so poor at communication? And why might PCGs do this any better?

Communication is a management tool

Getting an organisation to be good at communication is a management discipline, just as getting the organisation to be a good employer, financially robust or clinically competent. Much of the NHS has failed to acknowledge this and has failed to give it sufficient management attention over the past decade. Health authorities and NHS trusts have assigned communications, often limited to media relations, to a junior post or to no post at all. Thinking that a couple of good public speakers made for a communicating organisation, their results have been all too evident.

The world into which PCGs, as new organisations, are now becoming established, is an extremely complex network of organisations, groups and individuals, each of which has a part to play in the local health economy. The NHS is complex enough, but when national government, professional bodies, local authorities, further and higher education, research groups, regional bodies, voluntary organisations, pressure groups, local businesses, MPs, media, patients, public, carers, celebrities and opinion formers (to name a few) are added, the picture soon becomes bewildering. How PCGs communicate, or do not communicate, with all of these organisations, groups and individuals, will have a profound impact on the development of primary care.

If the picture quickly looks complex, two further layers need to be added. First, in each patch, there are already vast amounts of communication between all the existing local players. Even if your PCG had the time and resources to make links with all the relevant individuals and organisations, the pre-existing network of influence will make this more difficult. All local agencies will prejudge PCGs because each will make an assumption – fairly or unfairly – about what the new organisation is and what it will do. This complexity makes it essential that PCGs put some kind of communications action plan or strategy together.

Developing a strategy

The seven stages of developing a strategy are:

- plan
- map
- prioritise
- listen
- analyse
- engage
- evaluate.

First, the board needs to be clear about what this structured approach to communications is for. A communications strategy is not something created in a vacuum, but must be integral to the work of the PCG. What does your PCG wish to achieve over the next 3 months, 12 months, 5 years? Only when the development plan of the PCG has been formed and is clear enough to be written on a couple of sides of A4, will it be possible to structure PCG communications within the local health economy.

Second, the PCG must establish which organisations and individuals are necessary for the objectives of the PCG plan to be realised. Mapping key opinion formers for the PCG is essential. It is tempting to continue to communicate with the familiar: professional partners, known faces. Are these individuals and organisations really the ones the PCG needs to succeed in its objectives? If not, then which? Mapping the opinion formers, placing the PCG in the centre and placing the organisations, groups and individuals necessary to the work of the PCG around in a 'power map' quickly establishes the world in which you must operate.

Third, the PCG will need to prioritise. Which of your groups is necessary for the work of the PCG? Which are usual, but not essential? With limited resources, you must be clear where your maximum effort is needed.

Fourth, know as much as possible about each of these priority opinion formers. This is a matter of pooling individual knowledge from across the PCG and researching from other sources. If the local authority social services committee is a key player, it is not enough to know who chairs the committee and what political party they belong to. Do you know this person's interests, his or her voting record, recent speeches, network outside the council? What do you know of the other members on the social services committee and its officers? Can you profile the key individuals? Much is likely to be publicly available, or easily researched, and all will be relevant.

Target key individuals:

- prime contacts in local groups
- local opinion leaders
- product champions
- movers and shakers
- honest brokers
- enthusiasts
- blockers.

Fifth, you can do the same for the 'outliers', those who have the power to block your plans or hold them up. This is often the category in which the media are placed. How much do you know about the local media? You may know the local health correspondent, but do you know who writes the leaders in the local newspaper and what is their attitude towards health services? What are the special interests of the news editor and the editor? Who commissions the features, the opinion pages? Who is advertising on commercial radio, and what does this indicate about their audience? Analysis and knowledge gathering are the key to your success and these activities should be continuous. The more you have 'mapped' your possible 'blocks', the more effective will be your approach to them.

Sixth, you must be clear about why you are engaging each key audience. Your purpose is to communicate to improve their understanding of your objectives as a PCG, to engage their interest and to win them over to your position. In short, your purpose is to change attitudes and thus behaviour. And the only sure way to do this is to engage your key audience, face-to-face, with practical and concrete examples of the matters that concern them. Organisations employ a large range of communications techniques, sophisticated mass campaign methods, mailshots, mass advertising and, in the public sector, newsletters and leaflets. These are useful vehicles for raising general awareness and limited understanding of issues. Public meetings – another technique well loved by the public sector – may increase understanding and public knowledge. But if you wish to make behaviour change and shifts in attitude towards particular issues, then your intervention must be face-to-face, one-to-one. Nothing in this activity requires large expenditure, but it does require time and energy. Inviting the editor of your local paper for a drink after work is cheaper, more pleasant and certainly more effective than sending 100 000 leaflets to your PCG population (*see* Figure 22.1).

Finally, evaluate your efforts by getting feedback on what they think you are trying to do. Is change occurring? What do they say about what is happening?

Effective communications for PCGs is a tool of effective management.

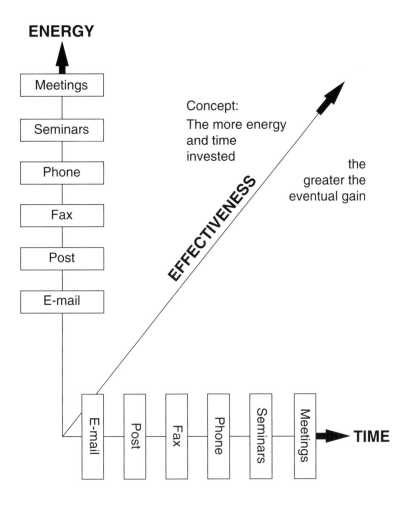

Figure 22.1   Jenner's Communication Law.

It requires time and thought, but is not out of reach of any PCG in the country. The benefits of getting it right are to contribute to the clarity and success of the plans and aspirations of the organisation. The costs of getting it wrong could be stasis and stagnation and an increasingly isolated future as the pace of change and the complexity of the local health economy move ever onwards.

CHAPTER 23

How to develop an information and IT strategy

Mark Couldrick

The formation of PCGs has coincided with a fundamental shift in the Department of Health's attitude to IT and primary care. In *Information for Health* Frank Burns shifted the focus of the NHS information strategy away from the previous obsession with financial and managerial information to the central premise that investment in computing should benefit clinicians and patients.[1]

Some particular elements emerged from the subsequent guidance:

- connection of all GP practices to NHSnet, subsequently revised to include provision of a connection on every GP desktop
- that information for PCGs be derived as a 'by-product' of normal clinical activity
- the development of fully integrated electronic patient records (EPR) and electronic health records (EHR).

The connection to GPnet is an essential pillar of the new information culture. It opens up the resources of the World Wide Web for use within surgeries. It will provide access to the National Electronic Library for Health (NeLH).

The extraction of morbidity data from GP clinical systems has huge potential but requires the routine use of GP clinical software for full consultation recording. The EHR, a longitudinal record of an individual's health based in primary care, and the EPR, an electronic record within a particular organisation, establish the primacy of computer-based medical records.

Implementation of information for health

Those involved in PCG IT will need to manage their most precious resource – time – carefully. The agenda is huge. After years of central neglect, primary care IT has become central to the whole NHS IT strategy. Given the underfunding of GP input it is crucial to direct energies at those areas which will result in changes, while ensuring that primary care's voice is heard where it needs to be.

Finances

Most of the new money for the implementation and development of Information for Health is being distributed from the centre via the much quoted 'modernisation fund'. This money is allocated at health authority level and much is ring-fenced for specific projects (e.g. GPnet connection). It is important for PCGs to negotiate with health authorities to identify those resources which will be best devolved for administration at PCG level. As a consequence of differential access to funding, many practices will need significant investment to bring their IT infrastructure up to date.

Local structures

The implementation of Information for Health has been charged to the chief executive of each health authority who has to develop a local implementation strategy (LIS). This will usually be led by the health authority's IT department and supported by a committee composed of the IT leads of the local trusts, PCGs and social services. Much of the agenda will not be under the control of PCGs but the voice of primary care needs to be loud. The PCG IT lead is likely to be the only representative with experience of primary care IT and it is an area where local PCGs may want to co-ordinate their actions to avoid duplication and to maximise resources. Certain areas of work are given particular emphasis.[2] PCGs should:

- plan over time to increase the use and scope of clinical recording within existing practice systems and identify a clinical lead to co-ordinate this work. This is work which will be best led by clinical governance with support from IT leads, particularly concerning Read codes and co-ordination of IT training. It is also important for the costs associated with increased data management to be recognised
- develop, within PCIPs and through contributing to the LIS, plans to

ensure that modernisation funds are appropriately deployed to:

- develop primary healthcare team systems and provide training and support either by running training course or supporting practices financially to identify their own training needs
- collect comparative data (e.g. MIQUEST), dependent on ensuring good information management within practices and the development of a culture of information sharing. The CHDGP[3] project offers excellent guidance
- implement decision support systems (e.g. PRODIGY). PRODIGY will be financed centrally and made available to all GPs through their system suppliers.
- respond to NHSnet targets, usually managed at health authority level. There is however, a huge training and information need to ensure maximum use is made of the resources on the net and to develop the use of e-mail to improve efficiency
- utilise electronic prescribing aids, e.g. ePACT.net, and work with local prescribing departments – PCGs may decide to buy in time.

Information management

The single most important task for IT leads is the development of information management within practices. This is crucial for both PCGs as organisations and increasingly as a core role for GPs. It is a task which satisfies the demands of several interlinked agendas and should be undertaken in partnership with clinical governance.

Data needs to be collected from:

- clinical contacts – consultations, new patient checks, specific disease management clinics
- referral letters
- hospital letters
- lab results
- radiology.

Data needs to be captured by:

- clinicians entering data during consultations
- entering data extracted from hospital letters (new or changed diagnoses, investigations, results, scanning letters)

- summarising existing notes
- electronic lab links
- electronic data interchange.

What data to collect

- Basic patient information.
- Basic data (e.g. date/time, primary healthcare team member involved) on patient contacts or health events (e.g. referrals, prescriptions).
- Problem (e.g. symptom, indication, diagnosis, morbidity).
- Episode type (e.g. whether first ever or a subsequent diagnosis) for calculation of incidence and prevalence.
- Referrals.
- Prescriptions.
- Test results and findings.
- GP interventions.
- Health promotion and risk factors.
- Disability/functional status for defined diseases.
- Source of data/author (e.g. hospital, GP, lab result, nurse).

It will be crucial that data is recorded in a retrievable way. This means the use of Read codes.

PCGs will need to facilitate this process by the development of core data sets of codes covering the main disease areas. It will be sensible to concentrate first on those areas which feature in the HImP and which are given emphasis in NSFs.

Benefits to the practice

- Improved patient care – easy call and recall, repeat prescription review, research, audit.
- Clinical governance – consistent data recording will make the extraction of practice 'performance' data easy, thus reducing the burden of administration.
- Reaccreditation – data collected for one purpose can be used to satisfy the demands of another.

Practices need to consider whether there are any benefits in the maintenance of both electronic and paper-based records. The development of the EHR would appear to make paper records obsolete. The new information strategy includes a plan to remove the legal obstacles to this.

Benefits to the PCG

- Consistent data recording across a PCG will facilitate the use of tools such as MIQUEST[4] to extract information from GP clinical systems. Information extracted from primary care can be used to inform the commissioning process and monitor progress towards the HImP.
- Collection of data from different clinicians will allow comparison against local and national bench marks.
- Measure performance against standards set by NSFs.

Costs and training

- Clinical staff may need to acquire/enhance keyboard skills.
- Training to maximise use of the clinical system.
- Training in basic PC skills.
- Data capture and recording takes time – consultations may initially need to be longer, letters need to be marked for coding, scanning takes time.
- Summarising has a directly measurable cost.
- Major savings in staff time will not be made until full electronic data transfer is possible.
- Costs associated with data management need to be flagged in the PCIP.
- PCGs will need to find funds to support and incentivise practices in this area.

Data management should be part of a wider strategy of practice IT development, which embraces the new information culture. It will be increasingly important for clinicians to acquire IT skills which allow them to embrace the need to access information and increasingly communicate electronically.

Table 23.1 illustrates a model of practice IT development.

Information to support clinical activity

The wider use of GP clinical software within the consultation and the provision of a web-enabled PC on every desk gives clinicians access to a huge source of information. PCGs will need to consider the training needs both to ensure maximal use of clinical software and also to develop the skills to critically access the knowledge base.

There is an information paradox:

Table 23.1 Model of practice IT development

Component	Level 1	Level 2	Level 3	Level 4	Level 5
Patient consultation	Paper clinical records only	Commitment to use clinical computer records	Post-event data entry by staff Data entry at point of service delivery	Full consultation recording	'Paperless' consultations supported by lab and radiology links, coding and scanning. Full electronic data interchange
Note summarisation	Paper clinical records only	Procedures developed for summarising patient records	Summarising in progress	Summarising complete for priority areas	Summarising complete for all conditions
Communications	No electronic communication	Local area network Internal e-mail	Health authority/ GP links	GPnet Path links External e-mail	Electronic referrals Electronic discharge summaries
Clinical coding	No clinical coding	Non-Read coding	Read clinical coding used in practice	Common Read clinical coding used by all clinicians in practice	
Access to the knowledge base	No web facilities within the practice	Some PCs enabled with Internet access	PC on every clinician's desk with web access		

- people are overwhelmed with information they do not need, but
- they cannot find the information they need when they want it.

The NeLH is a national project to help find a solution.[5]

In an attempt to maximise the benefit from referral to secondary care, many PCGs have entered into dialogue with local consultants to develop local guidelines. In addition NICE will be validating and disseminating guidelines. PCGs need to consider how best to ensure that this information is made available at the right place and time to actually effect clinical behaviour. Most GPs are overwhelmed with guidelines. A recent report in the *BMJ* demonstrated that a general practice in England could find over 20 kg of guidelines – a pile 2 ft high. Network technology and hypertext make possible much-improved management of information and PCGs will need to work with local library services to improve the delivery and relevance of information accessed by practices.

Communication

The GPnet project aims to provide every GP with an NHSnet connection on his or her desk. In time, it will obviously be necessary to provide the same access to nurses and PAMs. The project is complex and has suffered from unnecessary confusion. Clarity about such issues as call charges are now being resolved, but technical concerns about the messaging standard adopted for clinical messaging remain (X400).

However, while working through the difficulties, PCGs need to be thinking how best to use the technology.

Websites

A PCG website has the potential to save a lot of trees. It can be used to improve communication with both clinicians and patients. Many topics can conveniently be included on the site:

- information about the PCG (geography, constituent practices, etc.)
- information about board members
- contact details
- board meeting agendas and minutes
- proposals concerning movement to trust status and information about local consultation
- pages for nurses, PAMs and doctors
- information about local non-principals groups
- clinical information, local guidelines, formulary information
- copies of local referral forms and protocols ready to download as required.

Most of the information can be placed in the public domain. Otherwise it is technically simple to password-protect restricted areas of the site.

Some PCGs have developed intranets. These are wide area networks (WANs) which link practices within a PCG. The advent of free ISDN access to the NHSnet and thus to the World Wide Web make the need to use this route to connect practices less topical.

e-mail

The use of e-mail offers a different way to communicate, which can offer some advantages. It remains to be seen whether e-mail will become used for clinical queries between doctors, but it certainly offers the potential to open up communication between the PCG and its constituent members. Even a message informing practices of new information posted on a PCG website offers significant time and cost savings over the posting of vast numbers of minutes and letters. There will be a need for a cultural shift which will require investment in training (particularly in the use of the delete key).

Discussion groups

Newsgroup-type fora offer interested members of a PCG a chance to compare experiences, feed information back to the board, complain and share information. They are not difficult to set up but require a critical mass of IT-literate contributors to get discussions going. Once again this is a new area of communication that requires training and familiarisation.

Security, Caldicott and the Data Protection Act

Each PCG (in common with other NHS organisations) is required to appoint a Caldicott guardian. This was a responsibility identified in the Caldicott Report.[6] The Caldicott guardian is charged with ensuring that issues of patient confidentiality are considered whenever patient data are used. It is suggested that an audit of every NHS organisation is carried out, which for a PCG will include constituent practices. The audit should cover some of the following areas:

- consent of patients regarding use of information held concerning them
- staff code of conduct concerning confidentiality
- programme of staff training and induction
- contracts
- safe-haven procedures for information flowing in and out of the organisation
- security policy and identified security officer
- risk assessment and management

- user responsibilities, i.e. password management, protocol concerning unattended screens, log-in and log-out protocols
- controlling access to confidential patient information.

Potentially even more onerous will be the implications of the 1998 Data Protection Act.[7] This raises the following issues:

- consent for all 'processing' of data must be explicit – processing means using the data for anything other than the reason it was collected
- new classes of sensitive information are created which are subject to even stricter control
  - racial or ethnic origins
  - political opinions
  - religious or other beliefs
  - membership of a trade union
  - physical or mental health
  - sexual life
  - any actual or alleged offence or legal action.

The full implications of this act have not yet been explored but may well have an impact on data management and use of comparative data, particularly if small numbers of patients are involved and attributable to individual GPs.

Particular care needs to be exercised when patient-identifiable information is sent electronically. The NHSnet is too large to be considered safe for this purpose. It is likely that encryption of sensitive information will become the norm when data is transferred.

Technology

The biggest technical change in primary care IT is the widespread development of networks. GPnet connection requires the migration from a hub and spoke dumb terminal configuration to a network of PCs running a variety of applications only one of which is the clinical software.

General practice IT is rapidly reaching the level of complexity, even in relatively small practices, which in the business world would require the employment of a network manager. There is a rapidly developing skills gap which health authority IT departments do not have the numbers or expertise to fill. PCGs will need to be involved in the development of local health informatics services. They need to consider ways to provide technical network and PC support to their practices. This may be done by direct employment of staff or by the development of local suppliers of services. Practices will need advice on back-up procedures, antivirus software and security. In due course, PCGs should explore the possibility of using their purchasing power to obtain the best prices from suppliers of hardware, software and services.

References

1 NHS Executive (1998) *Information for Health: an information strategy for the modern NHS*. HSC 1998/168. NHSE, London.
2 NHS Executive (1999) *Primary Care Groups: taking the next steps*. HSC 1999/246. NHSE, London.
3 *The Collection of Health Data from General Practice*.
http://www.nottingham.ac.uk/chdgp/document.htm
4 http://www.clinical-info.co.uk/miquest.htm
5 *NeLH Executive Summary*. http://www.nelh.nhs.uk/strategy.htm
6 The Caldicott Committee (1997) *Report on the Review of Patient-identifiable Information*. http://www.doh.gov.uk/confiden/crep.htm
7 *Data Protection Act 1998*, Chapter 29. http://www.hmso.gov.uk/acts/acts1998/19980029.htm

Useful on-line resources

NHS Alliance http://www.nhsalliance.org/
NHS Information Authority http://www.nhsia.nhs.uk/
The NHS IM&T Electronic Library
http://www.standards.nhsia.nhs.uk/library/index.htm
PRODIGY   http://www.schin.ncl.ac.uk/prodigy/
MIQUEST   http://www.clinical-info.co.uk/miquest.htm
CHDGP   http://www.nottingham.ac.uk/chdgp/document.htm
WISDOM   http://www.wisdom.org.uk/
COIN http://tap.ccta.gov.uk/doh/coin4.nsf
NeLH http://www.nelh.nhs.uk/

CHAPTER 24

How to keep within budget

Debbie Fleming

Introduction

In December 1997, the White Paper *The New NHS: modern, dependable* was published, which set out the government's vision to build a National Health Service 'fit for the twenty-first century'. Part of this vision included the establishment of primary care groups aimed at involving clinicians in shaping and delivering improved health and healthcare for their population.

Along with the introduction of these new organisations, there was also a requirement for greater efficiency through improved performance, new incentive arrangements, capped management costs, improved budgets and sanctions when efficiency and performance are not up to standard. Therefore, in playing their part within the brave new world, PCGs have had to face the same pressures as any other NHS organisation over the past year – and one of the greatest of these is the requirement to balance the books.

In this chapter, the arrangements for managing the budget within one PCG in Dorset are explained, and ideas as to how these might be improved are discussed. Most importantly, this section highlights a number of the key issues that must be taken into account if PCGs are to ensure that their resources are appropriately managed.

A little bit of history

For the financial year 1999/2000, health authorities received a single unified allocation of monies, covering Hospital and Community Health Services, General Medical Services (GMS) Cash Limited Funding for GP practice staff, premises and computers, and Family Health Services Prescribing. This unified allocation meant that for the first time, all health service provision had to be contained within the same envelope – there would only be one stream of cash-limited funds flowing through health authorities to PCGs.

One of the benefits outlined by the government in introducing the unified budget was to give clinicians greater control and flexibility over the resources that they receive. In the working papers, it was stated that this development would:

> *give GPs the maximum choice about the treatment option that best suits individual patients, free from the constraints imposed by artificially distinct budget headings. It will align clinical and financial responsibility so that those who prescribe, treat and refer have control over the financial decisions they make.*

Although there are varying views as to how appropriate it is for health professionals to allow themselves to be diverted from the delivery of health services by the need to address financial matters, it has to be recognised that financial consequences derive from every decision a health professional makes. It now falls to the PCG to ensure that these tensions are managed appropriately. From now on, any overspend in one area of the budget must be off-set by savings in another, and it is the PCG, made up of local health professionals themselves, that must face up to the difficult decisions that this inevitably involves. Balancing the books has therefore been a huge challenge for PCGs during their first year of operation.

Setting the scene

Bournemouth Central is one of 10 PCGs within the Dorset Health Authority operating at level 2. Covering a population of just over 81 000, it is smaller than average and has to work within very tight management costs – less than £2.20 per head of population.

The budget allocated to our PCG in 1999/2000 was £11 564 149 as detailed in Table 24.1.

Table 24.1

Budget	Amount
Management costs	190 440
Cash-limited GMS	1 131 306
Extended primary care services	605 476
Community nursing	1 114 141
Prescribing	8 522 786
Grand total	**11 564 149**

As well as these budget headings, the PCG was allocated £25 778 400 as its share of the total funds in Dorset for secondary care commissioning.

At present, no finance officer is directly employed within the PCG. However, the board has access to its own designated management accountant who is based at the health authority, and receives general financial support from the health authority finance department.

While there is no designated finance committee within the PCG, this role is undertaken by the GMS subcommittee. This group was set up to consider issues affecting individual practices, many of which concern the allocation of resources. This subcommittee considers proposals for the distribution of GMS and extended primary care funds across the PCG, and makes appropriate recommendations to the board. Similarly, this group considers the results of any internal reviews carried out by the PCG, such as a review of nursing services. In this way, the GMS sub-committee provides a forum for taking into account the impact of PCG policies on individual practices, whilst at the same time supporting the effective decision-making processes of the board.

The GMS subcommittee is made up of two GP board members (one of whom chairs the committee), one nurse representative, two practice managers, the chief executive and the chair of the PCG. This arrangement has worked extremely well and has proved a real asset in managing the financial affairs of the PCG as a whole.

Nevertheless, the budget that can give rise to most concern within the PCG is the prescribing budget. The monitoring of this budget is carried out by the prescribing subgroup which is made up of all GPs on the board, the clinical governance nurse lead, the chief executive and the health authority pharmaceutical advisor. This group develops the annual prescribing management plan, monitors expenditure on a monthly basis, agrees the action necessary to maintain expenditure within budget and makes formal recommendations to the board with regard to prescribing policy. By involving *all* GP board members in this way, no one is allowed to abdicate responsibility, and proposals are rigorously debated and tested. This in turn means that effective decisions can be taken speedily at board level.

The management budget is routinely monitored by the board, but decisions about expenditure or the virement of funds are generally taken within the PCG office. To date, this budget has not given rise to particular concern, other than in the same way as for many other PCGs – that is, the small management team is under considerable pressure to deliver the annual accountability agreement within such a tight management envelope.

Having highlighted the need to allocate responsibility for overseeing financial matters to a number of small groups within the PCG, it must be remembered that all board members should be kept informed and up-to-date with regard to budgetary issues. Although it is really only possible to work practically and effectively through smaller groups and subcommittees, it cannot be emphasised enough that all members must remain 'on board' if the PCG is to respond appropriately to all the financial pressures placed upon it.

Managing the budget

For PCGs to effectively manage their budgets, the following basic principles must be followed.

Make sure you understand how the budgets have been drawn up

Although this may sound rather obvious, board members are not always clear as to how the different budgets within the PCG have been derived, yet this is very important if these budgets are to be effectively managed.

As might be expected, in setting up these budgets health authorities across the country took decisions as to how they should be devolved in different ways. Within our health authority, the Dorset Funding Group was set up to consider the various options available for each budget heading. This group then made recommendations to the PCG chair meeting, which took the final decision as to how this exercise should be carried out.

So it is important to remember that it is possible for a number of different principles to have been adopted for the devolution of the budgets held by a PCG. The amount of resource available under each heading will obviously vary, according to the methodology used.

However, many of the management appointments, and indeed some of the board member appointments for PCGs, came *after* these funding decisions had been made. This meant that there was a great deal of 'catching up' to be done for all those involved before they could reach the same level of understanding.

Given that there has been so much to learn over the past year, it has been hard to keep up with new issues as they unfold. As a consequence, catching up on previous events has been extremely difficult, and in many cases, simply has not happened. Therefore, it has been all too easy for individual board members to remain ignorant of the methodologies used for allocating budgets down to PCG level.

It is, nevertheless, extremely important for those who are taking decisions with regard to the use of PCG resources to have the background knowledge on how the baseline budget was put together. The methodology used may well impact on the way in which these resources are distributed in the future.

The situation is clearly much improved one year on, as boards have developed a greater level of understanding with regard to the business for which they are now responsible. It is encouraging to note how often phrases such as 'steady-state', 'weighted capitation' and 'GDP deflator' now roll off the tongues of board members!

Make sure you agree with the plan

It is often the case that those with no background in finance are intimidated by the thought of managing a budget, particularly when the sums are large, involving lots of 000s in different columns.

Nevertheless, the important point to remember is that the budget itself merely represents a *plan* as to the way in which resources are expected to be used over a given time period. The allocation of resources for that time period may well vary, with the budget set up to reflect the organisation's different expenditure patterns. For example, in setting up a management budget, one-twelfth of the budget is usually allocated for each month in order to meet this expenditure, as it is anticipated that management costs will remain fairly stable throughout the year. However, for another budget this would not be appropriate. For example, a budget which must meet varying levels of demand throughout the year should be divided up in accordance with the anticipated pattern of expenditure. Given that expenditure on drugs and other items directly related to patient care increase during the winter when the demand for services is traditionally higher, the budget for these items should be greater over the winter period.

Budgets are therefore likely to be set up in different ways, to reflect varying patterns of expenditure. The important thing is for board members to know what the plan is, so they can ensure that it is followed. This principle is particularly important when agreeing the delivery of savings targets. It is no good to simply cross one's fingers and hope that such savings will be made! Instead, plans have to be developed to release these savings, which will then be reflected in the budget, and the management task is to ensure that the necessary action is taken to deliver the plan.

Similarly, if board members are not convinced that the budget allocated to them is going to be adequate, they must develop alternative plans to address this – either by seeking additional funds from elsewhere or by identifying areas where expenditure can be reduced. It is no good starting the year knowing that your budget is insufficient to meet the demands you expect to make upon it. At the same time, this is still the PCG's responsibility – we cannot rely on luck or divine intervention to put such problems right!

The importance of monitoring and control

Having worked through the budget, understood its various components and how they have been devised, the next step is to ensure that it is properly monitored. There are a number of ways in which this can be carried out.

- Ensure that there is clarity regarding those individuals who are able to sign off expenditure. This is normally done by completing an appropriate form detailing the budgets for each authorised signatory and the amount of money that he or she is allowed to commit. Some limits may already have been decided by means of the health authority standing financial orders and standing financial instructions, but other smaller budgets will need to be considered separately.
- Give careful thought as to how far various budgets should be devolved throughout the organisation, or, indeed, down to individual practices. The answer to this question will clearly depend on the type of budget itself, the structure of the PCG and the calibre of the individuals working within it. As a general rule, it is accepted that people will take greater responsibility for expenditure when the budgets are devolved down to the lowest possible level. However, there are also a number of reasons for holding certain budgets centrally, and this is not always just about retaining control or minimising risk. For example, within our PCG, we decided to ring-fence a sum of money to support practice training. In this way, we were able to send out a strong message regarding the importance of training and development, as well as being able to use limited resources more flexibly and facilitate the monitoring of training at practice level.
- Make sure that proper attention is paid to the analysis of each month's budget statement, which shows the level of expenditure incurred against the budget that has been made available to meet it. Ensure that the reasons for any variances are clear to you.
- Make sure that regular financial reports are made to the board so that all members are kept up-to-date with the budget position and have a chance to challenge particular issues.

- Most importantly, ensure that speedy appropriate action is taken to address any over-spending.

All this serves to emphasise that the detailed arrangements for setting up and monitoring budgets across the PCG are vitally important in retaining financial control.

Ensure you get your priorities right

One of the biggest mistakes made by those new to budget management is that they often find themselves trying to keep a close eye on every-thing, to the extent that their performance is hampered in the areas that really matter. For example, like most PCGs our prescribing budget equates to around two-thirds of our total resource. It is therefore evident that the majority of management time and effort should be focused on managing the prescribing budget.

Unfortunately, in a world with so many challenges to face, it is tempt-ing to focus on some of the more visible budgetary pressures, despite the fact that these are relatively small scale. There are some managers who are reluctant to incur any additional expenditure against their budget – for example, releasing funds for training or booking temporary office support in the event of sudden staff sickness – because this has not been specifically accounted for within the management allocation.

This point is made with caution since there is no intention to move away from the common sense approach that 'if you look after the pennies, the pounds will look after themselves'. Indeed, this principle is very applicable to primary care. However, within a budget that runs into millions, there is usually some element of flexibility allowing for small scale, one-off expenditure. In the examples cited above, it could well be the case that the cost of *not* incurring this expense may be even higher than the amount initially requested.

The situation is frequently made worse by the fact that it is usually these same individuals who fail to keep a broad overview of the budget as a whole. They spend *all* their time worrying about the pennies, whilst some of the prescribing practices of individual GPs can be wasting thou-sands of pounds!

Much has been written about managing prescribing within primary care, and all PCGs have had to address this agenda. It is not the intention of this chapter to attempt to cover the same ground, but in the context of balancing the books, the message is very clear – controlling the prescrib-ing budget should be a major priority for the PCG as a whole. Not only is this the largest budget within the PCG, it is also the one carrying the greatest degree of risk, being made up of variable rather than fixed costs. A number of different actions can be taken to manage this budget effectively:

- developing a prescribing management plan, giving details on how this budget will be managed over the course of the year
- setting practice-level budgets
- keeping abreast of developments such as nurse prescribing
- establishing a local prescribing incentive scheme
- introducing formularies
- obtaining access to high-calibre pharmaceutical advice
- enabling the open sharing of prescribing data
- involving the local pharmacists whose own practices have such huge potential to skew the PCG budget.

To balance the books, we have to get our priorities right. Our time, effort and attention should always be focused on the areas that have the greatest potential to influence the success of the PCG financial position as a whole. The budget that gets most attention should be the one that equates to the largest percentage of our total resource, particularly when this is also the one with the greatest potential for variation.

The need for swift decision making

In taking responsibility for managing a budget, no matter how large or small the amount, there are bound to be problems and issues arising throughout the year that need to be sorted out. One of the difficulties for PCGs has been that given the early stage of their development, policies have often been devised as we go along. Members do not always know the way in which things should be done, and if they previously had this knowledge, the arrangements have probably changed! Instead, boards have found that they have to work things out for themselves, deciding the best way forward.

At the same time, there is also new emphasis on ensuring equity and maintaining openness, principles that derive from *The New NHS: modern, dependable*. Taken together, this places decision makers under far more pressure than ever before to make the 'right' decision – one that could be applied equally to everyone in the same way, and one which is open to scrutiny within the public arena.

In this context, what should the PCG do when faced with an overspend on a budget for complementary therapy such as acupuncture? How should we address the fact that one of our practices has received too low a share of the GMS budget, yet all the funds have been allocated? None of these issues are new in themselves, but the 'tool-kit' that enables board members to address them is still being put together. As a consequence, decision making within the PCG has sometimes been slower than it ought to be over the past year, due to either a lack of knowledge or a general uncertainty as to the best way forward.

Clearly, the ability to make decisions is key to effective financial management. In order to ensure that the books are balanced within the PCG, members must be prepared to take those difficult decisions that could previously be left to someone else. It is encouraging to see how this skill has developed over the past 12 months, with board members becoming increasingly confident in addressing difficult issues. Nevertheless, the danger of unnecessary prevarication is still there, and efforts must be made to guard against it.

Planning new developments

One of the most enjoyable aspects of life within the PCG is working to develop services for patients, and there is no doubt that all members find planning improvements in healthcare rewarding.

Despite a number of hurdles, this year has in fact been a very good one for PCGs. Not only were we allocated growth monies in both 1999/2000 and 2000/2001, we have also been sheltered from some of the harsher realities of life in the NHS such as efficiency savings. For example, when problems arose with an increase in the cost of generic drugs, PCGs were given extra resources to enable them to keep within budget.

Such a situation is very unusual. Ask any trust how often they have been baled out over the past few years, and whether or not they depend on such support from outside – the answer will be sobering. Although health authorities and trusts may well have worked together on a recovery package, this has generally involved agreeing on how to address the funding problems together, and confirming which services are to be cut back and how, so as to have the least impact on direct patient care.

In light of these lessons, the prudent PCG recognises that the only way to assure the ability to continue developing services is not to lose sight of the potential for savings elsewhere. By keeping one eye on the areas that are ripe for reorganisation, additional funds can be released within the healthcare system to finance new developments.

This is a new skill needing more development within PCGs, given that individual board members may not be used to undertaking such a role. It takes a high degree of confidence to overtly challenge the way in which resources are being used, to the extent that you are prepared to completely reorganise the way in which services are delivered, irrespective of the amount of change that this will involve.

Nevertheless, this is very much our responsibility and such skills will be essential if we are to truly introduce a 'primary care-led NHS'. It should never be forgotten that money is a very powerful lever for change, and we must have the necessary resources to enable us to deliver our agenda. Given that relying on a constant stream of growth money from outside is unrealistic, we must take steps ourselves to ensure that resources continue to be made available for reinvestment in patient care.

The primary care investment plan

Having considered some of the basic principles behind sound budget management and the funding of developments, it is useful to review the importance of balancing the books with regard to the primary care investment plan (PCIP).

All PCGs are required to produce a PCIP and within this document, there is a requirement for a clear financial framework. The main components of such a framework are as follows.

- Details of all available funds, both recurring and non-recurring, for the PCG. This should include the source for all new funds, and details as to how the existing budget allocations are to be rolled forward.
- Clarification of your financial assumptions – this will include details of the amount of development monies available to the PCG; the amount of efficiency savings that must be achieved; the uplift available for inflation; plans for holding any central contingency; and confirmation as to how any increases in pay and prices will be addressed.
- The identification of any known or potential cost pressures and how you plan to address these – for example, how will the PCG deal with the introduction of new drugs? How will it cope with the need to increase the use of drugs such as statins? What steps will be taken to deal with any additional costs associated with an increase in activity?
- Information as to how the PCG will ensure efficiency and value for money. For the vast majority, this will involve clarification on how the PCG will deliver the 3% efficiency savings target required by government, but it may be appropriate to highlight other plans such as those aimed at ensuring cost-effective contracts.
- Details regarding the management of issues at the interface between primary and secondary care. This is clearly important given the potential for costs to be transferred inappropriately from one sector to another, which in turn will have a detrimental affect on the wider

healthcare system. Plans should include information regarding the use of prescribing interface committees, policies for the introduction of new drugs, or arrangements for managing the financial implications associated with any shift in service.

- Information about the planned use of incentive schemes within the PCG, including the potential costs associated with running them and the mechanism for ensuring that these costs can be accommodated.
- A clear investment programme for planned new initiatives, highlighting the source of funds for each individual development, whether or not these resources are recurring or non-recurring, the planned start date, and the identification of any slippage.
- Details of the risk management strategy for the PCG and clarification on how expenditure will be monitored and controlled. Managing the financial risk to the organisation is one of the key roles for the board. As PCGs have matured, they understand more clearly the issues involved in contingency planning and risk management. For example, given the risk of overspending against the budget, a certain amount of money must be held as a central contingency. Similarly, the PCG will want to ensure that it has agreed a prudent timetable for the release of funds to support its developments so that the financial position of the PCG is properly safeguarded. In this way, the PCG can minimise the risk of over-spending, and ensure that patient care is not affected by some sudden unforeseen change in the level of resources available.

The commissioning role

Despite the fact that most PCGs have a large sum of money in their budget for purchasing secondary care, this is an area over which many of us feel little ownership. One of the most commonly expressed gripes over the past year has been from PCGs frustrated by the limited role that they have played in the commissioning process. There have been many complaints about the apparent reluctance on the part of health authorities to delegate this responsibility in the way in which it was originally envisaged. Certainly, it would appear that there has been a lack of clarity on the role that PCGs will be able to play in agreeing the service and financial framework for their local trusts.

It is not the purpose of this chapter to consider the role of the PCG within the overall commissioning process. However, it should be noted that as time goes on, it becomes evident that in today's NHS, even those previously involved in commissioning at health authority level have had to change their approach. The emphasis in securing cost-effective, high-quality secondary and tertiary services is now more about *agreeing a joint plan* with the relevant partners, along with appropriate mechanisms for its implementation.

Such a focus will obviously involve discussion on how resources should be used, comparison with bench marks across the country, and the agreement of appropriate changes in service delivery. However, it is by working together in partnership with others across the healthcare system that PCGs will balance the books in respect of their commissioning budgets. Adopting the old commissioning style, as a means of engaging with secondary care, will no longer be appropriate given the demise of the internal market.

So where do we go from here?

The development plan for Bournemouth Central PCG is now inextricably linked to its plans to become a merged primary care trust (PCT) for Bournemouth. In taking such a significant step, the PCG will be required to introduce strengthened financial arrangements. This is a welcome move, and one which we would have wished to pursue irrespective of the move towards trust status. However, without this impetus it may have taken longer for this change to be introduced.

The most important development that will assist us in balancing the books will be the appointment of our own Director of Finance. This will be a significant improvement for the newly formed PCT. No matter how effective the current arrangements for financial management, there will be considerable benefits associated with the appointment of one designated senior individual at board level, specifically responsible for ensuring the financial performance of the organisation.

A number of other features will be introduced as a consequence of the new organisational arrangements.

- The PCT will benefit from the support of a large finance department, available as part of the new Support Agency arrangements being introduced across the health authority.
- A new finance subcommittee will be established to support the work of the trust board and the trust executive.
- We shall endeavour to delegate more responsibility for individual budgets to a lower level within the organisation. In the same way as for the PCG in 1999, this will need to be accomplished in stages, once the levels below the board have the capacity and capability to cope with this level of responsibility.

Most importantly, as part of our organisation development programme, we shall be taking the opportunity to reflect on all that we have learned over the past year, to ensure that we continue to improve our performance in financial planning and financial management. Only by ensuring that we are able to balance our books appropriately, with all that this entails, can we be sure that we are truly acting in the best interests of our patients, and fulfilling our responsibility for improving the health of the local population.

> *Wine maketh merry; but money answereth all things.*
> The Bible, *Ecclesiastes*

Further reading

Lilley R (2000) *The PCG Tool Kit* (2e). Radcliffe Medical Press, Oxford.

Richardson F (1999) Take financial control and a giant leap forward. *Primary Care Report*. **May/June**.

Secretary of State for Health (1997) *The New NHS: modern, dependable*. Cm 3807. The Stationery Office, London.

Smith J and Baines D (1999) Managing a cash-limited prescribing budget in a PCG: opportunity or threat? *Health Service Management Centre Newsletter*. **5**(2).

PART 5

The future

CHAPTER 25

Towards PCT status

Geraint Davies

1 April 2000 saw the launch of the first 19 PCTs. These will act as templates for future trusts, very much as the locality commissioning pilots (established in April 1998) were templates for the PCGs that commenced in April 1999.

PCTs will be sailing in uncharted waters, offering opportunities and risks. Most of those taking the plunge in the first wave are groups who felt that they would be able to achieve more by becoming trusts. This is particularly so of the authors of the next two chapters, who are both firm believers and doers. Their different accounts will offer inspiration to any PCGs that have not yet decided whether to become PCTs. They will also provide a number of useful leads for those PCGs that have committed themselves to PCT status and who need to know the detail of what will be required of them.

The Hayes & Harlington experience

As one of three PCGs in the London Borough of Hillingdon, Hayes & Harlington PCG agreed in principle in June 1999 to move towards PCT status for April 2000. Its reasons for being at the forefront of this government initiative are covered in this chapter and hopefully our experience will be useful for colleagues considering a similar move.

This chapter sets out the process for developing the PCT proposal. From the outset, it was important that all the stakeholders felt they were active participants in this process. The stakeholders were the three PCGs, Hillingdon Health Authority, Harrow & Hillingdon Healthcare Trust, The Hillingdon Hospital Trust, staff and their representative groups, Hillingdon Council/Social Services Department, Hillingdon Community Health Council, the voluntary sector and the public. The ethos of the PCT development process was one of inclusiveness, ensuring that it was developed through an evolutionary approach and grounded in our strategy for improving health and developing health services.

A key theme governing the management process was to ensure that whenever a stakeholder raised a question/issue, it was proactively addressed.

The major questions/issues raised by stakeholders were as follows.

• Will it make any difference?
• What will it look like?
• Will all stakeholders be involved in the process?
• Have we got the experience and knowledge?
• Are we going too fast?
• How do we undertake a consultation exercise?

Background

Hayes & Harlington PCG is part of Hillingdon Health Authority, which is coterminous with the London Borough of Hillingdon. There are three PCGs within Hillingdon and they have a total registered population of 247 466. The respective registered population of each PCG is as follows: Hayes & Harlington 69 648; North Hillingdon 93 785; Uxbridge & West Drayton 84 033. There are 17 GP practices and 35 GPs within the Hayes & Harlington PCG. There is a high level of small practices within the PCG, namely 71% of the practices have either one or two partners.

Will it make any difference?

This was certainly the key question to be answered, not only in the initial stages of the debate, but throughout the consultation process. It was the litmus test to ensure that the reasons for proposing to create a PCT were valid to the local health economy stakeholders. The overriding principle was to deliver improved services to our local population and this was the starting point for us.

Health services within Hillingdon are provided by GPs, Harrow & Hillingdon Healthcare Trust and The Hillingdon Hospital Trust, while Hillingdon Council provides social care services, which support health services via the social services department. Currently there are administrative boundaries between these service providers that lead to delays in service delivery to patients. In addition, these divisions compound the achievement of seamless service delivery between health and social services. The opportunities offered by the establishment of a PCT, which could remove or lower the boundaries between health and social care providers, were seen as one of the main drivers for establishing a PCT.

The opportunities offered by trust status would help us deliver the recommendations of the community development plan produced in 1999. This plan recommended that there should be greater integration between service providers to enhance the services offered to elderly people within the borough. It was also a 'leap of faith' by all the stakeholders, not knowing whether the creation of a PCT would achieve this aim.

Once we had agreed on the vision for the creation of the PCT, we had a framework in which we could develop the proposal, and this provided the basis for the remaining questions to be answered.

What will it look like?

Once the vision had been agreed, it was necessary to agree on the model of PCT to best deliver the aim of improving the delivery of services to our patients. First, we explored the transition of one PCG to become a PCT. However, this model was based on a PCG serving a population of 100 000. The populations of the PCGs in Hillingdon range from the largest at 93 785, to 84 033 to 69 648. Therefore, it was questionable whether an individual PCG serving such a small population could have the management capacity to successfully lead the development of a PCT proposal or have sufficient resources to provide services to its residents.

To overcome the problem of each PCG's size it was initially proposed that we look at a formal merger of PCGs in Hillingdon to provide a configuration that complied with NHS Executive recommendations. However, the existing boundaries of the three PCGs were based on commissioning groups that were coterminous with the parliamentary constituencies. The PCGs were recognisable as discrete localities by their respective populations and these boundaries enabled decisions regarding health services to be responsive to the needs of the local populations. The PCGs had also established a federal system of working from their creation, which was partly due to their respective size and the need to avoid duplication of effort. For example, one PCG leads on the commissioning process with the local acute hospital trust on behalf of the other two and another leads on the implementation of the NSF for cancer. While all three PCGs have senior social service representation on their boards, the federal approach has enabled the development of a joint vision of the future between the PCGs/health authority and Hillingdon Council/Social Services Department. The existing arrangements were perceived by all the stakeholders to be delivering on the PCGs' agenda and working for the benefit of the local population. Therefore, it was agreed that there should be no formal mergers of PCGs to provide appropriate-sized organisations to meet NHS Executive recommendations.

The PCGs still wished to consider the development of PCT status within Hillingdon but the question was 'How?'. In our discussions, a potential alternative model evolved from the Hayes & Harlington PCG. The proposal was based on a pan-Hillingdon PCT that built on the strengths of the existing PCGs and provided the basis for the development of a Hillingdon-based solution.

This proposal was discussed with all the stakeholders in the local health economy and they were receptive to developing a PCT proposal based on the Hayes & Harlington PCG's pan-Hillingdon model. The details of the model were fleshed out during discussions between the PCGs, health authority and trusts in Hillingdon. The agreed model maintained the three PCGs as the foundations for the proposal, known as the 'engine rooms', and they would be transformed into locality directorates. The locality directorates would be responsible for the operational management of the PCT within their respective boundaries and would also have devolved responsibility for their respective budgets. Those community services that were transferred to the PCT from 1 April 2000 would be incorporated into the locality directorates with their respective management structures and budgets.

The proposed model was also seen as the natural development in the evolutionary process of the locality development in Hillingdon, namely from the commissioning localities, to PCGs and finally PCT.

The proposed pan-Hillingdon PCT model was accepted as the basis for establishing a PCT as it would:

- maintain the three PCGs as the foundations of the PCT
- build on the federal working arrangements between the three PCGs
- build on the knowledge and experience of the PCGs
- maintain local accountability
- maintain local flexibility
- be a natural stage in the development process in Hillingdon.

Will all stakeholders be involved in the process?

As stated previously, the involvement of all the stakeholders in Hillingdon connected with the establishment of the PCT was crucial to its success. The brief was widened to include some regional and national colleagues, namely:

- the three Hillingdon PCGs
- Hillingdon Health Authority
- Harrow & Hillingdon Healthcare Trust and The Hillingdon Hospital Trust

- health service staff, e.g. GPs, community/practice nurses, administrative/managerial
- staff representative groups, e.g. local medical committee, the health visitor, district nurses and PAMs Committee, local pharmaceutical committee, local dental committee and the local optical committee
- other health organisations in London, e.g. other PCGs and health authorities
- community health council
- voluntary sector
- the public
- London Borough of Hillingdon
- London Regional Office of the NHSE
- Department of Health.

This approach cut down on delays in the developmental process and enabled stakeholder questions to be addressed proactively. The value of adopting this style can be exemplified by the discussions with regional/national colleagues and GPs/community nursing staff regarding the proposed PCT.

The pan-Hillingdon PCT model does not comply with the recommended national model for establishing PCTs and it was essential that the views of colleagues at the Department of Health and the Regional Office regarding this proposal were assessed before it was actively progressed locally. Representatives of three PCGs, the health authority and the local community trust met with Department of Health colleagues to discuss the pros and cons of the pan-Hillingdon model. Our national colleagues endorsed our proposal as an alternative model worthy of exploration locally, but clearly no guarantee of approval could be given in advance of ministerial decision. Consequently, it was up to us to prove through the development and consultation process that there was confidence and support locally across the stakeholders for the model, via their involvement. We have also ensured that the ongoing development of our proposal has been discussed with national and regional colleagues at all stages to maintain their support.

Locally, this inclusive approach has enabled the GPs and community nursing staff to raise any queries they have regarding the proposal and these queries have been addressed quickly to ensure that the momentum of the development process has been maintained. The main questions raised by local GPs were in relation to their independent contractor status, management of the GMS and prescribing budgets and assurances concerning the continued maintenance of the PCGs as locality directorates. Community nursing staff raised questions in relation to the proposed management structure of the locality directorates and the PCT, the training and education strategy, and confirmation of their existing employment rights within the PCT.

The inclusive stakeholder approach adopted as part of our PCT development process has been a major key to its success in gaining support from professionals and the public alike.

Have we got the experience and knowledge?

Apart from the need to ensure a common aim and ownership to the proposal, it was essential to ensure that the proposed PCT had the experience and knowledge to not only lead the consultation process connected with the proposal, but also had the potential management capacity to manage the PCT.

Prior to becoming a PCG, the GPs in Hayes & Harlington were members of a locality commissioning group, as were the GPs in the other two PCGs in Hillingdon. In addition, the Hayes & Harlington GPs were a commissioning pilot with responsibility for managing its devolved prescribing budget. These commissioning groups had some of the hallmarks of the PCGs' structures, such as a management team consisting of both clinicians and managers, a GP chair of the management committee and devolved budgets. The collaborative working arrangements that were required to make the commissioning pilot a success provided the local GPs and managers with invaluable experience and was a vital foundation for the putative PCG. At the close of the commissioning pilot, the Hayes & Harlington locality had managed its devolved prescribing budget to turn a 1% overspend in 1997/98 into a 5% underspend in 1998/99.

From experience gained through the commissioning pilot and locality groups the Hayes & Harlington PCG was established in shadow form from July 1998. During this shadow period, the PCG was supported by the health authority to develop and undertake an organisational development programme. The programme aimed to provide the PCG with the opportunity to develop the board and its individual members via teambuilding exercises and establish the aims and objectives for the PCG from 1 April 1999. It was also during this period that the proposal to develop a Hillingdon-based PCT from 1 April 2000 started to gain momentum.

The shadow period between July 1998 and March 1999, and its associated organisational development programme, enabled the PCG board and its members to gain experience of their potential future roles from April 1999. The PCG chair and vice chair were elected by the board members and they used this period to develop 'how' their roles would be undertaken. In addition, the clinical governance, prescribing, commissioning and health improvement leads for the PCG were nominated and they also used this period to establish how their respective roles would be implemented.

During the shadow period, it was agreed that the interests of our local population would be best served if both the PCGs and the health authority shared a common aim. In light of these discussions, it was agreed that they would work in true partnership to deliver their common management aims of providing health services to their population and developing the PCGs.

To support these agreed aims the PCGs and health authority agreed on their respective responsibilities and it was agreed to establish the PCGs at level 2. The PCGs would become the operational arm of the health authority with devolved responsibility for managing the commissioning process, primary development, and GMS and prescribing budgets. The proposed budget amounted to 90% of their respective devolved budgets and the health authority agreed that the PCGs required the appropriate management infrastructure to deliver this level of devolved responsibility. The PCGs subsequently received a management allowance of approximately £7 per head, compared with the national recommendation of £2.75 per head. The PCGs could afford to develop and appoint effective management teams, who in turn accepted and delivered an ambitious work agenda, which has given the PCGs invaluable management experience. This knowledge was essential to support the PCGs in their progression to the next stage of their development, namely PCT status.

To enable the PCGs to meet their devolved responsibilities and to avoid duplication of effort a federal working arrangement was established. Each PCG has taken a lead on a key priority on behalf of the other two, namely commissioning services and implementing the NSFs for cancer, coronary heart disease and mental health. This federal system has enabled the PCGs and health authority to gain invaluable experience of working on a collaborative basis, which in turn has enabled all parties to support the proposal to create a pan-Hillingdon PCT.

The PCG chairs were supported in their roles by a PDP, the details of which were mutually agreed by them and the health authority chief executive. The PCG chairs were supported on their respective training programmes and they were empowered to undertake their roles. This style of working also created a close working relationship between the chairs and the health authority chief executive, which was mutually supported, and helped in the development of our joint vision for the PCT.

In addition, I and my two fellow PCG chief executives were full-time members of the health authority executive team and we met with the executive directors on a weekly basis to manage the PCGs'/health authority's workload. This approach enabled us to build a working relationship with the health authority senior management team. Another outcome was that we were able to discuss and develop our vision for the future in a non-threatening environment and the result was the proposal to create a pan-Hillingdon PCT.

The combination of the historical management experience and the knowledge gained during 1999/2000 has provided the PCGs with the necessary management teams to not only deliver on their respective 1999/2000 objectives, but also play a vital part in the development of the process of the Hillingdon PCT proposal.

Are we going too fast?

This question has been asked throughout the development of the PCT proposal and the subsequent consultation period by members/representatives of all the stakeholders, especially the PCGs. There was concern that the PCGs had been in existence only since 1 April 1999 and we were considering another organisational change a year later. An associated argument was that the PCGs had not had the opportunity to develop the appropriate skills to manage the workload of a PCT. However, as previously stated, the inclusive nature of the PCT development process allowed the concerns of the stakeholders regarding the pace of change to be addressed and the following counter arguments to be made.

The main counter argument to this question was that the PCGs were already responsible for managing 90% of their potential devolved budgets. The PCGs were established to be the operational arm of the health authority with responsibility for managing the commissioning process, primary care development, and GMS and the prescribing budgets, while the collaborative working arrangements with the health authority virtually put the PCGs in control of 100% of the budget and they advised the health authority on the specialist commissioning.

In addition, the full involvement of the PCGs in the management of the health authority's workload provided their management teams with a vital opportunity to gain invaluable experience of managing a corporate agenda. This was strengthened by the federal working arrangements across the PCGs/health authority. The PCGs' management teams had developed the appropriate management skills to indicate that they were ready to take on board the full devolvement of the management agenda required to be a PCT. The proposed PCT model supported this style of working and the PCGs/health authority saw it as the only option for developing this proposal in Hillingdon. All parties were also in agreement that the establishment of the PCT should be progressed as soon as possible, as its development was seen as an inevitability and there was the belief that it would make a difference.

At the end of the consultation period in December 1999, all the key stakeholders supported the proposal to develop the pan-Hillingdon PCT from 1 April 2000. However, there were concerns raised from Harrow & Hillingdon Healthcare Trust regarding the pace of change implementation and it was agreed that the transfer of services into the PCT would be handled on a phased approach throughout 2000/01.

How do we undertake a consultation exercise?

The Hillingdon health economy is an area that is used to dealing with implementing changes in the healthcare system and undertaking consultation exercises. Over the past three years it has dealt with consultations dealing with the reconfiguration of services across the Mount Vernon Hospital and Hillingdon Hospital sites; the potential relocation of the regional plastic and burns unit; and changes to paediatric services at the Royal Brompton and Harefield Hospitals. These consultations involved a series of public meetings along traditional NHS lines.

In the PCT consultation, we invited the public to 'open evenings' whereby they could discuss how the PCT would change the face of their local care. NHS managers, doctors and nurses, frontline acute and community staff, and colleagues from social services staffed stalls so questions could be asked directly.

In addition, there were a series of stakeholder meetings, which allowed representatives of the project team to discuss the proposal with staff and their representative groups. In all, there were four public consultation meetings and 60 stakeholder meetings.

It was also essential to ensure the consultation document was written from the perspective of 'how' the PCT would improve health services for our local population and maintain local accountability.

The production of the consultation document and the management of the public exercise were undertaken by a steering group supported by a project team. This steering group's members were the chairs of the three PCGs, health authority and Harrow & Hillingdon Healthcare Trust. The Hillingdon Hospital Trust and the community health council were also represented. The consultation process was led by a project director, who was seconded to this role from his post of health authority chief executive.

The consultation process was managed on an inclusive basis, similar to that adopted for the development of the PCT proposal, and this approach ensured that the issues raised by the stakeholders were addressed. The outcome of the consultation process was that an application document was produced which reflected the views of the local health economy and its stakeholders. We received 64 written responses, of which 61 supported the proposal. The remaining three letters raised minor concerns that were addressed in the application document.

Role of champions

The role of champions in developing and leading any management change process must not be overlooked. The proposal to develop a PCT within Hillingdon was championed initially by the chairs/chief executives of the PCGs and the executive of the health authority. These individuals developed the early thinking of the proposal, these early thoughts were discussed and further developed with all stakeholders.

It was essential for the success of the PCT proposal that leaders of all the stakeholders championed it from the beginning. This support not only ensured its ownership, but more importantly credibility among these groups.

Conclusion

The result of the process was that we in Hillingdon were able to produce a PCT proposal that reflected the views of the local health economy stakeholders and provided a Hillingdon-specific model.

CHAPTER 26

The view after the first fence

Chris Town

Vision, courage and inclusiveness are the hallmarks of North Peterborough PCG's readiness to move to trust status at the earliest opportunity. It is also the consequence of the right forces being present at the appropriate time. Not that this was entirely by chance. Fragmentation due to the internal market had already given way to co-operation and collaboration as the health authority, fundholders and provider trusts engaged in meaningful dialogue to develop an understanding of each other's circumstances and viewpoint in planning for future services.

The publication in December 1997 of the Government White Paper *The New NHS*[1] set out a vision for the future of the NHS which was broadly welcomed locally. The advent of PCGs was seen to be a legitimisation of our developing philosophy and an opportunity for still broader involvement of both professionals and the public. Rapid maturation was the result of inspirational leadership and enthusiastic endeavour in pursuing the widely and strongly held belief that this change offered further opportunity. If we grasped the nettle we could make a real difference and focus on the real issues in creating and delivering a local agenda for improving health and providing better healthcare.

To deliver effectively on an improvement agenda would require breadth of ownership of a common vision, with a climate in which everyone felt their views could be aired and would have some influence. The health authority provided the initial leadership. To facilitate development of this vision, a series of workshops and seminars was arranged, with invitations to everyone from all local healthcare organisations who was interested to explore different ways of working and to consider the implications of and opportunities provided through the proposed changes.

This principle of inclusiveness prevailed throughout the PCG formative period. Natural groupings were nurtured as boundary consultations cultivated groups that wanted to work together on readily identifiable issues. Shadow boards were created at the earliest opportunity and health authority commitment was clearly demonstrated, with PCG project management becoming the remit of directors of the health authority. Project teams were set up through secondments from across the various sectors of health and the emerging PCG membership was already becoming a more cohesive unit with many common goals, a desire to develop a corporate identity and a strong, though not universal, wish to adopt co-operative ideals. In November 1998, all the North West Anglia Health Authority PCG shadow boards took part in a facilitated time out and, in separate group discussions, determined, with the health authority, the responsibilities that would initially be delegated. Through this event value sets were agreed and mutual understanding encouraged.

There was early realisation that aspirations would be most readily achieved through trust status and, with the advantage of a community trust that shared this vision, the PCG was conceived as a transitional arrangement that would rapidly progress to independence as a PCT. Again the health authority was most supportive, paving the way for early transformation by agreeing realistic management resources and an establishment to suit independence. Perhaps assisted by reorganisation of health authorities locally, the PCG was able to engage a chief executive with experience appropriate to our aspirations and broadly skilled management staff, allowing much responsibility for the population's health services to be delegated. It is also through the advantage gained by the appointment of an energetic and involved chair, whose compatibility and teamwork with the chief executive has done much to promote the success of the PCG, and through enthusiastic involvement of key professional players that we have reached this youthful maturity.

Initial work as a PCG has demonstrated to all the advantage of working as a larger corporate body for the benefit of patient service improvements and increased professional involvement and development. Since its inception, North Peterborough PCG has expressed commitment to being a 'learning organisation'. This is reflected in the early implementation of PDPs and in the approach we have taken to clinical governance which, with the closely associated educational programme, has been viewed positively and encouraged sometimes isolated clinicians to meet and discuss clinical issues with a greater number of colleagues in a safe environment. A mentoring scheme has also been introduced to allow confidential exchange of concerns and pressures.

The conviction and commitment of North West Anglia Healthcare Trust (NWAHT) should not be understated as this has significantly assisted the process of bringing the two organisations closer together. Following a series of open meetings, support for the principle of early PCT application allowed the healthcare trust to reconfigure services to form multidisciplinary clinical management teams based on localities matching local PCGs. Integration has been further promoted with a representative from the clinical management team and PCG senior management team attending the other's meetings, which has helped in the understanding of the different issues experienced in the community and primary care and has assisted the convergence of the two cultures.

In developing the PCG, we have been working closely with neighbouring PCGs and intend to continue organising joint events and training opportunities where appropriate. An organisational development group, comprising representatives from the three local PCGs, NWAHT, Peterborough Hospitals Trust, NMET and GP postgraduate education, has been in existence for the past 12 months and has discussed many aspects of these plans.

Increasingly, the PCG is developing its corporate identity and is being approached by its constituents for advice and support on a range of issues from developing patient groups to employment issues and IT. Planning and decision-making structures have been implemented to engage a large number of our current and potential membership and partners. Through operating on a subgroup and working-group basis there are currently practice managers, community nurses, practice nurses, lay members, pharmacists, optometrists and PAMs, as well as 22 out of our 59 doctors, working alongside board members and PCG managers on various plans for the future. Relationships are also being developed with the voluntary sector and with a variety of community groups to ensure their appropriate inclusion in planning and delivery of services.

Perhaps most importantly, through wide involvement, communication has been enhanced and the objective of seeking trust status more commonly agreed. To ensure that this was understood by all staff, before the application was put together an extensive series of meetings was arranged with all the key professional stakeholders in both primary care and the community. Entitled 'Listening and learning', the main principles of becoming a PCT were discussed and community staff in particular were asked to consider possible models for providing their service in the proposed PCTs.

Building on the 'Listening and learning' exercise, a full-day conference, again involving all stakeholders, was held in partnership with Fenland, South Peterborough and West Norfolk PCGs and NWAHT. This focused on the full range of services provided in the community and developed proposals for their future management. These proposals feature in the consultation document as the preferred future service arrangements and the full draft script was tested against the professional representative bodies, staff side and CHC.

Although we have been successful in our bid for trust status, we have been sensitive to shortcomings and have learned several lessons from the process. The focus of attention was on breadth of inclusiveness and much time was devoted to meetings and presentations to rehearse the arguments and accommodate concerns where possible. In retrospect, there was a need for continuous update and reinforcement communication to maintain the momentum and keep issues alive throughout the consultation period. We should also have recognised that more work to overcome inertia was needed with some groups of consultees. Discussions with practices tended to be in mixed groups, although the GP board members did arrange an 'all-principle' meeting to consider the advantages and disadvantages of trust status. With mixed messages arriving from national bodies, allegiances were tested and a significant number of GPs chose to be neutral when balloted. As PCTs, like their forerunners, are based on practice populations, success relies heavily on active participation of GPs as well as other clinical professionals. We are fortunate to have enjoyed a willing input so far, and to ensure that this spirit continues we will need to demonstrate clear advantages from this new way of working.

For the future we will be seeking ways to remedy these shortcomings. Continuing involvement of professionals in decisions about their services and a re-evaluation of needs and priorities will pave the way for consideration of re-engineering services so that delivery occurs at the closest safe, convenient, clinically effective and cost-effective location for patients. This may well mean the development of an alternative delivery of services in the community and in primary care, enabling clinicians to use their skills in a more rewarding and more productive way. Integration of community and primary healthcare teams provides the opportunity to consider new ways of achieving our objectives with involvement of a broader professional base for frontline advice and care. Patient involvement in the important decisions around prioritising and expectation management will allow concentration of resources in those areas perceived to be most appropriate and will thus more clearly describe the roles and responsibilities of our clinical teams.

Reference

1 Secretary of State for Health (1997) *The New NHS: modern, dependable.* The Stationery Office, London.

CHAPTER 27

Summary and conclusions

Michael Dixon

PCGs and PCTs represent our hope for the future. Some would say that they are our only hope for the future. They are the end stage of an NHS that has tried to evolve into a modern health service, while at the same time keeping its basic principles intact. Those principles have been evident throughout the chapters of this book. They include: a commitment to equity and fairness, to accountability, to cost-effectiveness, to involving local people and health professionals, and to collective working and partnership. They also include a fearlessness towards changing things, when change can bring about improvement.

Most of those who have contributed to this book believe that the NHS now has a workable structure. Yet the success of this new system will depend less on those structures than on the motivation and skills of the people who will work within them. Good structures can only facilitate their work. It was therefore the intention that every chapter in the second, third, fourth and fifth parts of this book should be at least co-authored by someone who was working at the coalface. The chapters themselves reveal enough energy and light to launch a rocket, but putting a rocket into space may prove to be easier than reviving an NHS that had begun to sit on its laurels – a utopian system in theory but one that was not delivering in practice.

Health

The New NHS will be challenged by many of the problems that arose from the culture of the early and mid-1990s. A national philosophy of 'women and children first' had been changed to one of 'everyone for himself'. We asked not 'What can I do for myself?' or 'What can I do for those around me?', but more simply 'What can the NHS do for me?'. Indeed, during the early and mid-1990s, we were told that a society as such did not exist at all. The result was the beginning of a very sick and uncaring society, where the difference between rich and poor rose to pre-war levels and where it become both acceptable and conventional to all but ignore the needs of those most deprived.

But sick societies produce sick individuals. The health of individuals is inextricably linked to the social, environmental and economic wealth of the culture in which they live. That is why health has to be one of the first priorities of PCGs and PCTs. Indeed, it is an area where PCGs are already beginning to show their mettle. For the first time ever, public health planning involves both professionals on the ground and the very population that is the object of those plans. Furthermore, the implementation of those plans is now much more the responsibility of local health professionals rather than arm's length professionals preaching from ivory towers. PCGs are beginning to link with other local planning teams and have produced joined-up solutions to problems such as local road safety and teenage pregnancy.

PCGs and PCTs thus represent a vital element in a social revolution that is beginning to question whether we need to live in a society that is disengaged, in a culture that is obesogenic and a country that quite clearly does not offer equal opportunity for all. Indeed, a society where many feel permanently alienated. The rapid development of exercise prescription schemes at local gyms, of Sure Start and the spontaneous eruption of farmer's markets in rural towns are all important symbols of a search for better health, more social engagement and local empowerment. New services and sources of information such as NHS Direct may help to enable individuals, but significant health improvement will also depend on fundamental societal change. If PCGs can develop as John Bewick suggests, then they will become a vital element in bringing about that much-needed change.

Better health services

Some may see this as too long-term and fanciful. For them, the success of PCGs will depend on early visible outcomes. It will depend on improving the health services that we have and on making them more accessible and of better quality. In these areas too, PCGs and PCTs hold all the keys. They have an important role in making services both more appropriate and cost-effective in meeting the needs of their local patients. In their commissioning role, they will need to ensure that both acute and community trusts are more sensitive to the needs of the local population. Much will be achieved simply through the new culture of people talking to each other, especially GPs and specialists, even before care pathways and LTSAs have been fully formulated. The PCGs will also need to look at new solutions.

That is why the pioneering work of PCGs such as South Bradford and

Southampton East Healthcare is so important. The new model of 'intermediate care' being introduced by them and other PCGs will revolutionise the interface between primary and secondary care. Patients in primary care will be seen sooner, receive treatment locally and within a more holistic framework. When they need to be referred on to a conventional specialist, then the timing of their appointment will be more appropriate as intermediate care will become a point of triage between generalist primary and increasingly specialist secondary care. Changing the nature of services will be easy where there is available growth money. Where money is tight, primary care will need to work with secondary care within the unified budget to agree how both can orchestrate better services. Care pathways will help but innovations will get off the ground quicker if they can be pump-primed.

Making services more available, more appropriate and more cost-effective is only one side of the coin. The other is to ensure that those services are used both by patients and health professionals as cost-effectively as possible. This is where demand management comes in and it is not simply about cutting costs. Whether it be scoring or quota systems for orthopaedic or ophthalmological referrals or introducing guidelines, the overall aim is to make sure that people are treated according to need.

Improving quality of care

One of the most rapid areas of development for PCGs, however, has been the focus on governance in primary care described by Steve Gillam and Nick Bradley. Hitherto, there has been a strong emphasis on clinical quality and the focus has been on improving average standards and dealing with poorly performing clinicians. This will change as we begin to look at quality through the eyes of the patient as well as the professional. We will start looking at those aspects of healthcare and consultations, which may not be strictly clinical but which have everything to do with outcome and wellbeing. No longer the 'library molluscs' described by Gillam and Bradley, we will, in the words of Roy Latham: 'begin to look beyond the scientific angle and take in the patient experience'.

In time, we will be less tolerant of the deep-rooted culture of disorganisation, whether it be in primary or secondary care. Why should patients be left in the lurch as to when their operation or outpatient appointment might be? Why should these appointments be cancelled at short notice or why should patients be subjected to a disorganised series of investigations, which often take an unnecessarily long time? In future, will we allow someone to remove the uneaten meal of a disabled patient in hospital without anyone realising that he or she was unable to feed him- or herself? Indeed, will we allow a whole raft of things that are done simply because they have always been done that way and because no one has ever noticed or been prepared to question the status quo. If local people and professionals are really allowed to take power then these things should become a thing of the past.

Involving patients

The involvement of patients is essential for all the reasons that Donna Covey has put forward in this book. It will, however, be a complex and multidimensional issue as Debbie Freake and Ruth Chambers point out. If they are to become properly informed, responsible and accountable, then lay members and the public will require far more input and enablement than they have had to date, a point made by Roy Latham. Yet if it is a 'peoples' health service' then the people have every right to make the decisions. Those decisions may be more visionary and bold and will therefore necessarily involve greater risks than professionals might like. But as professionals, we must now be prepared to think the unthinkable. As Ian Wylie and David Jenner suggest, it may be more important to invite the local newspaper editor out for a drink than to scribble laudable health information from your garret, which may never be read or understood.

Involving professionals

Then what about the professionals themselves? Virtually all of them have mentioned how their new role in primary care is being paid for at the margins by themselves, their families and those who support them in their daytime jobs. Indeed, they have all but given their time in contributing to this book. Mike North gives a vivid account of the scale of this human sacrifice. It is an account full of humour and integrity, which carries all the hallmarks of the NHS. The scale of this human sacrifice is illustrated dramatically by Tim Hinds, social services representative on the Slough PCG: 'The sharp end of change is over-reliant on the goodwill, energy and commitment of individuals who are already in full-time employment. This has already produced burn-out. Slough is not the only PCG to have had turnover in the GP membership of its board or of its chair within the first year'.

It is part of an excellent tradition that the NHS runs on goodwill, public service ethic and the principle that everyone must muck in. We must not lose this goodwill factor but it sometimes begins to look like exploitation of the workforce, especially when we are asking so much more from it in terms of output, quality and accountability. The NHS must get its act together, as Alex Trompetas suggests, and look after those who work within it as well as its patients. The PCGs and PCTs are a good place to start this process. If we are to root out poorly performing clinicians, then we must focus even more on the causes of poorly performing physicians, which may range from poor training and support to bad working conditions or lack of a proactive occupational health service. If people don't want to work in the NHS, if it is losing personnel and if days off sick are far higher than in the private sector then these are crucial quality indicators that cannot be ignored. The new health message must apply both to the patients and to the professionals who are trying to look after them.

Primary care trusts

So what of the future? Will PCTs be more of the same but better? Offering increased opportunities for joined-up thinking, allowing the possibility of integrated health and social care budgets? Eventually – why not? – completely integrated budgets for all health-related services at local level? This could lead to the provision of a properly integrated service where primary care itself and primary care and social care all act as one. Is this the 'nirvana' that PCTs are leading us to? Geraint Davies and Chris Town certainly believe so. They are managers and very good ones too.

Some GPs, however, see PCTs as an establishment plot that will enable managers to line manage them. They fear that trusts will recreate those very walls that they have been pulling down in the name of collective work and corporate responsibility. They say that PCTs may become like health maintenance organisations in the USA – resulting in inequity of care with large management overheads; that the focus will return to secondary care just as it has in the US system; and that the NHS will become a consumerist organisation deaf to the needs of the people for whom it was created.

Such scenarios are unlikely, mainly because there is hardly anyone in the NHS who wants to see them come about (though there may be some who would like to have a little more control over GPs). The current NHS is a system in evolution and PCTs can be confidently expected to evolve within the founding principles of the NHS. They are based on populations and patients registered with GPs. This makes them quite unlike health maintenance organisations as they will take on responsibility for every local person.

PCTs have been created with a subtle tension in their governance arrangements. This will be most obvious in the relationship between the board chair of the PCT, the chair of the PCT executive and the chief executive. There will also be a subtle tension between meeting national priorities and taking on local ones. This tension will ensure that PCTs are never truly top-down nor truly bottom-up. The PCT chair will rule the roost but the chief executive may find him- or herself squashed somewhere between local professional democracy (coming through the PCT executive) and the central imperatives of an NHS. Some see this triumvirate as an unholy compromise – British and messy. If David Jenner, a PCG chair, already finds himself on a 'medieval torture rack' then it seems unlikely that becoming chair of a PCT executive will make life any easier. But the creative tension has a purpose, which is to bring about much-needed change within the NHS. It reflects the raw truths of a people's health service rather than a cosmetic solution to a management conundrum.

The first and ever-present tension for many PCGs, however, will be when to become a PCT. That is whether to develop fully first as a PCG or whether to join the early stampede to become a PCT in order to keep up with the others. Again Tim Hinds of Slough PCG has some wise words: 'When organisations are in change, the introspection that goes with it can shift attention from operational necessities or the opportunities of the bigger picture'. The HSMC report *Getting Into Their Stride* showed that many PCGs feel that a period of consolidation and stability is necessary before applying. This message was echoed in an independent report produced for the NHS Alliance entitled *From PCGs to PCTs: work in progress*. For others, however, it may be a question of 'If it were best that it were done, it were best done quickly'.

Conclusion

The funding issue will never go away. PCGs and PCTs will ensure that the money available is used to best effect. But the money available, however much, will never be enough. We will need to engage in an open debate with the people as to what sort of health service we all want and how much we are prepared to pay for it. Those who say that the issue can be dodged by introducing widespread private insurance or making patients pay for themselves are misguided. Both lead to more expensive healthcare and both lead to a system where the care you get is dependent in part on the amount that you can individually pay for it. These are not the principles of the NHS. A hypothecated tax could be one solution. Whatever it is, PCGs and PCTs and the professionals within them should never be blamed for deficient services if they are not given sufficient money to run them. If we compromise on funding as taxpayers, then we must be prepared to accept compromise in our role as individual consumers of the health service. We cannot have it both ways. As this book goes to press, there is the good news of substantial extra funding for the NHS. It will greatly ease the pressures on PCGs but also increase their responsibility to show local people, patients and taxpayers that the extra money was well spent.

PCGs and PCTs are the end result of an NHS that is continuing to go through fast evolution and change. As a result of apathy, unaccountability, demoralisation and underfunding, the NHS has allowed itself to become a second-rate service. We should be shocked and shamed by reports that foreign nationals are now told to fly home as soon as possible if they should become ill in this country. Throughout the UK, this negativity is now giving way to energy, commitment, inspiration and originality of thought. A new determination, individuality and sensitivity that are all in the best traditions of the NHS. These are written all over the pages of this book. We are fortunate that the NHS is still an organisation where people are prepared to provide extra time and extra sweat simply for the reward of seeing their patients being better cared for. That makes PCGs an unstoppable train. There is simply no going back. They offer the hope of making the NHS a really first-class service. The promise of restoring the NHS to something that is once again worthy of being regarded with envy by the rest of the world. A better health service, a better society and a better country altogether. All three are completely interconnected.

Cynics will say that *we* are dreamers. That is whether it is the *we* of those who wrote the chapters of this book, the *we* of those who are trying to make PCGs and PCTs happen, or the *we* who may not be actively engaged in PCGs and PCTs but simply want to see them succeed. To the cynics, to those who want a private health service or those who do not want to pay for a public one, to professionals or managers with vested interests, to health planners with centralist agendas, to those who do not believe PCGs or PCTs will succeed, to those who do not want them to, we say this. We say this too to the planners, advisors and policy makers, who are making decisions in the New NHS. We say this particularly to those who will be responsible for implementing the NHS Plan:

> *We have spread our dreams under your feet;*
> *Tread softly because you tread on our dreams.*
> WB Yeats

Further reading

Audit Commission (2000) *The PCG Agenda*. Audit Commission, London.

Dixon M (2000) *Primary Care Services and the New NHS*. NHS Handbook. JMH Publishing.

Kent A, Kumar A (1999) *Development of Needs of Primary Care Groups*. NHS Alliance Survey Report 1999. Available on NHS Alliance website www.nhsalliance.org

Marks L and Hunter DJ (2000) *From PCGs to PCTs: work in progress*. Produced by Medical Management Services for the NHS Alliance and available from www.nhsalliance.org

National Association of Commissioning GPs (1997) *Restoring the Vision*. Can be seen on NHS Alliance website www.nhsalliance.org

Implementing the Vision (2000) Executive summary can be viewed on NHS Alliance website www.nhsalliance.org

Smith JA, Regan EL, Goodwin N *et al.* (2000) *Getting Into Their Stride: report of a national evaluation of primary care groups*. Health Services Management Centre, Birmingham.

Index